BRAIN PAIN

Our "Invisible Wounds."

Traumatic Brain Injuries and Post Traumatic Stress

Father
Khe Sanh

Son
Baghdad

Anthony E. Jones, Major, USAF Ret.

Praise for *Brain Pain*

"Brain Pain is an absolutely fantastic book and needs to be read by all, especially medical and mental health personnel."
Rear Admiral Joan M. Engel, 18th Director of the United States Navy Nurse Corps

"Brain Pain is the personal, first-hand account of U.S. Airman, Tony Jones, who was 'blasted' multiple times in Iraq by exploding rockets. He survived the near fatal hits, but the injuries he suffered to his brain forever altered his career, future, and mind. Depression, suicidal thoughts, addictive pills and excruciating pain became his new enemies in a battle that few can see, except those who have suffered similar injuries and their loved ones. In his book, Brain Pain, Jones reveals what it took to live through those attacks and rebuild a meaningful life. Training taught him how to be a warrior on the battlefield, but fighting for his mind required new weapons of war. Drawing on his faith, family, and the example set by his father, a Vietnam vet with similar war wounds, Jones shares his experiences in hopes other brain injury survivors will also find healing and the will to live a purposeful life."
Mollye Barrows - Journalist

"We often say, 'Thank you for your service. Thank you for your sacrifice.' But do we really know what that means? Brain Pain, a brave war fighter's painfully honest telling of what it means to serve in the military and pay a lifelong price, is a must-read for anyone who wants to understand what the words service and sacrifice really mean. Truly inspiring!!"
Kate LeBoeuf - Daughter of a US Air Force veteran

Praise for *Brain Pain*

"You may know that traumatic brain injury (TBI) has been a huge issue affecting not only pro NFL players but also the more than 2.4 million veterans who've served in the "Global War on Terror." Tony Jones, whom I feel lucky to call a friend and mentor, has written an outstanding biography detailing just how much sacrifice is entailed in "taking one for the team" by sustaining such an injury...and also the kind of drive, passion, and determination it takes to turn such a challenge into a strength. Tony also honors his parents by telling the parallel story of his father in Vietnam, and of how his parents met, which I found touching. Highly recommended whether you want to understand TBI or you're just interested in a unique veteran's life."

Bryce Rogow – U.S. Marine Combat Medic

"2017 will be listed as my 46th year in the professional nursing arena. Upon reading Brain Pain, I had a clinically clearer picture and understanding of just exactly the effects of the traumatic brain injuries our veterans are experiencing and their confusion and feeling of hopelessness that is experienced because we the professionals are simply stated, falling short. It is not good enough to just try. I wish I had a clearer insight that this book has brought to me before I retired as a Nurse Practitioner. My medical/nursing decisions would have taken so very much more into consideration for a path that may have been more positive and resolute than the borderline negligent pathway(s) that we have offered to all patients with TBI."

Jacqueline Barfknecht, Nurse Practitioner, Ret."

COPYRIGHT

LIBRARY OF CONGRESS CATALOGING-INPUBLICATION DATA has been applied for. Brain Pain; our invisible wounds. Traumatic Brain Injuries and Post Traumatic Stress / Jones, Anthony. 1st ed.

Brain Pain; W.G.A.w reg.1769227
Author; Anthony E. Jones, Major, USAF Ret.

ISBN-13: 978-0692768624
ISBN-10: 0692768629

First Edition – Nov. 11, 2016
Second Edition – Oct. 25, 2017

DEDICATION

To my father, who led by example, and showed me courage.

To my mother, who is an unsung hero and wife of a warrior.

*To all my family, friends and advocates who
have helped me navigate the new me.*

For those who have paid the ultimate price.

RESCUE 25:17: The path of the downed warrior is beset on all sides by the propaganda of the enemy and the tyranny of evil men. Courageous is he, who in the name of camaraderie and justice shepherds the isolated through the valley of darkness, for he is truly his brother's keeper and the finder of lost soldiers. And I will strike down upon thee with great vengeance and furious anger those who would attempt to capture or kill my comrades. *And you will know my call sign is* **"T-DAWG"** *when I lay my vengeance upon thee!*

ACKNOWLEDGMENTS

I never intended to write a book, but my research and the experiences from my journal slowly became this memoir. *I was never comfortable with the idea of publicizing my life, but the lessons I can relate are more important than my privacy.* Thank you to my parents, Walter and Anna, and my sister and brother, Pam and Marcos. We are "Team Jones" and I am so proud to be a member of this team!

I want to acknowledge my family, friends, and contributors who helped me in more ways than I can remember. From their love and support, to being my advocates, to helping me navigate these new waters, to contributing to this book, and mostly – for believing in me.

Sincere thanks to the following: Kate and Rob LeBoeuf; Shelley Cooper; Eric Borden; Chess Crosby; Richard, Farah and Sophia Emanuele; Rick McMillion; Tiptida Jandawan; Gisselle Bermudez; Steve Moloney; Jon, Mary and Thomas Eckel; Duff Kaster; Bill McCoy; Randy, Hannah and Charolette Moulton; Max, Roxanne, Landon and Payton Maxwell; Ben Jones; Eric Westfeling; Brendan Clare; Ron Lee; Jimmy and Sharon Hughes; Ted Fox; Jean Walsh; Bob Jones; Ernie Giovanni; Robbie Robinson; Doron Benbenisty; Darla Sekimoto; Dr. Valerie Galante; Laurie Willmott; Suzanne Jones; Mrs. Colleen Rivas; General Patt Maney; Heidi Linn; Michelle Gaw; David Messer; Eric Fleischmann; Sandy Armour; Roland Katavic; Debbie Dilldine; Don and Julie Bieger; Edith and Mollye Barrows; and Anne, Tonya and Tony F.

AUTHOR'S NOTES

Walter "WK" Jones spent 22 years in the US Marine Corps before retiring. He joined the Marine Corps in 1953, served in Korea and 2 tours in Vietnam. He started off enlisted, being commissioned as an officer prior to deploying to Vietnam and retiring as a Captain. He then went on to join the US Capitol Police for 2 years before joining the US Border Patrol. Capt. Jones spent another 20 years as a Federal Agent, ultimately becoming a Pilot, flying over 10,000 hours in both fixed wing and helicopters. Service; Korea & Vietnam. Awards; Navy Achievement medal with "V" Device, Purple Heart, Combat Action Ribbon and Presidential Unit Citation.

Anthony "Tony" Jones, graduated from George Mason University, then joined the US Air Force in 1980, was commissioned as an officer, and then graduated from flight school earning his Navigator wings. He then served with the 8th Special Operations Squadron as an Electronic Warfare Officer, flying MC-130's. He served in Desert Storm / Desert Shield and Operation Iraqi Freedom. During Iraqi Freedom, he was the Director of the Personnel Recovery Cell in Baghdad.

He now owns Core Group Security, which conducts investigations, operations and training in Executive Protection and Technical Surveillance Countermeasures. Service: Desert Storm & Iraqi Freedom. Awards: 2 Purple Hearts, Army Combat Action Badge, Defense Meritorious Service, Meritorious Service and the Joint Service Commendation medals. He lives in Las Vegas, NV.

CONTENTS

PROLOGUE

"BACK HERE"

Running late as usual. In Baghdad everything runs late. It's almost midnight, dark and the heliport ramp is buzzing like a hive of bats, churning out of their tunnel. The heat rising up from the ramp reminds me of the many hot nights back home at Nellis Air Force Base, in Las Vegas, my home, where I spent many late nights, on the ramp with the pleasantly toxic smell of jet fuel.

My vest, plates, camel back, rifle, pistol, ammo magazines and helmet seem fairly light tonight. Must have been all the coffee. We've been waiting for almost three hours and I'm soaked with sweat.

It was past midnight when we boarded the Black Hawks. Two teams, two birds. A smile came across my face as I felt the hot rotor wash and smelled the jet fuel permeate my senses. I had experienced hundreds of these moments far from home, in third world countries, that always felt and smelled the same. Hot and fuel ridden, with dread in the air. I loved it.

As we took off and climbed out into the Baghdad night, I looked down at the snake-like traffic slithering through the darkness, like blood pulsing through its city veins. With one hand I put in my ear bud, attached to my iPod. With the other I pulled off the Velcro flaps holding my rifle magazines and tucked them away. Then I did the same for my pistols. I then went to my iPod and turned on my motivation, "Its My Life," by Bon Jovi. Smiles.

BRAIN PAIN

The loud buzz of the gunners test firing their mini guns gave me a sudden shot of adrenaline, as well as another smile. Looking down, I could see the Tigris River, and with the weapons firing it was eerily similar to one of those scenes in "Apocalypse Now." My smile slowly dissipated. The lights of the city quietly dissolved into darkness. An hour and a half flight. Two hours on the ground. In another hour and a half we'd be back in the Green Zone for breakfast. I was now a command officer, not a door kicker, and this was simple site exploitation. We were looking for Intel on a taken soldier.

The thumping and bumping of the helicopter became a rhythmic rocking chair as we flew along. My thoughts wandered to a particular ISOPREP (Isolated Personnel Report - private information on the service member) card of a passed warfighter. I had read it after his Black Hawk went down, I couldn't get it out of my head. Reviewing them was part of my job at the Personnel Recovery Cell. Who'd be reviewing mine?

Out the door to my left, I saw the flares ejecting, then the RPG flew by. The Black Hawk pulled up abruptly and just as quickly nosed downward. Then came the plinking of bullets hitting the aircraft. Believing we were going in, I grabbed the door handle with all my strength, trying to open it as we began autorotation.

Many years of flying had given me pretty good situational awareness, which told me I had only seconds before impact. As the pilot powered up, I knew we were going in. At the last second I grabbed for my rifle between my legs. Then my face smashed into the rifle stock, knocking me out.

Coming to, I grabbed my face, blood squirting everywhere, dozens of mini-explosions zapping around my head. As I wiped away the blood, I reached up for the door, then down for my weapon. It was then I felt the carpet.

Feeling around more, trying to orientate, I grabbed my chest. I paused in the darkness, things not making sense. It was then I realized I was naked, lying on the floor, in the darkness - in the hall of my condo. My face was bleeding, my heart exploding and my brain was on fire!

The nightmare pulled me from my bed, causing me to run down the hall, still asleep, straight into the corner of the hallway leading to my bathroom. My nose was cracked wide open. I grabbed a towel,

ANTHONY JONES

held pressure, then downed a shot of Patron.

After pulling on some clothes, I grabbed the Patron and went out onto my deck. The air of Las Vegas was hot and dry, the same as "over there."

Hours later, I watched the sunrise over the mountain behind my home. The bottle was empty. I was "back here."

BRAIN PAIN

CHAPTER 1

DEFECTIVE

In high school I did a report on Ernest Hemingway's short story, **"Soldiers Home."** It was also an attempt to understand my father's post-Vietnam experience. (He'd been hit several times during the siege of Khe Sanh.) The story follows a young World War I soldier home after the war. He returns to a home and community where he no longer fits in or is understood. Society keeps on churning, yet he can't see his place in it. He's lost his ability to love, and his irritability dispatches those close to him. He's survived; being the best soldier he could, yet he longs for the sense of clarity he once had.

Finally, I get it. When the uniform comes off, you hang up a piece of your soul, right next to that box everything else goes in. Dad and I had survived similar combat experiences. We had both survived multiple explosions. Mine in Baghdad, his in Vietnam.

I survived, but I didn't return with my old brain. I left it "over there." When your mind starts to go, your abilities diminish. The time it takes you to process and calculate thought swells. Time slows as your memory catches up. Your brain betrays you with convoluted and incorrect memories, if any at all. There's a certain discomfort those around you feel. They can't see it, but they know it. Just by interacting with you, they realize you're slower. Even more so, because they can't see, they fear it. It's the **"Invisible Wound."** Acquaintances start to disappear, friends tread lightly and colleagues try to understand what you've become.

BRAIN PAIN

Socially, I'm now a different person. While everyone around me is sharp and quick-witted, I stumble trying to make a point. I call this, "**Access Dyslexia.**" Meaning, it's harder for me to access the information in my brain and when I do, it's often the opposite, backwards or something strangely close to what I'm looking for. When I'm trying to make a point or argue a position, I can't hold my own in any conversation, discussion or argument, especially a debate. I think that I know in my head what I want to say, but I'm unable to access it quickly and retort, or I just lose the thoughts altogether. The harder I think, the more confused I can get and the more physically painful it becomes. Then that smoldering firestorm of pain in my brain intensifies, overwhelming me into mental retreat. Agh! Agh!

Then, *frustration* sets in. The more frustrated I get, the worse the direction my mind takes. *"Chaos"* just noticed its opportunity; sliding into my brain through the cracks. My mind explodes with hypervigilant thoughts, like a stuck record, sparking out of control. Frustration is at the heart of *Chaos*. It starts with a simple brain fart, and then intensifies when my memories hide out. Frustration grows to anger; my heart rate increases, my blood pressure rises then a firestorm of electrical shocks manifests into an explosion of Brain Pain. Peripherals disappear and the focus tightens as the anger bursts forth exponentially. With me, there are the constant mini-explosions of pain, churning and spiking, enabling my *Chaos*, confusion and disarray. *Suicide?* Yep, he's visited me too.

I call my nemesis, **Chaos.** Dad calls himself **Defective.** To look at us, and the hundreds of thousands like us, you wouldn't know. The shrapnel scars have long healed, but it's an on-going battle.

For a long time I chose not to engage. I second-guessed myself constantly, trying to figure out if my memories and decisions were correct, because so often they're not. Until the gift of clear thought, learning, processing and predicting, is taken away, you don't appreciate it. You take it for granted. I did. My best friend Richie told me that for the first few years afterward, "I seemed to think I had TBI written on my forehead." My self-doubt was leading me down a path to complete social isolation. After a lifetime of living with the results of my fathers' Vietnam experiences, I was now living with the results of Baghdad. My father lives with his Traumatic Brain Injury (**TBI**) and Post Traumatic Stress (**PTS**,) as do I.

Chaos is the sum of TBI and PTS, i.e. headaches, anxiety, lethargy, irritability, anger, memory loss, frustration, depression, alcohol and drug abuse and bad choices. *This leads to weakening links in what I call our mental health "Chain," or our newly damaged mind.* *Chaos* eats away at the links in this "Chain." A healthy "Mental Health Chain" is the result of having proper morals, values and ethics, reinforced by well thought out choices.

The links in our Chain are constantly assaulted by headaches, depression and anxiety, which leads to anger, irritability, memory loss and frustration, which leads to loss of trust and feelings of betrayal, which leads to poor decisions, which lead to a dissolution of family and friends, which leads to bad financial decisions, which leads to personal destitution, which leads to overwhelming disappointment, which then leads to their perceived last choice, suicide. *Chaos attacks this Chain until a damaged link snaps;* 22 veterans a day. This process has been repeated over and over with way too many NFL concussion veterans as well.

Most can relate and understand the ramifications of the recent NFL concussion crisis, because the of the lawsuit played out in the media, and because of the movie "Concussion." The ***next concussion crisis*** will come from the aging Vietnam veterans who were not diagnosed and forgotten, and the Iraq / Afghanistan combat blast-induced veterans. Remember, many of the injured are A-Type personalities, having experienced prior concussions growing up in high school, college and military training. Multiple concussions can lead to a higher probability of Alzheimer's, Dementia and ***Chronic Traumatic Encephalopathy (CTE).***

CTE has been found in nearly every former NFL player's brain that has been examined posthumously by autopsy. ***Recently published reports have shown that CTE was also found in 4 of 4 deceased US military combat veterans exposed to a blast or multiple blasts in combat.*** *This is literally just the tip of the iceberg.* The first concussion crisis was sports related; the next will be our warfighters. It's catching up with us.

My father was blown up 4 times in Vietnam. He and hundreds of thousands of blast-exposed veterans were forgotten, left out in the cold. *I parallel this with what was done in the past with many NFL veterans.* They were denied and left on their own. We never tracked blast victims from Vietnam, but they did track NFL players and their concussions. *Through my research, what I've noticed,* with concussion experienced athletes, is the slow deterioration throughout their careers and afterwards, mostly leading to deteriorating marriages and businesses, sometimes ending in suicide. More than likely, the same occurred with Vietnam blast exposed veterans.

What's occurring in the NFL and other sports, regarding final recognition of concussion injuries, is just now being looked at with those grouped from the Vietnam War, 40 years ago.

The Iraq and Afghanistan wars have **birthed a new group** of blast related **TBI** recipients, who over the next 40 years will have to be dealt with. As many as 320,000 war veterans are estimated to have some form of TBI, and upwards of 60% of those were combat and blast related. This is the next *"Combat Concussion Crisis."*

Close to 20% of Iraq and Afghanistan veterans may have **PTS**, over 500,000 war veterans. Over forty years later, 4 of 5 Vietnam veterans also report recent symptoms of PTS. My father is one. As we age, other maladies will come along in life and how we handle those will be tested. Many of the injured are already working from a mental health deficit. *Also, many don't ask for help.*

I've learned it's not getting better, but with treatment, it's not yet getting worse. I fight my fight, **"Doing The Work** (DTW)," wondering if and when I'll deteriorate? Some estimates are that TBI victims are 50% more vulnerable to the onset of neurodegenerative diseases such as Chronic Traumatic Encephalopathy, Dementia, Parkinson's and Alzheimer's.

I've also learned I have a voice, something I can share with others about moving through this. I had no desire to write this. No desire at all. Although I've always enjoyed writing, all my passions have dissolved. In-depth thinking manifests pain, which can bring me to my knees. *Putting this on paper was physically painful, redundantly painful.* But the pain is going to be there anyway. Might as well get the most out of it. There are lessons here. *My story relates how I "Do the Work" to strengthen my mental health "Chain."*

Two people stood out as I wrote this. The first, legendary Chicago Bears football player **Dave Duerson**, 50, who called his headaches *"Starburst Headaches."* The other, **Lt. Col. Raymond**

Rivas, 51, who was my age when first blown up in an explosion. His headaches took over his life. My neurologists called mine TBI, Post Concussion Syndrome, Chronic Migraines, SUNCT, even Cluster Headaches; but since first being hit, I've called it, **Brain Pain**. Calling them "Headaches" just minimizes their description.

Everyday, as thoughts get jammed in my head, hundreds of electrical shock-like explosions occur in my brain. It's 24/7. Literally hundreds of thousands since being hit; first thing in the morning until I finally make it to sleep. Nine years out, they are still there. Whether they're smoldering in the background, or sending bolts of lighting though my skull, there's not a day that goes by that I don't endure them. Like an electric fly zapper, snapping and tasering my brain, scattering any coherent thoughts I might have at that time.

My memory fails me on a regular basis. I can't remember significant events, days or weeks in my life. I have the photos, but it's like there's a stranger in them; not me. I just can't remember. I'm lost inside my brain, trying to find my way out.

Having just turned 60, I want what I can remember; my memories, thoughts, and values; where I've been, what I've done, to be preserved for the future. Five, ten, fifteen years from now, this journal, which turned into a manuscript, is my way of preserving the stories of my life. Maybe someday, in my old age, somebody will read them back to me.

No "woe is me" here. I made the decisions that got me here. My soul told me that this was the table I wanted to play at. They're offering you Baghdad. Hell, yeah! That's my table. There's my chair. Let's play! My soul also knew the consequences. I've known them my whole life. I learned them early on. I learned them while my father was at Khe Sanh, Vietnam in 1968. I learned them on the day the Green Sedan full of Military Officers in their full-dress uniforms pulled into our cul-de-sac. The "Notification Team." When that officer stepped out of that car and stared directly into my eyes, the game was real.

*There are **lessons** here of understanding and coping with this "Invisible Wound."* I grew up in the same house with these wounds, and then they moved into mine. Everything here is my story, true and the best recollection of my memories.

I wanted to tell this story from my perspective. No ghostwriter.

BRAIN PAIN

In other words, I had to "Do The Work (**DTW**)." My "Defective" brain translating MY thoughts into MY words. *I will end up repeating myself, but this is my new brain's voice and I appreciate the readers' understanding of this.* **Don't expect Hemingway, but do expect the honest and raw voice of the damaged mind of a warfighter.**

Putting these words down has been a cathartic and healing process, reinforcing and strengthening my resolve. It has also been painful, both emotionally and physically.

Since, this memoir is about how we fight TBI and PTS, I'll be discussing only our blast related deployment events.

This isn't a combat story; it's more of a "**back here**" story. *This is my perspective of how I fight what I call, Chaos.* It's my nemesis that could, one day, kill me. It has tried. It's a fight for my life. As with any fight that's worth fighting, you've got to come up with a plan: a plan of how to train, prepare, adapt and survive. *Chaos* is always there, lurking and waiting for an opening.

This is my management plan or my long-term management strategy. No simple "One, two, three and you're good." It's a continuous new lifestyle of "Doing The Work."

I'd grown up the son of a Marine, a combat veteran of Korea and Vietnam. I had already seen and lived under the umbrella of Traumatic Brain Injury and Post Traumatic Stress. Then it happened to me.

My dad's nightmares are still vivid in my mind and seared into my character. The lessons of my childhood motivated me to *"nip this in the bud."* I had no desire to be *Defective* too.

We are just now acknowledging blast related TBI's, but much like football concussions, the real manifestations are yet to be realized; ten, twenty, thirty, forty years from now. This will be the *next concussion crisis.* **The PTS crisis could be even worse.**

There are thousands of professional athletes, hundreds of thousands of military warfighters, and millions of civilians, fighting this injury. This is my journey, but it could easily be the journey of so many others, civilians and military, who suffer with TBI and PTS...

Chaos has found cracks in my armor.

ANTHONY JONES

Dad with his hand over his heart during the raising of the flag, during the siege of Khe Sanh, Vietnam. Once a Marine, always a Marine!

CHAPTER 2

KHE SANH

"Preparation"

It was 1967 and Dad had been in Khe Sanh, Vietnam, for several months. The famous "Siege of Khe Sanh" was some of the heaviest fighting going on to date. The nightly TV news never let us forget it. *Back here*, my Mom kept us busy allowing us to be the kids we were. Yet, the reality was we were young warriors in training. Those constant reminders on the news never allowed us to really be kids. Then one day, a day I'll never forget, the Marine Corps green sedan pulled up and turned into our cul-de-sac. It was just after Christmas. I had just gotten off the school bus and was walking towards our apartment. The Marine Officers stepped out, in full dress uniforms. One of the officers turned to me, his eyes catching my eager stare. They were in full military dress and I instantly knew what that meant. They were the "notification team." He saw that I was standing on the walkway leading to our apartment door, then looked to me and slightly shook his head. He had silently told me he wasn't here for us. I can remember the guilty tears running down my cheek as the men walked over to another home and knocked on the door. ***My father was alive and their father was dead.*** I wasn't prepared, I was a kid.

BRAIN PAIN

My father and I both survived our second combat deployments with eerie similarities. Me in Baghdad, and my Father is on a mountain plateau in South Vietnam called Khe Sanh. *Preparation, training and adapting can equal survival.*

Dad was born a survivor. Raised poor, when push came to shove, he made it happen or made it work. He was good at anything and everything he wanted to be good at. Baptized in the Marines as an Infantryman and Artilleryman, he rose through the enlisted ranks, into the officer corps, retiring as a Captain. Next, he joined the Border Patrol and after another twenty years, retired with over 10,000 fixed wing and helicopter flight hours.

Growing up, Dad and his older brother, Ben, both worked the farms. Extremely close, they were tall, handsome and built like bulls. During his teens, he moved to Norfolk, Virginia, living with his sister, Hilda, and her husband, Roger. He got a job at Birchard's Dairy, where Ben and his future wife, Yula, both worked. Being the youngest, it was a matter of survival. Dad excelled mainly due to his ability to fix machines, keeping them running. By now he had developed an abundance of redneck pride and values; family, hard work, perseverance, responsibility and the ability to make broken things work.

There were dozens of moments that defined the future of my father's character, but the one that always stood out is the story of Uncle Joe Wall. You see my father saw his Uncle Joe develop cancer. He had no health insurance and died a horrible death. Dad vowed to always have medical insurance. That meant getting out, getting an education and finding a job with benefits. Easier said than done in those days.

He joined the Marine Corps in September of 1953 and in January of 1954, deployed to South Korea, on the Demilitarized Zone, with the NATO peacekeeping forces. The armistice between the United States, Korea and China had been signed six months earlier, in July of 1953, but failed to bring about permanent peace. Dad was assigned to a Marine Artillery battery, which also had service members from Australia, Canada and Britain attached. As an artilleryman, the experience, training and preparation he honed for eighteen months on the hills of South Korea would, years later, serve him well on a mountain plateau in South Vietnam.

After overseas training he returned to the states and was stationed in Camp Pendleton, California, where he continued advanced training. This is the area around Oceanside in Southern California. It was 1955. Shortly after he got there, he met my mom, *Anna.* She was 21 and he was 20. She was Mexican-American, born in Houston, Texas, but raised in Mexico. She was also a chorus girl in a traveling musical production. Her father passed away from a cerebral hemorrhage and her mother of Tuberculosis. Her father's name was Elpidio Serato Cortes, and her mother's, Julia Cortes Quijano. She has no memories of them and was raised by her brother and sisters. *Another survivor.*

It was at the musical show that they first met. Dad was instantly smitten with her, as she was with him. He was Western European looking and 6'2" and she was Hispanic and 5'5". (It was also during the mid-nineteen fifties and racism was a huge issue) He was James Dean and she was Lena Horne. Dad pursued her relentlessly until they were married and next year I was born.

There was nothing my father couldn't do. *He's a jack-of-all-trades.* Starting off as an enlisted man, he shined at his job and was selected to become a temporary Officer when the Vietnam War began. Because of a shortage of educated young Officers, a need developed for experienced enlisted Non-Commissioned Officers (NCO) to become commissioned. With orders to Vietnam on the way, he accepted an Officer's Commission. A very large promotion

In preparation for his deployment, we all moved to on-base housing at Camp Pendleton. Dad had hurt his back and was going through physical therapy, before he could deploy. We knew what was coming, but rarely discussed it.

Dad was our protector. *To me he was John Wayne.* Tall, handsome, strong, confident and smart; all the things I wanted to be. A few years earlier we were in North Carolina, where my dad's family was from. We were in the woods, hunting. My uncles Wiley and Jerry were with us. I was quietly walking out in front, when out of nowhere a boar came charging towards me. I froze. Dad then calmly raised his gun and shot him dead, just a few feet in front of me. It was actually probably a escaped pig, but I was a kid and everything was monster sized to me. Either way, he's a badass, he's John Wayne, and I wanted to be just like him.

BRAIN PAIN

Once dad left for Vietnam, my mom, Anna, became our support system; both mother and father. I was in the fifth and sixth grade, my sister **Pamela**, the fourth and fifth, and my younger brother **Marcos**, pre-school. I was eleven years old and had already moved ten times. It was the height of the sixties. Peace signs, flower power and rock music were the scene. The Doors, Jimi Hendrix and the Beatles were the sounds. I was into model cars, my sister just finding her fashion sense and my baby brother was bouncing around, a mile a minute.

We got used to Dad being gone. Traveling on what we called, "maneuvers" (war games), as well as being a member of the Marine Corps Rifle and Pistol team, took him on the road a lot. Initially, we didn't understand war. The more we started learning about it, the more we realized men were dying and some fathers were not coming home. As our father left, the news on Khe Sanh wasn't at the forefront, but later news about it would become an addiction for us as we grasped for any information on what was happening there. *The realization would set in as the daily body counts were growing.*

Dad had always been a big news fan. When he was home his priorities were his job (providing for the family), his shooting team, his golf and reading and watching the news. Towards Christmas of that year, the fighting was growing heavier and heavier, and the news and TV dinners were the nightly staple. *Later, in February and March, the height of the "Siege", news coverage of Khe Sanh populated 25% of all media.*

The importance of Khe Sanh was related to its position amongst rugged mountains that formed a natural boundary between South Vietnam in Laos. The North Vietnamese were using the Ho Chi Minh trail to resupply their troops in the South. Unbeknownst to many, the Ho Chi Minh trail ran all through and around Laos and back into South Vietnam. The weather was hot, rainy and humid and the terrain was rugged and unforgiving. The importance of Khe Sanh came down to two basic reasons: One, to interdict and interrupt the resupply along the Ho Chi Minh Trail and Two, to conduct secret intelligence gathering missions into Laos against the North Vietnamese.

From 1962-1964, Vietnamese engineers built an airstrip atop the plateau we commonly came to know as Khe Sanh Marine base. In October of 1966, General Westmoreland had the Khe Sanh airstrip upgraded and placed the first Battalion of Marines there. Khe Sanh would soon become the base from which the Marines attacked and engaged the North Vietnamese on the border and in Laos.

It was October of 1967 when my father, 1st Lt. Walter K. Jones, arrived at Khe Sanh. It was one of the most remote outposts in Vietnam. By now he was a career Marine. Already 15 years into his military service and the Assistant Operations Officer of the First Battalion, 13th Marines, Ninth Marine Amphibious Brigade. Initially, there were minimal contacts and sparse incoming fire. Although they were taking casualties from reconnaissance missions and perimeter probes, the main attack was still months away.

His commander had discovered that Dad was an experienced artilleryman and surveyor, and they desperately needed surveyors, so he was tasked. This meant surveying the inner and outer perimeters, training, making repairs, reviewing the fire direction computers, simulating firing positions and shooting for accuracy. The air was thick with boiling humidity. The ground was layered with red clay and green foliage covering it like moss. The red clay filled thousands of sand bags, and the foliage was cleared to build out the base. Everyone knew something big was coming. The perimeter was constantly being tested. The enemy (North Vietnamese Army, NVA) was knocking on their door and preparation was at hand. *Everything my father had learned in Korea would now pay dividends.*

Dad's always been a stickler for details. *"**If you're going to do it, take the time to do it right.**"* As he began to survey the base, looking at its strengths and vulnerabilities, one of the first things he noticed was that the water supply point was outside of the perimeter. This didn't seem right, since the enemy could easily block it or poison it. He went to the command bunker to mention it to one of his friends. He said, "Who's the boy scout who set up the water point outside the perimeter?" His friend's face tightened, then out from a room divider came Colonel Lownds, the base commander. A brief introduction and ass chewing ensued. Well, to say the least, Col. Lownds had it in for him from that day on. Although the water point supply was never poisoned, it was constantly being blocked and cut off, increasing the need for air support to bring in more water. First impressions? Dad can be brutally honest, but he was usually right.

Continuing his survey, Dad recommended the TACAN TRN-17 radio antenna be moved outward toward the perimeter. Positioned near the heavily populated base headquarters, the antenna needed to be moved outward, where it was less populated because it was currently in the middle of the base and was sure to be a target when they were attacked. This was no normal radio antenna; it was on top of a deuce and a half, a cargo truck, with another twenty-foot protrusion on top, which looked like a water tower, making it an easily visible target. If the enemy could destroy it, the base would be unable to call in support. They could lose most communications. Once the siege began, it was constantly targeted. All of the relentless targeting was damaging the command post as well as the surrounding buildings.

All of the tension in the air and premonitions of being attacked after months of suspected build up, was explosively shattered the morning of January 21st, 1968, as the siege of Khe Sanh began. That morning the shelling began around 5:00 am as the People's Army of North Vietnam began a massive artillery campaign against the Marine Corps outpost.

The sleeping bunkers were 2 to 4 feet underground. The holes would be dug out, sandbags placed around them, with makeshift roofs built of plywood, mud and more sandbags. Marines are the epitome of adaptation. To improvise, adapt and overcome. These words embody my father. He is an expert at surviving; water, food and shelter. Improving, fixing, sharing and trading it.

Dad, sleeping in his bunker, was awoken by a barrage of artillery, rocket and mortar explosions. The continuous thunderous explosions blasted red clay, mud and sand super-sonically through the air creating a red-brown mist over the entire base. The smell of the moist dirt mixed with heated explosive smoke was choking him.

Simultaneous explosions had announced his call to action as he charged out of his bunker, running, under fire, the 200 yards to the Fire Direction Center (FDC). *This was when he was first hit*. An incoming round landed approximately 25 feet away. The concussive wave blasted sand - like shrapnel through his uniform and into his skin, and sent shrapnel into his left ankle. Picking himself up, as Marines do, he made it to the FDC, manned his station, barked out orders and returned fire. Simultaneously that morning, the North's artillery had also hit the main ammo dump. When the ammo dump exploded, so did around 50,000 rounds of ammunition, mostly artillery. If there is such a thing as hell, that's probably what it looked like. The fight of their lives had begun and their day of reckoning was at hand. This is what they prepared for.

He didn't realize that he was hit until later. Only when his boot became warm and soggy did he notice the blood. "On 21 January, 1968, the Khe Sanh Combat Base came under an intense enemy mortar and rocket attack. Although the Fire Direction Center received several direct hits from the enemy fire, First Lieutenant JONES demonstrated outstanding professional ability by skillfully supervising his men in controlling effective counter-mortar fire from five separate artillery positions." This was an excerpt from Dad's awards certificate. *He did what Marines do, get up and back in the fight to protect his Marines.* He lived through his first massive artillery barrage and first hit. There would be more to come. Twenty other Marines died that day.

From that morning, the siege would be almost nonstop. As an artilleryman, keeping your guns up and working was a invariable priority. They would get shelled and the guns would get damaged, then they would go into repair mode. Repair mode meant they would assist the wounded, then diagnose and repair any damaged guns and get them firing back, as well as addressing their constantly changing tactical options. *Fight. Bleed. Repeat.*

The attack was also a distraction for the Tet Offensive, which was the foremost battle, planned by the North Vietnamese. The North believed the US Forces would be required to use more troops defending Khe Sanh, thus making it easier for them to take the southern cities they were actually after. Ho Chi Minh, the Vietnamese President, was near death and they wanted a victory before he died. Normally, during the Vietnamese New Year, there was an agreed upon truce in the fighting. The North broke the truce, catching our forces off guard, launching major attacks on multiple southern cites deep inside South Vietnam. Although US Forces retook all the cities weeks later, it was a psychological victory for the NVA because it showed Americans here at home that the war was far from over.

During the day, the shelling would start and stop, the sky would fill with flack, the fog would come and go, they would tend to the wounded and dead, and fire out up to 6000 rounds a day, versus 800-

BRAIN PAIN

1000 rounds incoming. Deafening sounds, horrific sights, nauseous smells, sulfuric tastes and everything gritty and wet to the touch. It was a constant sensory overload, testing the will to survive as well as the fortitude to move through, multi-tasking to each one's limits. The North Vietnamese Army (NVA) had a total of over 24 battalions (20,000) to the US's 6 battalions (5,000) at Khe Sanh Combat base. It was a maelstrom of fighting and bleeding. *Fight. Bleed. Repeat.*

There was occasional down time during the siege. After all, the North Vietnamese thought they could take Khe Sanh and were persistent to say the least, feeling the timetable was theirs.

A week into the siege, the only working generator used to power the Fire Direction computers got hit. This barrage of incoming fire lasted almost an hour, battering the area around the TACAN antenna, the intended target. There were two generators. One was already down. This now meant both were down. When the computers don't work, the outbound fire isn't accurate and timely. Without the computers, the computations must be done manually, which takes more time. The faster their guns become accurate, the faster they can silence the enemy's artillery. The generators needed to be fixed.

Dad ran to the freshly damaged generator, diagnosed the situation, ran to the broken generator, cannibalized it for parts, ran back, replaced the parts and got it running – all while under fire. This took almost an hour. Generators up, computers up, accuracy back on target, enemy eliminated quicker. *Improvise, adapt and overcome.*

Towards the third week in February, **Dad was hit again.** He was moving to cover, as incoming began, when a artillery round hit about 15 feet away, on the opposite side of the sandbags. The blast sent shards of rock, shrapnel and sand at him, tossing him to the ground and knocking him out. Once he woke up, there wasn't much time for recovery because he needed to get his guns up. The adrenaline pushed him through and he made it to the FDC. Afterwards, the Corpsmen would spend several hours scraping out the sand from underneath the skin on his face. That day he just happened to have his glasses on. They were sandblasted. Had he not had them on, it would have blinded him. Close calls were the norm. If you lived, you moved through and forward. *Fight. Bleed. Repeat.*

Incoming artillery, mortars and perimeter probes weren't the only threats; there were also threats inside the wire (secure perimeter). Khe Sanh Village was just south of the base. It was full of local nationals, with an Army Special Forces (SF) camp next to it. The SF camp had been set up by our forces, to protect and assist the locals. Khe Sanh base employed many of the local nationals to help them out with cleaning, maintenance, logistics and building. One day, Dad noticed what he called the "Big Villager." This was a Vietnamese worker who was about 30% larger than the average Vietnamese. He didn't fit in. Instinct told my Dad something was amiss. He reported this to intelligence and the next day they caught that "Big Villager" pacing out the camp.

Accurate measurements from inside the base could lead to accurate fire from the enemy's artillery. But the enemy's long-range guns weren't accurate. The Fire Direction Center, the Command headquarters and the main radio antennas were high value targets to the enemy. The "Big Villager" managed to escape, but later when an attack on the perimeter occurred and was repelled, his body was found. When his body was laid out, Dad recognized him. He was a Major in the North Vietnamese Army.

In the morning, the thick, wet fog would cover the NVA's mountain top positions and they wouldn't have a good view of the base, so the Marines had a very short window of time to get some work done until it burned off. At night, the NVA couldn't see either; so, another window of time was available. That doesn't mean the night was quiet. After dark, the snipers and the perimeter probers would come out. Some of their snipers were competent, but most weren't. The perimeter prober's would search for weak spots in the perimeter, attempting to exploit any weaknesses.

Towards the later part of the siege, the enemy dug trenches closer and closer in towards the base perimeter. They dug the trenches deep and narrow, making them hard to see and harder to target. They dug tunnels as well. One night, two Marines on perimeter security heard something peculiar. They couldn't tell where it was coming from, until the ground caved in below them. Faced with two-surprised NVA, the Marines eliminated them. *From then on, dogs were used around the perimeter to sniff them out.*

BRAIN PAIN

Being overrun was in the back of everyone's mind. An Army Special Forces camp had been there since the summer of 1962. It was along route 9, a highway that ran south and around the east side of the Khe Sanh hill, just south and west of Khe Sanh village. The camp was just out of range of the Marines' artillery guns, but having been there for six years already, they were dug in. Unfortunately, two weeks after the siege began, February 6th, the camp was overrun.

Being overrun and taken prisoner was a real possibility. They were under constant attack and under siege. There was no doubt the NVA were coming and no doubt they'd be dealt with. This was the Marines' marker in history. *Most of them, like my father, had already come to terms with it and would decide to not be taken - to go out fighting.* **To this day, being captured is the running theme of his nightmares.**

Dad was always an out-of-the-box thinker and under these conditions, he definitely had a lot of time to think. Surviving will prioritize everything clearly. If he was told something couldn't be done, it gave him all the more reason to figure out how to do it. Now that the siege was going strong and they were getting hit daily, he wanted to figure out how to use every piece of equipment available to them. He was constantly coming up with ideas; whether asked or not.

The 4.2" mortar, or four deuce, batteries weren't being used much. Mortars are short tubes, fired at steep angles, so the projectile flies high and comes down directly on the enemy. They're lightweight, adjustable for azimuth and distance, and very mobile. Dad had trained on these in Korea and more extensively at Camp Pendleton, after his return.

Initially, because of the dense jungle, reconnaissance units would occasionally get lost. You could use the four deuce to airburst a round in the general direction, then through communication with the team, have them orient on either the sound or the visual, fine tuning it down to a fix on their location. It worked, getting them oriented for extraction. Not standard use, but definitely, out-of-the-box, thinking.

Hunger pains were the norm so there weren't many fat Marines. Due to all the fighting and anti-aircraft artillery, the base had a very hard time getting re-supplied. The food got low, only C rations (much like today's Meals Ready To Eat – MRE'S) for a while, and each Marine was delegated two meals a day and approximately 8 to

16 ounces of water. The sparsity of food and water often led to constipation. You could go days without any relief. One day, after a few days of constipation and a lengthy round of incoming, Dad was finally overwhelmed with the pain of needing to go. He was in the Fire Direction bunker and this would mean running through the incoming artillery and mortar rounds, to reach the latrine. Finally, during a lull in the incoming, he said, "Screw it!" and made the run. *Just as he got there, another mortar round hit it.* They found him underneath the debris, bloodied, where the latrine used to be, a pounding headache, ringing in his ears and several shrapnel tears in his vest and his legs.

During any siege the trash is going to pile up. With that trash is going to come rats. Here the rats were growing to the size of cats. There are several documented cases where Marines had to be medevac'd due to being attacked by these giant rats. Dad remembers when one woke him up by pulling out a chunk of his hair for its nest. Marines became adept at their counter-rat tactics, with spears, blowguns and homemade arrows. I'm sure a few saw the round end of a 45 caliber. There were also rock apes just outside the perimeter. They were endearingly called this because they loved to throw rocks at everyone, including Marines. *To this day, monkeys fascinate Dad.*

The last several months during Vietnam had been a time of many firsts for me. My first time surfing, skateboarding, the first time I confronted a bully, and my first kiss. All the stuff normal kids do. What normal kids *didn't* do was watch daily news reports of their father's firebase get pounded over and over. We'd look at all the TV reports and look to see if we could spot Dad in the background. We'd wait until the end of the news hour, holding our breaths to see the body counts and where the unending battles were being fought. Is one of those dead my father? We'd also endure the nightmares of our father not returning.

Half a world away, the news was always a day late. It was the norm, watching Walter Cronkite and the devastating situation that was the siege at Khe Sanh. Even back then, the news could be graphic. At the end of the news they would review how many soldiers had been Killed In Action (KIA) or Wounded In Action (WIA,) and we would pray those men in the green car would never show up at our house.

BRAIN PAIN

The morning of **March 4th, 1968**, was a Monday. It started off as every other day had. Incoming all night, then quiet time, both sides getting some sleep and food, then more incoming. As the next incoming began, around eight or nine in the morning, my dad was hit for the fourth and final time. He was coming out of a bunker to join the fight. *This time a rocket landed 10-12 feet away.* Shrapnel fragments pierced the sandbags, protecting him to his right, and peppered the entire length of his right leg. The concussion from the blast knocked him out, and a large three-inch piece of metal shrapnel stuck just above his right knee, cutting into his right femoral artery.

Some very brave Marines pulled him to cover, and then another brave corpsman found his leaking artery and pinched it off. The concussion and blood loss forced him in and out of consciousness. He was moved to the regimental aid station where he had multiple blood transfusions from other Marines. This bought him some time. Later that afternoon, he was loaded into the back of a CH-46 medevac helicopter. This process was a dangerous one, in itself. These incoming medevac helicopters were constantly under fire. The pilots were flying into a smoke filled and smoldering hot zone. Automatic weapons and anti-aircraft artillery filled the sky. They had to observe the area and judge their timing, because it all had to be done at high-speed. These missions were to resupply food, water and ammo, as well as medevac the wounded. Once the pilots committed, they knew they would be drawing enemy fire. Down and land, hold, then up and out. For the pilots, the holding is always the hardest part.

The aid station was a deep bunker built close to the airstrip, where the wounded were pre-positioned. When the helicopters touched down and the signal given, the medevac detail, already waiting in trenches or behind bunkers, two men with a stretcher, would run out to the chopper, load, then run back. *Dad's last memories were of the initial climb out.* Due to the anti-aircraft artillery, the pilots powered up and out as fast as they could. Dad later discovered that, during ascent, their helicopter had taken multiple hits. He was medevac'd back to Da Nang and woke up there. The surgeons saved the leg, put his arteries back together and pulled out as much shrapnel as they could. Much of it was left in to work its way out later and he was eventually flown out to Saigon, then Japan.

ANTHONY JONES

It was Monday, March 4, 1968, the 47th day of the siege of Khe Sanh. The siege lasted for another 30 days, for a total of 77 days. That morning three others died. Lance Cpl. Dennis Mutz, Lance Cpl. Roger Yamanaka and Pfc. Donald Saunders. [1] During the siege, more bombs fell on Khe Sanh than the entire eighth Air Force dropped on Berlin and Frankfurt, from 1944 to 1945. *It was also the fourth and final time 1st Lt. Walter K. Jones was hit.*

After returning from his first-hand experience of the Vietnam War, TV anchorman Walter Cronkite announced gravely, *"For it seems now more certain than ever, that the bloody experience of Vietnam is to end in a stalemate."* After this, President Johnson stated, *"If I've lost Cronkite, I've lost middle America."* Soon afterwards, he decided not to run for a second term.

There was no formal military spouse network or support system, but they all supported each other. Everyone in our cul-de-sac knew one another. It was an informal, ad hoc support system. The **wives** experienced collective anger, fear, frustration and stress of raising their families as single parents. They took care of each other. Mom was having coffee with one of the wives when the mail arrived. Dad sent a simple postcard saying he was fine, and his new address. No other details. The other wife noticed the postmark was from a Hospital in Okinawa, Japan. Together, they contacted the Red Cross, and got through to the hospital in Japan. Dad was caught off guard when he answered the phone and it was Mom. He was back home within a week.

Mom answered the door when the knock came. It was the Green Sedan, with the Marine Officers in their dress uniforms. The official "Notification Team." They nervously completed the notification, that Dad had been wounded and that he was in stable condition. She said, "I know, he's sitting on the couch." The notification came late, to say the least. He had lost 30 pounds, but he was home, telling jokes and complaining that our hair was too long. We were happy with that.

Dad's physical injuries almost put an end to his career. If he were unable to run, he wouldn't be able to pass his physical training (PT) test. His Medical Evaluation Board (MEB) tried to move him out of the Marines, *but he worked overtime to rehab* his legs and ankle. Several months later, he was able to pass his PT test. *He showed us how to do the work, overcome the challenges and press on.*

BRAIN PAIN

He had been blown up four times and knocked out twice. *There were no tests for Traumatic Brain Injury (TBI) back then and the mere mention of an Anxiety Disorder, now known as Post Traumatic Stress (PTS), was a career ender.* **PTS made you look weak.**

Dad earned the Navy Achievement Medal with the combat "V" device for Valor, the Purple Heart, the Combat Action Ribbon and the Presidential Unit Citation, the same valor required for the Navy Cross. There were no celebrations; no, "Thank you for your service," remarks; parades or ceremonies; just a welcome home from his family, lots of his favorite home cooked Mexican meals and the beginning of a lifetime of fighting new battles.

He fought for his life and the lives of other Marines, survived, and returned home. So many hadn't. He had a family to care for, so he moved through the negatives and went on with life, never once complaining. Survival, love of family and love of country are traits I inherited. Training, preparation and adapting were traits taught to me by my father. *I had grown up in his shadow, and the darkness Vietnam had left him with.*

Even as a kid I knew that adapting *back here* would mean a lifetime of overcoming the twin specters of mood swings and anger as well as a litany of other new challenges.

Dad and mom on the couch after his return from Vietnam. He made it.

26

CHAPTER 3

BAGHDAD

"Pedaling fast"

One of my earliest memories was of my father placing me on a tightrope of fear, and then pushing me through. We were living in Hawaii when *he taught me how to ride a bike.* I was barely four years old. Some people have good memories about this, some people don't. I don't. But what I do know is that's where it started. That's where my training and preparation began. Being forced to master something, so unnatural and so quickly, with threatening urgency, is exceedingly intimidating as a child. But, there was no choice. I was a Marine's son. ***It was time to pedal.***

My dad put me on the bike, barked out his Marine Corps orders, guided, pushed and yelled at me to **"Pedal now**!" I would pedal, try to balance, then fall, and then repeat. My dad was young and didn't know how to train a kid. He did know how to train Marines, and that's how he trained my sister and me. *What I didn't realize until years later was that* ***the real lesson was about-facing your anxieties.*** The earlier I learned this, the stronger I'd become. ***Pedal. Bleed. Repeat.***

Within 30 minutes, I could ride a bike. From that very early lesson I began my training. I had learned one of the most important lessons in my life: moving through my anxieties. I pedaled harder and faster, adjusting my weight, balancing, and maneuvering not to fall. Success meant the pleasure of riding a bicycle, and failure meant the angst of my dad yelling and pain of hitting the ground. Fear of failure replaced my fear of falling. Choice was simple - pedal fast.

I have come to believe that everything you've ever learned, including cultural traditions, education, your genetic heritage, all the training and preparation during your life, is subliminally manifested as your instincts. When that little voice calls, listen. ***"Trust your instincts, there's no time for second guessing."*** It's the one tidbit of advice on combat from my father and it would later save my life.

In 1978 I received my bachelor degree in Criminal Justice from George Mason University. I had grown up the son of "John Wayne," our protector, so becoming a "protector" myself, just like my father, seemed to fit my direction. I'd already served 21 years as a Marine Brat, so the Air Force and traveling the world, appealed to me.

We are an extremely patriotic family and the military was in my blood, so after college, I applied too, and was accepted into the Air Force Flight program. After getting my Officers commission, I went off to flight school, getting my wings in 1980. Next, I was off to Electronic Warfare training, then Survival School, Water Survival and then to Survive, Evade, Resist and Escape (SERE) School. SERE school is where they teach you how to resist torture, as well as learn communication and escape skills. The prevailing enemies at the time were the Russians and other communist countries, so many of the Vietnam era torture techniques were used. I was sleep deprived, water tortured, stuffed into a small bamboo box, and much more. This was an authentic experience.

In April of 1981, in the mountains of the northwest, I experienced one of the most memorable moments in my life. On a rainy night, after several weeks of SERE training, my peers and I were paraded outside. Cold and bewildered, we endured a lengthy communist orientated speech in the darkness, then suddenly, lights came on and we were told to turn around. In the brightness of the searchlights was the American Flag. *Our purpose waved brightly in the skies and Patriotism flowed through our veins.*

After this, I ended up at my new Squadron, the **Eighth Special Operations Squadron**, at Hurlburt Field, Florida. This was in Fort

Walton Beach, near Pensacola, on the northwest panhandle of the Gulf. My newly assigned aircraft was an MC-130, an Air Force Special Operations cargo aircraft, nicknamed the "**Combat Talon**." It was famous for the covert operations during Vietnam. It was the same unit that flew classified teams into Iran for "Desert One (1980)," Grenada for "Urgent Fury (1983)," Panama for "Just Cause (1989)" and Desert Storm (1991). More recently in Iraq and Afghanistan. The mission was low-level delivery and insertion of Special Operation Forces behind enemy lines. At this squadron, I would join my new Air Force family, meeting some great friends and mentors, like Lt. Col. Thomas Mosley, Lt. Col. James Hobson, Capt. Rick Gentry and Lt. Eric Fiel. I was surrounded by excellence and met some of the greatest people and took on some of the greatest challenges in my life. I was now an "*American Airman*."

In 1984, I was selected to become a Special Ops Air Liaison Officer, ALO, attached to a Joint Special Operations Command (JSOC) in Little Creek, Virginia. It was temporary, for the annual exercise "Ocean Venture." *It was exciting because I got to work from a ground component, having always viewed operations as aircrew prior to this.* I worked with four Army Special Forces Operators and three Navy SEALs. One of those operators, *Dave Messer*, a Special Forces Vietnam Veteran, would become of one my best friends and mentors. The experience working these Joint Operations, would come back to assist me many years later in Iraq.

In August 1990 Saddam Hussein invaded Kuwait. At that time, I was an Instructor at the **Combat Aircrew Training School** at Nellis AFB in Las Vegas. My schoolhouse colleagues and I were deployed throughout Saudi Arabia to train up as many of our C-130 and Helicopter crewmembers as possible. This was my second trip to the Middle East. The first one was training (Jordan) and this one was real. I can remember briefing after briefing, and how we made the distinction that we were facing one of the most formidable military forces in the world. At the time, Russia was supplying Iraq with state-of-the-art equipment: radars, aircraft, surface to air missiles, long-range ballistic missiles, etc. *The buildup took months, and then the war was over in a blink of an eye.*

After returning, we spent much of our time rewriting the books on our portion of Operation Desert Shield/Desert Storm. We took lessons that our brothers had learned and rewrote the operational directives to get it all down while fresh in our minds. The deployment left us feeling as if our service had made a difference.

Those years at the schoolhouse allowed me the opportunity of surrounding myself, and interacting with some of the **best Airmen** in the Air Force. These guys were the best at what they did. Hopefully, some of that rubbed off on me. I was at the top of my game, riding my bike through a motocross course of ups and downs, with cliffs on both sides. *Pedaling fast and balancing on the tightest of trails. Thanks Dad!*

When the United States went to war with Iraq, in 2003, I was a Major in the Air Force Reserves. I spent 12 years on active duty, with the Eighth Special Operations Squadron in Florida, flying as a Electronic Warfare Officer (EWO), and later as an Instructor EWO with Combat Aircrew Training School in Las Vegas, NV. I spent another 12 years in the reserves where I worked for Joint Forces Command (JFCOM), as **Personnel Recovery Officer**, assigned to the Joint Personnel Recovery Agency (JPRA). As a civilian, I was a Personal Protection Specialist and Investigator. My company "**Core Group Security**" provides high net worth companies with bodyguards and corporate security solutions. I had been preparing and training, either in the military or on my own, most of my adult life.

By 2006, most Americans had tired of the Iraq and Afghanistan war and called for the US to get out. But in January of 2007, President Bush announced the "**New Way Forward**" regarding an increase of troops being deployed there. This would increase the number of American troops in Iraq by 30,000 US warfighters, providing additional security to Baghdad and the Al Anbar province, the western part of the country where the Marines were.

Back in the US, the media called George W. Bush's plan "**The Surge**." Prior to this, there was an extremely violent sector in Iraq, with thousands of civilians being killed each month and death squads roaming the streets of Baghdad. "The Surge" was primarily in response to the extreme increase in violence. What most Americans did not understand was that "The Surge" did indeed work and the violence did decrease with the arrival of the additional troops. When the death squads were dispatched, the violence and deaths significantly decreased. By July of 2008, the violence had decreased

ANTHONY JONES

to its lowest level since the spring of 2004. It made sense; more troops would have a stronger military presence to prevent and quell new violence, giving us the ability to effectively train more Iraqi Army soldiers to take care of their own country.

It was the summer of 2007 and I was on my way. Our C-130 had broken on a searing hot tarmac. I had spent so many hours in a C-130 Hercules that I knew when the engines pulled back to idle, we had broken. Been there, done that. We were already strapped in the seats, soaked with sweat, when the loadmaster gave us the news. We needed to depart the aircraft, while they brought the part out and repaired it. 110 degrees in the shade, 120 degrees inside the back of the C-130 and 130 degrees on the tarmac. It was time to hurry up and wait. After thousands of C-130 hours, this was a phrase I was exceptionally familiar with. *But, this time I was sitting on the ramp in Kuwait, with a ticket directly into Baghdad.* I was happier than a tornado in a trailer park.

The night I arrived in Baghdad was a blur. But the next day it seemed all too familiar. August 28, 2007. It was about 100 degrees at night, but I was used to that. To me, it felt like the average, end of summer day, in Las Vegas, Nevada, my home.

Camp Victory was the largest US base in Iraq. It was located 3 miles from Baghdad International Airport. Twenty-seven miles of T-barriers, or concrete walls nine feet high encircled it. It was also the location of Al Faw Palace, one of ninety-nine that Saddam Hussein built during his tenure. It was built as a country club, casino, zoo and hunting and fishing lodge for Saddam and his entourage. It was also there to commemorate the victory of recapturing the Al Faw peninsula from the Iranians during the first Gulf war. It's a massively beautiful Middle Eastern citadel, complete with a trough, bridge and lake. It had boat docks for the ski boats, was stocked with four-foot-long fish, complete with paddleboats and jet skis. It was adorned by the Arabic symbol for Saddam Hussein's name that looked exactly like Mickey Mouse's face and ears. Hilarious. Everywhere you looked, there was the Disney character image of Mickey Mouse, which made Saddam Hussein look, to us, like a cartoon character.

The Al Faw Palace also became the headquarters of the Multi-National Force-Iraq (MNF-I) and housed the Joint Operations Center (JOC), where I worked, that controlled and oversaw Operation Iraqi

31

Freedom (OIF.) Walking around Camp Victory reminded me of the many bases I had stayed on during Desert Shield/Desert Storm in Saudi Arabia. Back in 1990 we were based out of Saudi Arabia with our targets being north to Iraq. Now I was in the middle of Iraq, in the capital. The difference was that this area had seen significant combat. There were reminders everywhere, buildings peppered and pockmarked from bullets, artillery and shrapnel. It was a surreal, but sobering reality.

I'd been deployed many times throughout my career and it all seemed familiar. The same dust, dirt, tents and trailers we had back in Desert Storm, but this time I was sitting smack-dab in the middle of Saddam Hussein's Palace Gardens and his now-converted country club grounds. We had come a long way since Desert Storm with pre-paid calling cards, phone booths, snail mail and MRE's (meals ready to eat). Now we had Pizza Hut, Taco Bell, Cinnabon, a base exchange, dining facility, television, bootleg movie stands, state of the art gym, Internet and cell phone service - for a price. Some things hadn't changed though. *My mom's gift boxes were still filled with her special oatmeal cookies.*

At the Joint Operations Center (JOC), I was the **Director of the Personnel Recovery Coordination Cell** (DPRC). A Command Air Force Officer reporting directly to, and working for the Army. My boss was Colonel Eduardo Gutierrez, Air Operations Commander. The Army controlled the majority of rescue assets in Iraq. We managed, analyzed, coordinated and oversaw all actionable rescues and recoveries.

Several months earlier President Bush had started "The Surge" and General Petraeus was named as the new Commander MNF-I. Gen. Petraeus was a West Point graduate, a Ranger school graduate and by the age of 46 had achieved the rank of a One Star General. In 2003, when the Iraq war begin, he commanded the 101st Airborne Division in Baghdad, Iraq, and, later, in Mosul. He was widely known as an expert on the Vietnam counter-insurgency, and had continued to develop his ideas throughout the first years of the war. His "Winning the hearts and minds" of the people position and calling for more troops finally led him to be named Commander of MNF-I in 2007.

The "Surge" or buildup of troops had not been lost on the insurgents. There were over 200 suicide and car bombs exploded per month, as well as hundreds of Indirect Fire (IDF) rounds, launched into US held area. The Al Faw Palace was constantly in the sights of the insurgency. It contained the Coalitions Command Center for all of Iraq. *That year there were an average of 400 attacks per month.*

Explosions and sirens were just part of our day and rocket attacks and "Dets" were commonplace. "Dets" were intentional detonations of enemy explosives that were found or captured. They were usually thunderous explosions, supposedly scheduled, but that rarely seemed the case. Rocket attacks were known as IDF attacks, meaning they weren't generally accurate or precise - more like throwing a baseball into a basketball goal, from half court. More than likely you'll be close, but not accurate. They were also not recorded unless they produced casualties.

Camp Victory had several Counter-Rocket Artillery, and Mortar (C-RAM) systems surrounding it. The first time I saw one was a few days after arriving. During a nighttime attack, the alarm claxon sounded. I put on my armor and went outside to get next to the T-barrier. As I looked up, a line of tracers snaked upwards and around the nighttime sky, filling it with lead. Basically, it was a radar controlled Gatling gun on steroids. It looked like a line of zippered mini-explosions, until it contacted an incoming round, which produced a much louder airburst. Hypnotized, I saw it hit an incoming rocket and explode. *It was really quite beautiful.*

On Sept. 10th, 2007, I had flown up to the Embassy in the Green Zone for a meeting with my Air Force Commander, Col. Williams. Later that afternoon my second meeting was with a group of Private Security Contractors, then off to the Embassy pool for lunch with a group of those 3 letter spook types (CIA). We brought our lunch outdoors to a poolside table, which had a pretty good view. In the middle of conversation, an incoming round landed a few hundred feet away. Nobody moved or flinched. Then the alarms sounded, and one of the guys looked at me and said, *"There's no time to run, so eat up."* And I did, as three more rounds landed in the not too far distance. I remember thinking, "Damn! That's a good club sandwich." that day. By the time I got back it was past midnight, and on the way out, I took a photo of myself sitting in the famous, iconic chair given to

BRAIN PAIN

Saddam Hussein by Yasar Arafat. I was still a tourist. Back at the bunk, I was able to get a few hours sleep as my second week came to an end.

The next day was **September 11, 2007**. It was mid-afternoon and I had just finished briefing my shift, then to a Commander's briefing. I was thinking of heading to the gym. There was a 9/11-remembrance service in the main hall, where by chance, I met up with one of my Rescue Controllers, *Bryan Callan*. He's a Warrant Officer, an Apache Pilot and an exceptional controller. Afterwards, since we were headed the same way, we walked out together. We were done, or so we thought.

Bryan was headed back to his trailer and I was headed to change and hit the gym, then dinner. Walking out of the palace daily was always a surreal experience. We walked out under these huge columns, across an ornamental bridge over a man-made lake, filled with four-foot-long fish, passing through a gate, and then emptying into a huge parking lot. We made it past the parking lot, just past the large concrete bomb shelters, where we said our goodbyes, then I went left and he went right. Minutes later, our lives would change.

It was just past 3:30 pm and shift change was ongoing. The parking lot had more people in it than normal and the buses were unloading dozens more. As I began to cross the street, a bus came around the corner, and then passed in front of me. Behind it was a Hummer that an acquaintance of mine, was driving. We spoke briefly, and then I began crossing the street. *As I stepped onto the sidewalk, an earsplitting roar came from overhead.* I heard what I thought was a F16 flying over me at about 200 feet. As I looked up into a clear and beautiful sky, I was momentarily dumbfounded. ***Shit, there are no jets flying over Baghdad!*** Little did I know, that would be the last clear, pain-free thought I would have. Then came the piercing explosion. **BOOM!**

First, the concussive wave passed through me, knocking me off my feet and slamming me to the ground. Simultaneously, air began filling every orifice in my body. *Like sticking a compressed air hose up my ass, in my nose and mouth.* There had been no sirens, no returning fire from the C-RAM radar controlled Gatling guns, just, *BOOM!*

A 20-foot hole in the ground spewed shrapnel and asphalt supersonically in all directions. Time slowed to a stop as the concussive wave and super heated air hit me, and I was almost 100 feet from center impact. In that split second I saw chunks of shrapnel cracking by my head and hitting the SUV next to me. It went from blue sky to a deafening, ringing roar of black sulfuric smoke and sandy beige mist in mere seconds. Opening my eyes, dark gray smoke filled my view. I couldn't hear, just a loud rumbling-distorted sound. As the smoky cloud cleared, I started to make out the devastation. *Time was still slowed down for the next 15-20 seconds, I just tried to orient, myself and assess the area around me.*

I'd been there long enough to know that when the shelling starts, it comes six to a dozen strong. Most likely, there were more on the way. The roaring growl in my ears slowly faded into a ringing, which distorted into screams. **Screams** *of death, fear and pain, which snapped me back to real time.* I stumbled getting up and realized I wasn't bleeding, but there were others who were. I staggered around trying to assess who was the worst, *and saw one warfighter who was squirting blood like a sliced radiator hose.* That meant he was in the most danger. I pressed my knee hard into his crotch, putting pressure on his femoral artery, slowing the leak. I then pressed my hand on it, holding pressure.

On my shoulder holster where I carried my weapon, I had attached a medium sized medical pouch. It went everywhere my gun and I went. When I opened the pouch, everything fell to the ground. I grappled around trying to get my gloves, gauze and bandages together, while yelling at him as he yelled at me. *Balancing my knee in his crotch (femoral artery) to slow the bleeding, I poured Quick Clot (a blood clotting powder) into the wound, then packed it with gauze and wrapped it with a Israeli bandage, making it as tight as possible.* I have no clue what he looked like, but the image of his leg and the wound are still vivid in my mind.

My mantra is, "*move through*." Two words I've always used to get me going. Thinking, "move through" over and over in my head, then screaming out questions and orders, helped to steady me. The screaming was because none of us could hear. We were all screaming and using hand signals to communicate the best we could. Those already in our vicinity, other uninjured warfighters, began the treatment and triage of the wounded. We were all working in the open and kept waiting for more rockets, *but not one left*, they all stayed on point. As we used up what was left of the gauze, others cut up uniforms. As quick as shreds of uniform were cut, they were handed out and placed on wounds to stop the bleeding. We then set up a triage for the most severely wounded. It was only minutes before the first vehicles arrived and they were loaded on board.

*It had been a **240 mm**, Iranian made rocket.* It's about the size of a large oxygen tank and carries over 100 pounds of explosives. One Third Country National was killed and thirteen others were wounded. CWO3 *Bryan Callan* had survived as well. He was just outside of the parking lot, but the blast had given him a concussion, later to be diagnosed as TBI. It was all over within three to four minutes.

I called into my office for a head count and was told all my people were accounted for. My adrenaline was surging. My head was pounding and my ears were ringing. Other than checking in, there's not much to do afterwards. You're still fueled up and your mind keeps reviewing it over and over. Now the shakes came, as I faltered, robotically, back to my trailer to change my blood-spattered flight suit. I'd walk fifty yards; lose my balance, dry heave and repeat, until I reached my trailer. The concussion I'd just incurred began taking its toll. After changing, still dazed, I went to the nearest bus stop. *I got on and found a seat and spent the next half hour or so just riding, watching life through the window.* I eventually ended up at the Support Hospital, only to leave with a bottle of Ibuprofen. ***But, there was an ecstasy going on, and I was alive to feel it!***

My insomnia began shortly afterwards as the nightmares began taking their toll. I knew I needed to sleep, but because of the nightmares, I fought sleep. *The incident had been on Tuesday and by Friday, the Brain Pain was born.*

The mixture of headaches, ringing in the ears, nightmares, and memory confusion was becoming my new reality. *Not wanting to become one of those **whiners**, I just sucked it up; max'd out on the Ibuprofen and Tylenol PM.* The doctors added some Naproxen for pain and some Seroquel to sleep. The Seroquel just made the nightmares more vivid, so I tossed those. The common theme of the nightmares was me possibly faltering, hesitating and stalling during combat. Something I hadn't done yet, but until you're tested you're never sure how you'll react. There's always self-doubt.

"*Eat up*" the spook, told me, so that's what I did. It was just part of my new and ever evolving world.

A month later, on **October 10, 2007**, I was headed back to my trailer with my dinner in hand, intending to eat at my bunk. Suddenly, I felt an explosion. The alarms sounded. I hit the ground and as I lay there, the next explosion was deafening and close. I looked up to see a truck driving by that had taken a direct hit. I got up and ran towards the vehicle. I could hear the screams and moans as I approached. As I arrived, so did several other warfighters. Gas was the first thing I smelled. The gas tank had been penetrated by shrapnel, but luckily hadn't caught fire, yet. We extricated the injured as the gasoline started to pool, then carried them away from the danger area and immediately began assessing their wounds, applying pressure and bandages. *Luckily, I had restocked my medical pouch.* It was a Deja Vu moment.

This time the shelling was ongoing and we could hear other rockets exploding around us. Three were injured. We searched for the blood, looking for wounds, and then we found the shrapnel holes and began plugging them. I remember finding a leg wound, cutting off his trouser leg, and he went for his weapon, pointing and flashing it dangerously. His rage, confusion and adrenaline were skyrocketing. Luckily, another soldier talked him into releasing it. His fury wanted retaliation against his attackers, not us, but he was understandably disoriented. *I recognized this fury.* It had been on my face weeks earlier.

As I looked around, time slowed again. One of my most *prideful moments* in-country was when, *as rockets were still impacting around us*, I could see the young faces of warfighters who **did not** run away to shelter, but instead ran out into the open to help others. *I am still so proud of them.* Amongst them, I recognized a face. It was my Rescue Controller *Bryan Callan*, who not only worked for me, but had also been hit back on September 11th, during the attack on the Al Faw palace. He was administering an IV to another patient. Soon other vehicles began to arrive and we loaded the wounded into those. They were then taken the short distance to the CSH, or Combat Support Hospital. The incoming rounds that day were from Iranian

BRAIN PAIN

107 mm rockets. They're about three feet long like a smaller oxygen tank, with three pounds of explosives. That day, two warfighters, Specialist Samuel Pearson and SSgt. Lillian Clamens, were killed and 40 others wounded.

For almost a month since the September 11th explosion, it'd been difficult to sleep. *The hangover-like headache and ringing in my ears had not stopped and there was a new and uncomfortable pressure circling my head.* I had to sleep, so I continued my sleep protocol of Tylenol PM, which seemed to help. It was a local trick that had been passed down. I also tried to work out extra hard, and then go for long walks, trying to wear myself down.

Thursday, **October 25, 2007**. I woke about 5:30 am, grabbed my shower kit, and then walked over to the showers. Somewhere, a few miles away, a group of insurgents had parked a truck. The common methodology for an improvised rocket launcher was to fabricate the launching rails onto a flatbed truck. Twelve pieces of angle iron would be mounted in the bed of the truck, with the rockets laid inside them, at a 30-45 degree angle, and attached to washing machine timers. They were covered with tarps and under the cover of night driven to the launching point, which was already recon'd for azimuth and distance, then parked. The tarp would be removed and the timers set to 5-10 minutes, as the insurgents made their escape.

The sun was rising; the air was fresh, crisp and slightly moist. Next, like most days, I waited in line to get to a shower stall. Once I got underneath the water I began to wake up. My mind started going through the checklist of meetings and briefings I had later in the day. Normally I shaved in the same trailer, but for some reason I decided to take a walk over to the next trailer and shave there.

As I walked out of the shower trailer and into the morning's rising sun, the last thought I had, actually put a big smile on my face. I realized, "It's Groundhog Day." There are no days off while in country and every day begins to seem the same after a while. I was walking between the T-barrier and the trailer, about to open the door, when I heard the ever so slight whistling of an incoming rocket. No boom, alarms or other warning. *Instinct took over, my adrenaline spiked and I pushed myself backwards and balled up, towards the ground. **I didn't make it to the ground.***

As the explosion occurred, all my senses went into overdrive. My mind went into hypervigilance mode and once again time slowed to a frame-by-frame juxtaposition of sight, sound and feeling. A 107 rocket went through the corner of the trailer 15 feet to my right, and hit the concrete wall, exploding back out towards me. My last thought was *"Shit!* ***This is how I die."*** as I could clearly see *hundreds of pieces of shrapnel* approaching my eye view.

I'd been hit and knocked out. Everything went to black; like the frames of a movie, coming to an abrupt end. It was then, during the darkness, *I felt a warm loving embrace from beyond.* It was one I had felt before. ***Somehow, I was shielded.*** Out of all the pieces of shrapnel I saw approaching, only a handful hit their mark.

I was protected and in my mind, I heard the words, ***"It's Okay."*** It was a comforting, loving, warm and enveloping reassurance that now was not my time. What I experienced in that minute or so of darkness, was a journey in it's own. It was a sense of love and comfort. ***More on that later, but I recognized the voice.***

Soon afterwards, I came too, choking on the heated smoke. My mantra of *"move through"* pushed me forward. Adrenaline and anger became my motivation; a mindset of confusion led my direction.

My feet and arms moved, and my crotch was intact. So far, so good. Once again, my head was pounding and I couldn't hear except for the unfortunately familiar, growl type buzz. It was the first round of the incoming and I knew there would be dozens more. My trailer was a few feet away, so confused and in disarray, I stumbled over. I grabbed my vest and med bag and ran back out. I was practically deaf; not thinking clear and completely disoriented, but went into automatic mode.

There was dark smoke and debris everywhere. I lost my peripherals and my focus tightened. I couldn't hear, couldn't see well, but knew there were most likely still people inside the trailer. ***My throttle was stuck on open.*** I defaulted to autopilot and my training mode told me to get in there.

The reality was that my roommate **Major Eric Westfeling** had been in there when the explosion occurred and had *courageously* helped clear it. I ran right past him. I don't remember seeing or hearing him, so confused, I went into the trailer and cleared it again.

BRAIN PAIN

Afterwards, someone realized I was bleeding. A dark froth was also coming out of my nose and mouth. I thought I was bleeding internally. I am a medium brown Latin American, and my roommate, Eric, said I turned white. It's funny now. Later, I discovered the dark froth coming out of my mouth and nose was cerebrospinal fluid from around my brain, mixed with the dark smoke I was coughing up.

Someone stopped a vehicle alongside the road, shoved me in the back of it and told the driver to take me to the hospital. Here, they assessed me, along with another individual who was inside the trailer. They medevac'd us to the 28th Combat Support Hospital, Emergency Room, in the Green Zone. The shrapnel in my back was close to an artery. My face, mouth and eyes were swollen, but I could see and breathe.

As my medevac helicopter lifted off, the sun was beginning to rise and I noticed how beautiful everything was. I was gazing to the Heavens, yet I wasn't ready to visit. It was the most amazing and memorable helicopter ride ever. Lying on the stretcher, looking upward, I scanned the sky, the rotor blades, the pilots, the medics, the horizon, the landing pad, and all the action moving in front of me. I felt the sweet ecstasy of life and embraced the beauty of everything around me. *I was happy to still be here.*

As we landed, the medical crews came out and transferred another soldier and me onto the mobile gurneys. I had another surreal moment while rolling through the doors and underneath the ER sign. You see, a year earlier, during the summer of 2006, HBO produced a televised special called, "**Baghdad ER**." It was a very real documentary about the operations of the Baghdad Emergency Room, run by the deployed Combat Support Hospital personnel. Who would've thought that I would be rolling through this same doorway on a gurney, looking up at the same iconic sign?

While I laid on the gurney, many others came in with injuries that day. One was a little Iraqi boy who had multiple shrapnel wounds like myself. After a lot of crying, he finally caught my stare. He stared back and slowly stopped crying. I believe he saw my wounds, and that my skin tone was the same as his. As I smiled, he smiled and began to listen to the woman, speaking softly to him in Arabic, seeming to believe things would get better. I hope they did.

ANTHONY JONES

Once the doctors realized the shrapnel had not clipped the artery in my shoulder, they bandaged me up. Several hours later they released me and I caught a helicopter back to Camp Victory. It was late in the afternoon, but it was important for me to get back on "the bike," if only for a few minutes. ***Pedal. Bleed. Repeat.***

Bryan Callan picked me up and took me back to my trailer and I was able to get back into uniform. Earlier our First Sgt. had asked about contacting my next of kin. Since I was somewhat cognizant and knew it was bedtime back in Vegas, I opted to call them later in the afternoon, which would be wake-up time back home. I also wanted to ensure that my dad answered, not my mom. He did, with his usual jovial, *"What's up Boy?"* I couldn't help but smile, then I told him, "I'm okay, walking and talking, but I got hit this morning." Afterwards, he told me to *"**document everything**."* That advice would be instrumental down the road.

After well wishing's from colleagues, I wandered over to the Dining Facility. It was around dinnertime and I hadn't eaten all day and was still in the surreal excitement of being alive. As I wandered around looking at the selection of food, I saw the ice cream. Specifically, I saw a banana split. I couldn't remember the last time I had one, but this one was the best one I had ever eaten. Carbs never tasted so good. ***Eat up.***

Months later, I was medevac'd to Germany for MRI's, then back to San Antonio, Texas for brain scans. ***The "Brain Pain" had become too much to handle.*** The decisions my leadership dictated could be life and death. I found my anger turning into frustration, and my communication, memory, multi-tasking and processing ability deteriorating faster and faster. I knew something was wrong with my brain. I was forgetting things, missing meetings, yelling at my subordinates, talking too bluntly to my superior Officers. I lost two of my security access badges, only to find them both next to my bed, the day before I left. If I couldn't do my job properly people could die. Later, brain scans and neurological testing would corroborate these new developments. Insidiously, ***Chaos*** had found an opening, and was wiggling its way around my brain.

I was diagnosed with TBI and PTS. I stayed in the game as long as I could, but still felt some *kind of shame*, as if I had let someone down. ***I felt guilt.***

BRAIN PAIN

I was dealing with the onset of Post Traumatic Stress the best I could, but the headaches were relenting. Had I not had this "Brain Pain" I firmly believe the PTS would have taken a dissipating course. But the headaches were getting worse, day-by-day, and the mental trauma was feeding off that pain.

One of the most difficult moments I've had, was to acknowledge to myself and accept that I had a mental injury. *I too, now felt Defective.*

So often, I was tempted to disassociate with them, thinking they would heal, like a normal wound. They haven't so far. Growing up with my father's experiences reminded me to acknowledge this truth and to try to *"nip this in the bud."* That was my first step in my new fight to stem ***Chaos***.

Traumatic Brain Injuries are invisible, as is Post Traumatic Stress. *Your ability to interact in the world is dramatically weakened by this newly acquired "Achilles' heel."* If you're a warfighter, your spouse, family and co-workers tiptoe around you. If you're a football player, endorsement deals disappear. If you're a High School student, your future is jeopardized. Whether its from a car accident, fall, trauma or combat, we are just survivors trying to stay the course. ***Moving through and moving forward.***

A couple of months after my return, my awards ceremony took place. I was awarded the Purple Heart, Army Combat Action Badge, Defense Meritorious Service Medal, Joint Service Commendation Medal and some other ribbons. I don't remember much, other than the overwhelming support of my colleagues and other members of the Air Force family. I felt a swell of pride that day. That was enough for me. Three years later I was awarded my second Purple Heart for the September 11th, 2007 injury. The bureaucracy was catching up.

My story is not a combat story; its my journey before, during and *back here*. Subliminally my mind heard and learned from my Dad's advice. I had paid attention to my instincts. It got him through Khe Sanh, and me through Baghdad.

I had learned early on, how to **"Pedal Fast."** Now, *back here*, a new journey was beginning.

The tourist chair at the Al Faw Palace, the early morning of Sept. 11ᵗʰ, 2007. Later that afternoon I would be hit for the first time.

My parents and me, during the awards ceremony after my return from Iraq in 2008. I trained my entire life for my "moments."

BRAIN PAIN

CHAPTER 4

BRATS

"Doing the job"

Settle in, enjoy, pack up and move – then repeat. It's still all too familiar. We'd just be getting comfortable. Our rooms made up, finally fitting in with new friends, and then the infamous "orders" would arrive. They were written in stone. "**Orders**" were synonymous with heartbreak. They were pieces of paper ordering our father to his next assignment. Dad would get them, we'd pack, clean and be inspected. The Mayflower tractor-trailer would show up, and off we'd go. Onto our next base. *From day one, we learned a sense of Mission, Tenacity, Courage and Integrity.* Our life was a finely tuned operation, planned and executed with precision and timing. Team "Jones," the five of us. We had guidance, direction and emotional calluses. Our lives were a mission. We were the children of military service members and were "**Brats**." Home was wherever we were.

[2]"Brats" is a term earned by a childhood of service to our family and to our country. We are military dependants whose home is never a place but a mental state. Our childhood shaped us and made us who we are, mostly stronger, smarter and more emotionally capable than our civilian equivalents. *We moved so often that we developed advanced social skills and learned early on how to read people and*

adapt to their expectations. As "Brats," we hardened our emotions every time we left an assignment, then honed and used our social skills to fit into our new one. No matter what base we went to, we had something in common with our peers. **We were "doing the job."**

I can't count the road trips we've made together. Dad was on the Marine Corps Rifle and Pistol team and would spend most "summer camp" like time with his brother, Uncle Ben, and his family, or my mother's sister, Aunt, or "Tia" Carmen and her family. Fifteen cousins to get into trouble with!

My whole life I've been asked the question, "Where are you from?" I'd say, "The Corps." After the puzzled look on the questioner's face, would I explain that I was a Military Brat. There are few civilian corporations or organizations that are as inclusionary and intimately involved in the personal lives of their employees' families, as the military. *Military life came with many benefits, almost like a socialist society.* We had an ID card, medical care, a commissary, a base exchange, sports teams, bowling alleys, pools, free legal service, church, housing, and schools. All part of the deal.

Manners and appearances were life-size. If a kid got in trouble, his father's Commander would get the call, not him. You'd never see that with a civilian job. At 5 pm the flag was brought down and the whole base would stop. People stopped walking and held their hand over their hearts. If in uniform, they would salute. Cars stopped, and if you were riding a bike, you stopped. You answered the phone with your father's rank and name. "Lieutenant Jones' residence, how can I help you?" What you did and how you dressed, affected your father's career. If he couldn't handle his kids, then how could he command troops in combat? It was wartime after all.

"*The Great Santini*" was a 1970's movie starring Robert Duvall. It's about a Marine Squadron Commander during the Vietnam war and looks at how his "take no prisoner's" attitude, that served him well in combat, didn't work as well at home with his family. There's a great quote from the movie that always struck a cord. The family had just arrived at a new duty station, and Colonel Wilbur "Bull" Meechum, in uniform, was briefing his family. *"I know it's rough to leave your friends and move every year, but you are Marine kids and you can chew nails while other kids are sucking cotton candy!"* Then, *"Said bellyaching will end today at 1530 hours!"* It wasn't as

ANTHONY JONES

harsh as that, but our home was run like a finely tuned operation. We learned the chain of command before we could understand what it meant. *My dad started out enlisted, earned his commission as an officer during the war, then finished his career as an E-9, the highest of the enlisted ranks, retiring as an Officer, or Captain.*

By the time I finished 6th grade, we had already officially moved ten times and now were on number ***eleven***, not counting the motel stays. As kids, it really didn't bother us, because our parents were there to provide for and love us. All was well with my sister, little brother and me. Here in Virginia, I would enter the seventh grade and attend Quantico High School. It was a Department of Defense (DOD) school and included seventh through the twelfth grade.

*As the new guy, within a week **I had to fight**.* This time "doing the job" started in the hallway, but finished after school behind the tennis courts. Before this kid was finished explaining the rules (of our fight), I had already knocked him to the ground. ***As we grew we adapted. These were our survival skills.*** Afterwards the year went along just fine.

My parents were both born during the "Great Depression" which happened in 1929, but lasted throughout the thirties. My mother never knew her parents, surviving by the love of extended family. My father survived an abusive stepfather, learning his values from his mother, brothers and sisters. He was raised around family and love. They worked hard for everything they had. Because of this, we were brought up with good old ***North Carolina redneck pride****: values, hard work, love of family and country and the ability to adapt and be on the side of good and righteousness.*

After Vietnam, Dad's nightmares began. As a kid, waking to screams in the middle of the night, scared the hell out of us, but they explained it and we listened. Our father had made it home alive, there were so many others in our neighborhood whose didn't. ***Dad left as a light-hearted comedian, but returned distant, irritable and dark.*** Back then it was hard to categorize and understand all of this, but we're mini-Marines, so we adapted and moved on.

While Dad was in Vietnam, I met my first girlfriend, got much better at riding a bike, learned to skateboard and ride my first waves on a surfboard. I would also get in my first fight after standing up to a bully. I was scared shitless, but once I made the decision, it was on.

From then on, every new place we went, my sister and I would be the new kids, I would be bullied into a fight. *Once they knew I could throw a beating as well as receive one, we'd be good for the rest of that tour.* It was part of "doing the job." **Pedal. Bleed. Repeat.**

We were old enough to ask what he did, why did they send him, is he coming home, is he going to die, what would happen to us if he died? We had seen the loss of other families in our cul-de-sac. *Everyday* it was all over the TV, in our faces, in black and white. **Mom** answered all these questions as well as many more. She held down the home front. She had been through much more, going from home to home, family to family. She learned her survival skills much earlier than us, from her brother and sisters, aunts and uncles. Her adaptability, learned in childhood, flowed down to us. *The lessons we learned during that tour were lessons kids our age shouldn't have had to learn.*

Our father was alive. We were happy and we were off again to the next assignment. Dad was now a First Lieutenant and Officer, which meant we lived in the Junior Officer Quarters. Here, at Quantico, Dad would be attending the Marine Corps Communications School. Dad's MOS (his specialty) was as an artilleryman, but he was also a great marksman and being trained as a Communications Officer. By this time, he'd been selected to represent Marine Corps on a larger scale with the shooting team. He traveled a lot with the Marine Corps Rifle and Pistol team; always bringing home gifts.

As part of the shooting team, he had already won the Mid-Atlantic All Service Rifle and Pistol Championship, as well as the Gold Medal Division Pistol Championships. He liked shooting and it kept him home more than he would have been, had he stayed permanently as an artilleryman. We liked it when he was around more, especially after returning from Vietnam. **Keeping engaged and challenged kept the anger and nightmares in check.** It was at one of these shooting matches that he won my first guitar. I took to that like iron to a magnet!

It was also then that I noticed my dad's new temperament. He could snap and change personalities in a split second. It's something he's battling to this day. **Vietnam hardened him. Emotional calluses.** He became more of the disciplinarian, as were the majority of other Marine parents. Dad could throw you a single look, *tighten* *his brows* and it would stop us in our tracks. He'd lived through more hell in Khe Sanh than he ever let on. Kids shouldn't have to learn about those things and he protected us from them. *He fought hard for our way of life and never let on.* **He never once blamed anything on his injuries.**

There were no TBI or PTS diagnoses back then. Dad was a career Marine with a family to take care of. Like so many other families, what happened in your home, stayed in your home. There was no support system, no way to talk to your father while he was deployed. **No** counseling when he returned. **No** anger management classes. When the Marines sent a man to Vietnam, he returned a different one, a darker one. In order to survive, you have to become one mean son-of-a-bitch. *Our emotional calluses were thickening.*

Now when I snap and my Brain Pain overwhelms me, I try and remember. **Control that beast; don't let it control you.** That's what he tried to do. Marines are tough, that's why they are survivors. We were the children of Marines and were being trained to be just as tough. No matter how many moves there were, we always had more confidence than our peers. Even as kids we knew the value of life and liberty. After Dad graduated from Communications School, we received orders again. This time to Cherry Point, North Carolina, near Havelock and New Bern.

It was 1969 and we were in the South. This time we entered a civilian public school. My sister and I were the unknown new kids and darker than most. The South was still racially charged. The military was integrated by this time and race was never an issue on base. *The only color was the color of your father's uniform.* This new public school was different. The white kids weren't sure about us and the black kids thought we were white. Within a few days, I got shoved and the boy and I went at it in the hallway. We were sent to the office. Back to "doing the job."

It was a time when corporal punishment (the paddle), was accepted and used. Mr. Edwards, the principal, gave us, myself and Johnny Angel, a choice - ten whacks with a paddle or ten days suspension. The paddle made more sense. The suspension would lead to an ass whipping anyway, so we both took it and moved on. A few weeks later several African American girls ganged up on my sister, and I was fighting again. This one was practically an all out brawl. This "race" thing brought us up to speed on the times. Johnny and I were now friends, so he and his friends stepped in to help. Dad came down to school to let the principal know that these kids' bigoted behavior would not be tolerated. He's always had our backs.

There were good things also. We lived right next to the Neuse River. Dad had a motorboat and we did a lot of fishing and water skiing with our parents. I became very good at floundering but just mediocre at skiing. *My sister and mother (the hipster) and I watched American Bandstand and Soul Train every Saturday morning; also Ed Sullivan on Sunday nights.* We learned all the new dances and kept up with the latest fashion trends. I went to my first school dance and took my first trip to a fancy movie theater for a screening of "Gone with the Wind." For a while there, we were able to be regular kids, but the war was still going strong. After a year, Dad got his "orders" to Vietnam for the second time.

This time we moved to **Kenly, NC** where Dad's family lived. Dad brought a trailer and placed it on Grandma's, '**Neppie Jones Crumpler,**' farm. We had been visiting there for all of our lives and my Grandma, all my aunts and uncles were there. It was my first year in high school. North Johnston High School. Naturally, I would have to fight again, but soon the students accepted us and the year went by with some good memories.

During the second tour in Vietnam, Dad ran artillery battery, or Bravo Battery, south west of Da Nang. The war was still going strong and battles were being fought. Dad's brother **Jerry** was exempt from the draft because he was the son that was running the farm, but his younger brother, **Wiley**, wasn't. Wiley was drafted, sent to basic training, then onto two tours in Vietnam. Dad was already deployed to Vietnam when Wiley was sent there for his second tour. Because of the "**Sullivan Act,**" the rules were that you couldn't have two sons deployed to a war zone at the same time. Grandma asked Dad to look into this and he said he would. Dad is very adept with regulatory situations like that. He drove four hours up to Da Nang and tracked Wiley down. Wiley remembers when he saw his older brother storming down the red-clayed walkway to his Commander's office. He said Dad looked like "a bull getting ready to attack the Matador." Soon afterwards, Wiley gathered up his gear and was back on a plane to the states. *If one brother had to be there, it was going to be Dad.*

ANTHONY JONES

Back home in North Carolina, being a teen whose father was overseas; I started acting out, trying to fit in. I was hanging out with the wrong crowd and started smoking to be cool. The Physical Education teacher had watched me wrestle and noticed how agile I was. He was also the track coach. He asked me to try out and I took to pole-vaulting like riding a bike. Then he told me, to be on the team, I couldn't smoke. *That decision took my path in a much more productive direction. No smoking for me.*

For a dark kid in the South, with **racism** still around, prejudice followed me out in public. Not so much at school anymore, but out and around town. I remember being at the town's pool hall one day when the manager called me the "N" word and told me I wasn't playing in his hall, kicking me out. When I got home and my Uncle Jerry found out, it became a different story. Jerry was bigger than my dad, 6'3" and 250 pounds. His family had been in this town for almost a hundred years and everyone knew them. Jerry and I went down to the pool hall and he literally pulled the guy out from behind the counter by his collar; so hard that his feet left the ground, letting him know that I'd play here any time I wanted. No color, just the family version of "doing the job." *Wonder where I got that?*

Dad survived that tour and we now had orders to New York. He was taking an assignment as a Marine recruiter. My sophomore year was completed at Niagara Wheatfield High School, Niagara Falls, New York. Here, it was pretty easy going. I didn't have to fight hard this time, just a couple shoving matches. The area had a large influence of Native American kids, so my sister, my brother and I just blended in. I was a sophomore and my sister was in the eighth grade. We were also in public schools again. I joined the track team. My parents bought me my first of several Cat-a-Poles; the first fiberglass pole used for *pole vaulting*. I also found a talent for art and drawing. I started my first band, playing guitar and played my first gig at a school dance. I got my first of many *Fender guitars*, my sister got her first boyfriend and my little brother got his first Big Wheel. We were back this year to being a family or Team Jones, as we called ourselves.

It was the beginning of my Junior Year. Her name was Diana. It was an hour walk one way to her house. We would just hang out there in her yard for the afternoon, then two hours prior to dark, I'd head back out, walking home. She was blonde-haired and blue-eyed. She had come to all my track meets that past spring and we started hanging out over the summer. I was getting comfortable again and the thought that we would be moving soon slipped from my mind. As the child of a military member, this was dangerous. Once again, Dad got orders to Quantico. It would be our third time there.

The all-too-familiar Mayflower moving tractor-trailer came and we packed, cleaned our home and passed the inspection. The next morning, with the vehicles packed, we headed south. I remember it being a dark early morning. Tears leaked from my eyes as I put my arm around my sister, who was also crying. She also had a young love she was leaving behind. We've done this all of our lives, making new friends then leaving them. ***Heartbreak became another part of the "mission."*** Our calluses thickened as we sucked it up and moved through. I told Diane that I would write. I did, but it all dissipated soon and I never saw her again. That was part of the Brat life.

It was Quantico High School again. I'd gone to seventh grade here. It was a DOD school, meaning military dependents only. The upside was that we would probably graduate here because Dad was getting close to retirement and this would more than likely be our last military move. All dependants had something more important in common. ***We were Brats, survivors and warriors.*** All of the parents had been survivors of the Vietnam War in one-way or the other. The war was taking its toll on everyone; especially those who made it back alive. They carried the warrior demons back with them, as did we who made it back from Iraq and Afghanistan. If a parent died in the war, the family moved on to civilian life. They were gone from the base within weeks. We learned loss is inevitable and death is always around the corner. Our fathers had survived, so had our families. It was a common bond, a unique time.

Starting school at Quantico again, we were excited to see other Brats we had grown up with and to meet new friends with whom we would bond for life. We moved into on-base housing that was literally just across the street from the home we lived in several years earlier when my brother, **Marcos**, was born. I was a junior and my sister was now a sophomore instead of a freshman. Her scores and credits were good enough that she was able to skip a grade.

ANTHONY JONES

There are always cliques in high school. There are the sports jocks, the rockers, the stoners, the partiers, the slackers, etc. Quantico had them all. From grades seven through twelve we had just around 300 total students. My graduating class had just over 50 people in it. Everyone knew everyone and most of their business as well. Having spent the last couple years in public school, our social skills were tested again. *For me it was another fight and we were back on track.* For this one we had gloves on, during Physical Education class. The teacher made us do it safely, in the gym, in front of the class. It was fine with me. I didn't win, but didn't lose either. Once again, I was "doing the job."

Acting out in school and fighting wasn't uncommon. Children can be hard on each other, especially around this age. They were all the children of warriors and their fathers could be very hard on them as well. The fact was, the Physical Education teachers would give us gloves and send us to the gym, just to get it over with and keep it quiet. *They knew what we were going through*, and this dealt with the issues and minimized the damage.

Many Marines who survived Vietnam were hard drinkers. Luckily, my father never was. He's actually a bit of a teetotaler and rarely has more than one or two drinks. Some other parents would have us make their drinks for them when we were at parties. More than a few times, we saw the results of too much alcohol. I can't count the number of arguments and fights that broke out at the Officers' Club between husbands and wives. We'd sneak up onto the upstairs balcony for major events and wait to see the action.

That first summer I had a job as a weekend custodian at the Officers' Club. One morning we found a young Captain in the closet, desperately hung over, holding a gun in his hand. It seemed that he had planned to commit **suicide**, but ended up passing out with gun in hand. I took the gun slowly and called the father of one of my friends. He came down and quietly helped the young man out of the club. No one would find out about this. Marines can be fiercely loyal to each other because they give their all at everything they do.

It was the 70s and rock 'n' roll was the culture. In New York, I played guitar in my first band in front of my first auditorium audience. *That **guitar was my best friend** and through it I could express myself. It wouldn't leave me or move away.* At Quantico, I

53

started another band, called Mourning. We played at the local teen club called the "Hut," as well as at several school dances. In youthful turmoil, I would always retreat to the comfort of music, my solace. **It was the birth of my music therapy.** I kept busy, studying karate, skateboarding, and surfing during the summer. Two of my best friends to this day, Wes Edwards and Don Beiger, I met through skating and surfing. Virginia Beach and Cape Hatteras were our spots. My sister, **Pam**, was busy as well, playing on the girl's basketball team. My brother Marcos followed in my footsteps doing everything I did, just doing it better. He also had Dad's passion for golf, becoming State Champion before finishing Middle School.

Up to this point, I was a below average student. The many transitions had me focused more on fitting in than on studying. *Then something happened that started out somewhat surreptitiously, but ended up being **monumental** in my life.* My government teacher was Mr. Blatt. He spoke slowly and with a monotone. I just wasn't getting it. A few months earlier the movie, "Class of 44," a sequel to the "Last Picture Show," had come out. One of my favorite scenes was when a student used a 3x5 card with a string attached to it, and then to his belt, hidden inside a long-sleeved shirt and then into his palm. *This was used to cheat on a test.* The 3x5 card fit in his hand and had the answers written in tiny script, on it. When the teacher came around you would raise your hand for help, thus making the card magically disappear back into your sleeve. No harm no foul.

With a big final coming up, I needed help. I remember sitting at my desk doing an immense amount of research and cramming all that information on to a 3x5 card in a matrix format. I was up past midnight. The next day I wore my long-sleeved shirt with the 3x5 card inserted in my sleeve, a string hidden and attached to my belt. When I was handed the test, I waited for Mr. Blatt to go to his desk and sit down, but he didn't. He was wandering around the room and time was slipping by, so I decided to get done what I could. To my surprise, I knew almost all the answers and was one of the first to finish. I passed with extra time. *I was adapting, accidentally discovering my own "work arounds."*

This became a staple of how I studied. The 3x5 card was gone but I would condense all the information onto three to four pages, then down to one page; then memorize that one page in a matrix form, from left to right and top to bottom. "Work around." I used that method through College, Flight School, Squadron Officer School and Air Command and Staff College.

Having been **bullied** since I was a kid, I had to learn how to defend and stand up for myself. From that first bully back in Oceanside, I could not and would not stand by as others bullied those around me. Once you understand the psychology of intimidators, you see them for the weak individuals they are. I didn't start out campaigning for Homecoming King my senior year, it just happened. Since I wouldn't let bullying occur to the mostly younger seventh, eighth and ninth graders, they voted me King. It was a humbling experience and a rarity, since I didn't play football.

Marcos was growing up, too. I changed his diapers, watched him grow from a toddler, to a civil war buff, to a skateboarder, to surfing, to karate kid. He liked whatever I was doing, copied it and always excelled. We were kids wearing bell-bottoms and hip huggers. We had long hair and played rock and roll. I had a pretty good Afro going on. Our parents would both encourage our individuality and stand by our choices. Not only here, but for the rest of our lives.

As I look back on it, Dad had lots of patience with us. At the time, it seemed as if he were more like Robert Duvall's character, the "Great Santini." But my parents were only in their thirties, living through a war, raising children, all the while trying to enjoy some of their youth with friends. It's the same scenario replaying itself over and over in today's military. **Been there - done that.** I understand and empathize with the younger generation of Brats going through it today. It hurts all over again as I see this generation fight their own battles. As the years went by, we came to realize our parents really were our heroes. *Real Heroes*. They sacrificed everything to put a roof over our heads and food on our plates. They got up every morning and went to work, washing clothes, making lunches, etc. In our case, as Brats, they even put their lives on the line in far away places.

Dad instilled a great ideal in me; that we as children should strive to be better than our parents. In my case that's a hard one to follow, but I have spent my life trying. Dad also made it clear to me that as a man I would one day have a family and would need to provide for my family, thus needed to take advantage of the opportunities he afforded us, *ensuring that we did better than they did.*

Our parents served in Korea and Vietnam and we all had lived through this together. We were children of war. The offspring of warriors. We were Brats, earning that title with service to family and our country. **Our values were:** *1.) The line between right and wrong is clear, as is the line between good and evil. 2.) We always stand for good and righteous. 3.) Anything we do should be worthwhile and important.*

My parents both got out of unsatisfactory childhoods and they both made a better life than they were given. They didn't settle. They fought their way out. To understand where we are now and where we are going, we must know our past. *We must learn from our ancestors so that when we are called, we will ensure that our lives will have been most purposeful.*

There is a sense of deep loyalty in being a "**Brat**." Our parents had our backs, a "leave no man behind" loyalty. It's something we Brats have carried forward in our own lives. *A fierce loyalty to our family and those who became our friends. There is no other choice, you don't quit, and you carry on the mission.* For the rest of my life, everything continues to be a mission. You review the facts and options, come up with a plan of attack, and then execute the plan.

Today there is more recognition of these issues. I read somewhere that they don't yet know long term how these combat deployments is affecting our children. There are so many more resources available now than were for the children of WW1, WW2, Korea and Vietnam. The fact that we made it through and grew stronger than many of our civilian peers, leads me to believe that *today's military children should be even stronger* than us and will make us proud with their resolve.

We were Brats. "Doing the job" was more than a saying, it was a way of life. **Mission, Tenacity, Courage and Integrity.**

"Doing the job" would soon turn into "**Doing the work**." Dad showed us how to do the work, overcoming his challenges and pressing forward.

CHAPTER 5

TBI

"Welcome to '*Chaos*'"

When I'm staring at the ceiling in the darkness, fighting my way to slumber and searching out my thirty-nine winks, the constant shrill ringing is deep in my ears, piercing my core like the high-pitched feedback of a musician's microphone. Underlying this turmoil in my mind is a blackness of distorted voices preaching terminal suggestions. All of this is swirling beneath a cacophony of tiny explosions, parallel to the snaps of flies being terminated by an electric fly zapper. **Chaos - my nemesis.** It surrounds me 24/7, like a band of *mosquitoes* hovering over me as I navigate a slippery trail in some third world jungle. The constant bites are my reminder to maintain my focus on the wet rocks beneath my feet, because the trail is long and there are cliffs on both sides. They never leave, waiting to settle in and suck the rest of my blood. Chaos in the brain; pain that jolts me, racing thoughts that betray me and eat away at my soul. Waking, it's still there. **Chronic pain, *Chronic Chaos*.**

For the last 7 years, since first being blown up, my brain's been on fire, exploding daily with a *firestorm* of searing electric shocks and a constant heated, circling, bruising pain! There's no running away, no "off" switch. I move through, forward and constantly adjust my *management strategy*. I look fine, but inside my mind, there's that "Invisible Wound" that bounces around my brain, trying to take control of my inner "thinking" mind and thoughts. "**Chaos**."

I never believed in headaches. Flat out. It seemed like a sign of fragility or an excuse. The only reference point I ever had was a bad hangover. Even after a car accident in college and the many blows to the head while studying Karate, *I've never even had a migraine.* My brain seemed invincible. Our brain holds who we are within it. It's truly remarkable and we should never take it for granted, because when it's gone, so are we. It allows us to absorb our environment, calculate and process, move and communicate, to store memories and learn from others. With hundreds of thousands of Vietnam, Iraq and Afghanistan war veterans and countless millions of civilians already affected with TBI, the research and conversation needs to turn into action.

I always connected traumatic brain injury with car accidents and blunt force trauma until just prior to my leaving for Iraq in 2007. I read an article in my dad's **Navy Times** called the "**Signature Wound of the War**" that talked about "**Traumatic Brain Injury**" or TBI. After reading it, I remember asking him if he'd ever had headaches? He said he didn't, but knew of many others that did. That article stuck with me. Hundreds of thousands of Vietnam veterans came home with blast related concussions, yet this "Signature Wound" was being looked at like something new. The massive use of Improvised Explosive Devices (IED) and rockets not only resulted in extremity amputations, but hundreds of thousands more brain injuries.

The way the media played it out was as if our leadership was caught off guard. This was a slap in the face to World War I, II, Korean and Vietnam veterans. These types of injuries happened over and over in those conflicts. *Had they just forgotten?* They had been through this "*Concussion Crisis*" before but chose not to acknowledge it. Now, those prior war-injured veterans added to the current war-injured veterans, ended up overwhelming the VA system.

Growing up, I understood the advantage of being the underdog. No one sees you coming. Going from town to town, school to school, it seemed, more often than not, you were being set up for failure. But the benefit of being a Brat was that you could do anything, because you often had to. I was always looking outside of the confinements of the normal box. You're forced to find a work-around method to success, a way to search out your personal path. I knew I wasn't going to some Ivy League university. My goal was the degree. Later, I would discover that the name of the university you graduated from wasn't as important as the fact that you graduated. Almost debt free, I might add.

I enrolled in Northern Virginia Community College, commonly known as NVCC, as a Criminal Justice major. Once I made it past the first semester of too much partying, I fell into the groove. I learned how to maintain good academics and still have a social life. If there is one thing college did for me, it was to allow me to figure out balance. For the next four years, I worked at various part time jobs, played in my band, Mourning, on weekends and hustled doing custom auto paint jobs. I went to school full-time, every semester including summers. There was never a break until I finished. After getting my Associates degree from NVCC, I transferred all my credits to George Mason University (GMU), also in Virginia.

While I was still finishing my second year at NVCC, my dad retired from the Marines and began his second career with the Capital Police. He was still in his forties when he went through the Academy for the Capitol Police, then the Federal Law Enforcement Training Center (FLETC) in Simon, South Carolina. Although this job was close to home, there was never going to be any room for advancement, so he pursued his way into the Border Patrol. He was able to get an age waiver, tested and was accepted and sent to Yuma, Arizona, where he excelled at the Academy and began his first year as an agent. *My father's pace kept him **engaged and challenged**, and Chaos was semi-sealed away.* Anger and nightmares were still there simmering under the surface. But he had found a new mission and pursued it with a vengeance, like anything he did. He was "*Doing the work.*"

At George Mason, I fell into the academics and social aspect quickly. NVCC had fortified my studying habits. I joined the track team, pole vaulting and javelin throwing, and became a Fraternity President. One of my new friends I met in college ended up as a lifetime buddy, **Rick McMillion**. He's the only college friend I really ever stayed in contact with and we've been through a lot over the years. He played drums and I played guitar. There was a point when I thought music would be my career. I was a decent lead guitarist, but when I was honest with myself, I knew there were plenty others out there, as good and even better. I also continued to skateboard; surf and snow ski. I was the first one in our family to graduate from college; earning my bachelors. I was just a C+ student, but I worked my way through; hustling and doing a multitude of jobs, while going to school non-stop, including summers. I played in a band on weekends, did custom artwork on cars and vans, ran my fraternity, pole vaulted on the track team and was a social butterfly.

My brain was strong, clear, flowing with passion and ideas, and my social skills honed to a razors edge. Clarity, purpose and fun drove my life. ***Play hard, work harder***. *Chaos* wasn't even in my vocabulary.

My first major concussion *came right after college graduation.* I was on my way to my girlfriend's house. Just when you least expect it, life crushes you on a Friday afternoon. I was driving a small white Porsche 914. I had just entered an intersection when a woman driving a large Ford station wagon ran a stop sign and T-boned me. The last thing I remember is looking into her eyes, through her windshield, and saying, "Shit." Witnesses stated my head went through my side door window and I bounced onto her hood. Although I had taken several serious hits during karate, and several falls skateboarding, this the first time I was knocked out. *I don't remember having headaches;* just back pain, which went away after several months of wearing a brace and physical therapy. Youth and the ability to repair and regenerate, nice.

When Gen. Petraeus finally announced **"The Surge,"** in 2007, more people were needed to deploy to Iraq. I volunteered and received orders to Baghdad and I was looking forward to making a contribution again. Prior to the deployment I wanted to get as up to speed as I could, so one of the schools I wanted to get under my belt was Air Command and Staff College. This was the largest educational project I had taken on since college and Flight School. Like signing up to get your Masters, I couldn't help but wonder if I still had the brain for it. I opted for the correspondence program, which is done at your own pace and takes 12 to 18 months. Normally the program is done with 4 to 12 other Field Grade Officers, meeting once a week in a seminar environment.

My pace was vicious and confidence in my brain's ability swelled as I passed each exercise and exam. After work and on weekends, I was reading and studying. As soon as I received one module, I would order the next in advance, then cut down the learning objectives into a matrix of bullet points, again condensing them down to two pages. My version of the 3x5 cards or cheat sheets, just like in high school, college and Flight School. One right after the other, I'd complete the exercises and the exams. I completed the curriculum successfully in just over four months. I still had it.

Afterwards, *I actually remember thinking that my brain was still going strong for my age. I was **50 years old**.* Today, I realize that having completed this school was monumental. It gave me a baseline of comparison, a "**before TBI standard**" regarding the condition of my brain prior to my injury. This was a moment of *Clarity*. It was the *Clarity* I have been searching to find again.

Having 24-hour news formats on TV in 2007, the constant broadcasts regarding our losses in Iraq brought back memories of the nightly body counts in Vietnam. Because of my aviation career, I always thought my demise would be a plane crash. ***Never did I think I'd get blown up.*** Either way, *your ending* is always in the back of your mind and it should be when you're a warfighter. If there's ever a time for your awareness to be heightened, it's in combat.

The summer prior to deploying, I was busy with school and training. There's a long checklist of training that needs to be completed. Everything from combat training, cultural sensitivity to first aid/self aid. I also took several weeks off and went to a civilian tactical medicine course down in Los Angeles. I can't tell you what drove me to do that, other than I wanted to know as much about first responder medical training as possible in case I had to treat myself. Sometimes you have to listen to that little voice in the back of your head. In Baghdad, that training paid dividends, allowing me to save others.

You can't control the cards you're dealt, but you can control the game you sit down at. I had come full circle with success, failures, resurrection, integrity and purpose. I chose the game; trained and educated myself. I made choices and was now prepared to walk my talk. *Life was bright, my mind sharp and clear and purpose was fueling my direction.* I finally got that seat at the table and now it was time to see if I could play.

Just after my arrival in Iraq, I was given a power point brief on Traumatic Brain Injury and Post Combat Stress. As Director of Personnel Recovery Cell (DPRC), I then reviewed it with my team. It defined TBI as a form of concussion, resulting from a blow to the head or concussive blast wave that causes the brain to be shaken, squeezed or compressed within the skull. Unlike severe Traumatic Brain Injury, where there's a penetrating head injury with an obvious wound. Most concussions don't result in any obvious physical injury. However, they can result in brain functions being disrupted; a kind of "dazed and confused" feeling.

The irony was, that the briefing just kind of rolled over me, joining the rest of the checklist items I needed to absorb. Read it. Reviewed with team. Checked that box. Holy Shit! *Then it happened to me and it became the focus of my life's new investigation.* I'd gotten my "bell rung" twice, "saw the stars once" and went to black once. It was exactly as described in the briefing; a sudden manifestation of headaches, dizziness, nausea, vertigo, light sensitivity, memory problems, irritability and having a hard time multi-tasking. *Chaos* was laughing at me as it took hold.

The explosive shock wave doesn't target your brain, but your whole body. It was during my third or fourth visit to my ophthalmologist, when I got a better understanding of what happened to my eyes as well as my brain. As would be expected, my eyes were swollen and reddish in color, but after the redness went away, I still had yellow spots in the center of my vision. The ophthalmologist explained it simply. He told me that "***the blast over-pressured the fluid in my eyeball and that some of the capillaries had burst,***" leaking blood into the fluid and causing the yellow spot. He showed them to me and I could see those tiny, burst capillaries. It made sense. (Capillaries vs. neural pathways)

The brain is made of a gelatinous mass of billions of neurons, protoplasmic fibers, capillaries, veins, neural pathways and synapses, all inside a hard skull. It's surrounded and protected by a cerebrospinal fluid that acts as a cushion within the skull. If the concussive wave had burst the capillaries in my eyeball, surely it had done similar damage to other parts of my brain, affecting each of my sense modalities along with memories, emotional regulation and other cognitive functioning. Could other structures and functions within my brain have been affected by *the blast waves*? Could my emotions, memories and senses be misaligned? **Yes, I think so.** *Wow, a moment of clarity.* I had a clearer understanding of what happened to my brain. To this day I have a yellow spot and blurred, double vision in my right eye. It's another constant reminder.

Multiple concussions or blasts further increase damage possibilities. So many things come in to play; proximity of the blast, the size of the blast, open or closed shrapnel wounds. With sports injuries, it's the number of concussions a football player has had, the height a snowboarder fell from before hitting the ground, the angle it was from, the direction it was hit from, etc. The bottom line is when the brain's damaged; it's bad information in (senses), thus bad information out (emotions, movement and communication). What I mean by this, is that our senses have changed, thus so has the input to our computer (brain). If the information coming in is erroneous, so will be the information going out.

What I call my "**Access Dyslexia**" [3]may be better referred to as "Aphasia", which is a communication disorder that results from damage or injury to language parts of the brain. It's more common in older adults, particularly those who have had a stroke. Aphasia gets in the way of a person's ability to use or understand words. Aphasia does not impair the person's intelligence. People who have aphasia may have difficulty speaking and finding the "right" words to complete their thoughts. They may also have problems understanding conversation, reading and comprehending written words, writing words, and using numbers. *My frustration!* No longer able to be witty and quick, I came to avoid the social situations I used to enjoy. Isolation.

At the time, I didn't have the knowledge and tools to deal with all of this. It might seem that "*Isolation*" would make things darker and worse, but without the proper direction and tools, I found it better to take myself out of those situations I might become uncomfortable with. I stayed away from anxious situations and stayed within my comfort zone.

Social situations are where my "Access Dyslexia" seems to be the greatest. *My brains on **overload** and conversations are work.* Being quick and witty is expected of me, and trying to produce this weighs heavy. Conversation and interaction demands thought processing. During the processing, my brain can't find the memory/data file or folder and in an attempt to give a response, I spit out a word or group of words, which are generic at best, or opposite at worst. I feel stupid. All of my friends understand it by now, but inside, it's hard to handle. Simple conversation can be exhaustingly frustrating.

I've had to admit that I don't always trust my brain. My memories are often faulty. Growing up, I watched as my father's memories faltered too. He hasn't admitted this yet, but when he can't remember something, it's the start of his frustration beginning to boil. This is the same for me. When I can't access my memories or they are faulty, frustration takes hold. For me, debating a position is utterly fatiguing, most often ending with incorrect words coming out or not at all. ***The increased pace of thought overheats my operating system.*** The memories I'm searching for are gone or incorrect. Then, in the frustration of not being able to make my point or defend my position, I get angry. *Chaos* sinks it's claws in and takes hold, seeking the easiest way to take back control. I become louder, veins protruding from my forehead. **I've suddenly become my father.** ***Shit!***

Something else that started soon after my TBI was tongue biting. I literally cannot chew while doing something as easy as talking or writing. It's my "access dyslexia" of eating. I had never even thought about the process, as it always seemed automatic. Now, I have to stay focused on the slow methodical chewing pattern, because if I forget and let it go automatically, I will inadvertently push my tongue up into my teeth and bite through it, as I chewed food. I've bitten my tongue hundreds of times, bringing me to the ER twice and needing stitches. Who gets stitches in their tongue? Me.

The Brain Pain came to the forefront after my second hit. I remember telling my boss I felt like I had been ruthlessly pummeled by a bear. I hurt all over. The throbbing in my head was more intense than I had ever felt. My ability to comprehend what was going on was too complex to process without becoming exhausted. *I felt like my brain was using a dial-up modem, instead of a cable Internet connection.* I couldn't get back on-line and access my files. I would maintain through the pain and my various other problems by telling myself I'd be better tomorrow, or next week. My irritability was getting worse and my decision-making process erratic. I was holding a lot in, constantly checking myself and walking a tight rope all at the same time. I second-guessed every choice I made. Second-guessing has no place in combat.

There were constant themes in my nightmares; one was me possibly faltering, hesitating and stalling during combat or while under duress, and the other that I was dying of a Brain aneurysm.

The spikes of electric shock like pain shooting through my brain occurred even during my sleep. ***Chaos* was digging in**. In my mind there was no doubt something was wrong. I had been of strong mind and body for so many years and knew myself, pre-injury. I realized I was on a path of degeneration. Only you know what's going on inside your head and for the first time in my life, my thoughts and cognitive processes were askew. Several months earlier I had completed Air Command and Staff College in record time, and now I was living from a notebook and relying on sticky notes to remember. **Was I becoming *Defective*?** I wasn't going to be satisfied with that.

Just the Brain Pain itself, told me that there was something deeper going on. On the job, my priority was to utilize my team. As the Officer in Charge (OIC) of my section, I had to ensure that I carried out and delegated orders the best I could. As I lost confidence in my decisions, I asked my team for more and more of their input, bouncing everything off them. The Brain Pain and "Access Dyslexia" was taking its toll. As my memories weakened, I would get angry over not being able to access them. I was faking my way through. Decisions became a team effort. **Thankfully, I had a great team**. My deputies, Capt. Geozelious and Capt. Bieber, were instrumental in backing me up. They knew what happened to me, but you could see they didn't understand it completely. Hell, weeks earlier, I didn't either.

Another constant intruding into my life was ***the hypervigilance of thought***. I couldn't turn it off. Suddenly my thought process couldn't be slowed down by itself. My mind would constantly race, getting deeper and deeper into whatever topic is was stuck on. I liken it to you're in a parked car, but the engines still racing. Relaxing was practically impossible. My attention span is scattered, like changing the channel over and over, then stopping on one to momentarily focus, then onto another ten minutes of channel surfing, until you remember what you were looking for in the first place.

BRAIN PAIN

My first diagnosis was called "Post Concussive Syndrome," with a headache, but this was sheer pain. **From the first blast I called it, "Brain Pain."** I was far from being the only one with this. Brain Pain feels like a warm bruise pulsing around the exterior of the brain, while mini explosions of lightning crackle through the interior gelatinous mass inside my skull. I learned that the brain itself doesn't have any pain receptors, but the meninges, (branches of arteries or membranes that envelope the brain and spinal cord), the periosteum, (membranes covering the surface around the skull), and the scalp do. The brain is the sensor that perceives and reacts to pain in the body. The pain was inside my head.

As the various types of Brain Pain manifested, I named each of them, to relay to the doctors what was happening inside my head. I came up with analogies they could understand. I would describe the actual pain with four names: Washing Machine, Spike, Tesla and Mohawk. Both blasts were to my right side and to this day, that's where the majority of pain is located.

The *"Washing Machine"* is a constant, daily pain, much like a washing cycle that churns round and round. It circles the exterior of my brain with a throbbing texture of pain, much like a fresh bruise. Sometimes it's debilitating and other times it's just a warm constant annoyance, but its always there, 24/7. Nothing works for this one so I "move through." It's part of my morning checklist, right off the bat. Take a piss, check my head. Yep, pains still there.

The *"Spike"* is a sharp pain, like a mini-explosion that can occur anywhere in my brain. Right side, left side, center, bottom or top. The majorities come from the upper right hemisphere, which was the direction both blasts came from. It manifests with a sharp shock-like burst inside my skull. Anytime, anywhere, it will jolt me back into its grasp, reminding me who's the boss. Without any way of combating it, my natural reflex is to knock it away, literally, tapping. Morse code. SOS. ***Tap, tap, tap,*** pause, ***tap, tap, tap***, etc. *Hey, what's that guy doing hitting himself?* Out of nowhere, they instantly manifest. I don't have a choice nor do I care what anyone is thinking. I just tap. These can last 10-30 seconds and happen dozens of times per hour. For years, I tapped, trying to diffuse and disseminate it. It's awkward for others who see me doing this, so I've worked on just squinting and holding pressure on it. But shit happens, and there I go tapping again.

Recently, one of my doctors saw me doing this and explained to me that the light tapping on my scalp *confuses the scalp's pain receptors*. This made sense, so I found a palm sized vibrator to carry with me. The more I use my brain; i.e. arguments, debates, deeper thinking, the more pain that occurs. My scalp massager allows me to be a little more pro-active, prior to being lit up in pain.

The *"Tesla"* is named for the famous, "Tesla Coil," built by Nikola Tesla. This electrical shock sprouts around my brain like a burst of electrical energy searching for a conductor. It can go from the outside inward or vise versa. These pains occur dozens of times a day, but manifest more when I become sleep deprived. Sleep is an on-going battle. If the brain can't rest, it affects the processes. Good sleep equals good thinking. The fact is, we need to sleep so our brain can repair, reenergize itself and remove waste products.

Recently, there was a sleep study done by researchers at the [4]Uppsala University of Sweden showing that lack of sleep caused a build up in proteins, similar to those levels after a concussion. In other words, *Lack of sleep can have a similar effect on the brain as having a concussion would.* My point is that sleep is essential to a healthy brain, especially to those of us with a damaged one. Tesla pain lasts longer than the "Spike" and it interrupts my thoughts, body and life. But, that's what *Chaos* does, right? **Chaos is disorder, disarray and mayhem.** *Chaos* has no empathy. *Chaos* kicks you in the balls and then smacks you with a bat to the head when you grab them. *Oh, anyone watching? Don't care.*

Last is the *"Mohawk."* These are lengthy, sharp pains along the center of the top of my head, much like a Mohawk haircut pattern. They were more predominant in the early years and now just occasionally, 2-3 per week. They come out of nowhere unexpectedly. Good days, bad days, they bring me to my knees. Shooting straight up from the core of my brain, they split my skull down the center, disabling me instantly. It's as if *Chaos* is going in for the kill, the final "Coup de Gras!"

Almost everyone exposed to an explosion will have some sort of hearing loss and a constant ringing in the ears or **tinnitus**. My doctor told me if it's still there in 3-4 months, it'd be there forever. If you've ever shot a gun and forgot to put on ear protection, you'll understand what the ringing is like. It's still there and it's constant.

BRAIN PAIN

The evenings are the hardest. As things begin to quiet down, I lose the noise and shuffle of the day, the ringing in my ears rises to the surface, becoming louder and louder. My Brain Pain comes on suddenly in the midst of the ringing and hypervigilance of thoughts. It rises above the ringing, and to the forefront. It's one negative compounding onto another; anxiety provoking more anxiety. Trying to relax and rest becomes an enormous effort in itself, making it hard to finally shut down and sleep. *I wish I had special earplugs for the noise in my brain.* I normally take the easy way out, sleeping meds and a cocktail. *Will I wake?* I also become excessively aware of too many things at once and can't focus. Did I take the correct meds? What did I get accomplished that day? Is my heart-beating irregular? *Is that pain in my head going to erupt in a brain aneurysm tonight? Spikes, anxiety, tinnitus and nausea. Agh!*

Vertigo and nausea are also results of concussions. After my return I spent almost a year going through one form of balance therapy or another. I've fallen dozens of times and just recently, while standing up playing my guitar, vertigo struck and I fell straight down to the floor, catching myself at the last minute. It's hit me several times while driving as well. Every time, I was fortunate enough to have someone with me who took control.

Combined, these issues constitute my "Brain Pain."

After a blast, the second thing I did, after seeing that my legs and arms were intact, was to **grab my crotch**. *It was still there!* But many warfighters are not so lucky and may discover they had damage in this area. **Sex** is a topic rarely discussed, yet it is one of the largest motivators in our lives and one of our most important drives. Sex is a brain function. As the brain repairs itself, sex drive is placed on the back burner, or at least it was for me. Physical intimacy became too much work, again *easily being overwhelmed*.

Almost half of those with TBI will see a drop in their libido, and more than half of the men will have *Erectile Dysfunction*. *And yes, I have this problem.* My mind over thinks everything.

Most of those affected will have difficulties, specifically, with experiencing orgasm, in part related to the physical damage to the brain, depression, medications, etc. There is a loss in confidence,

68

passion and trust. Loving is but a memory. Physical intimacy, a longing replacement that doesn't always work.

Relationships take effort. Partners need attention and when you can barely take care of yourself, it can be *overwhelming* to give just the basic attention to a spouse, girlfriend or child. The interaction and constant explaining your feelings or lack of them, takes its toll. I had lost all feelings of love, even lust, after my injuries. I had no yearning to be attentive to those I cared about. I knew I loved my family and friends, but it was a clinical type, whereas I knew how I used to feel, so I played the part, until after several years, I found a new pathway to my underlying emotions. For me it was Horse Therapy that led me to trust again, and be open to my emotions. I'll talk more about that in a later chapter.

Also, as I struggled through my lack of loving emotions, I was constantly bombarded by the symptomatic anger and irritability of TBI and PTS. When your brain is in pain and you're walking around depressed and withdrawn, it's not easy to conjure up a reassuring smile to let those who love you know you're okay.

My memory often fails me and it can easily lead to an argument with someone close to you. I remember it one-way and they remember it another, more often than not they're right. But, my perception of my reality, memory, is my reality. I'm holding on to my memories with a death grip, wanting to believe I'm not losing my mind. Simple things like thinking your spouse or girlfriend moved your keys, because you're sure you left them in your spot, can blow up. So many times, I've been a hundred percent sure my memory was right, only to discover it wasn't. Loosing my mind?

All of those normal triggers that put stress on normal relationships grow exponentially with us. Money, doctor's appointments, grocery shopping, the cars, the children, the needs of the family, etc. Most of the time, you're able to fake your way through, while the pain and depression smolder under the surface, before one day, finally exploding into a breakup or divorce. *Chaos*?

My father calling himself "*Defective*" didn't happen recently. That first came out of his mouth after my parents got in a fight in the late eighties. The verbal argument was so intense, I had to intervene. I had to step in to "change the subject / change his mindset" which worked, and as he stood there in his silence, staring at me, I felt as if he wanted to say he was sorry, but what he uttered was *"I'm just Defective."*

I've also been through this with most of my wounded warrior mentee's. I'm a Wounded Warrior Program Peer Mentor, advising the younger wounded warfighters, through my experience. I can't count the times I've been called for everything from intervening between couples, to having to bail my guy out of jail, to having to escort my guys to court to keep them calm. Most relationships will pay the toll. Many don't survive.

Watching a documentary about returning wounded warriors, one section that stuck with me, was about a husband who returned to his family, a wife and several children. The "noise" of the household, literally and figuratively, was *overwhelming*. After months of trying to work it out, he finally had to get his own apartment. His own space. *I couldn't have done it either*. The "noise" of family interactions; needs of the individual family members; the assumption by them *that since they don't see your injury, you're "ok";* as well as the passion and love that's disappeared, would've been too all consuming. Time to disengage to my solace. I'm still single.

I remind myself that I chose to sit at this table.

Relationships usually have emotional highs and lows, but with TBI and PTS, most intimate encounters quadruple the thought process, more often than not, ending up with minimal arousal for the affected warfighter. I feel as if I've lost my passion; feeling love for very few. The sense of longing for a companion has been placed on a sidebar. My relationships have paid the toll.

With me, it was the normal needs, like the giving of my attention that comes with a girlfriend. Nothing in comparison to marriage and children. Social events became too intense. I had a hard time with memories, so when she remembered things differently, I had to trust her recollection. *I constantly doubt my own memories*. Her version would seem to be to her advantage, making it easy for her to manipulate an agenda, or me just thinking that. **Trust**. Yeah, I have a hard time with that one too. I chose to disengage, to isolate myself socially. I chose to not date and to focus on myself.

ANTHONY JONES

With TBI, the medical community can only tell you so much, so it's often left to us, the patient, to research and understand what's happening inside our heads, as well as find **alternative** treatments. With so much time on my hands after my return, I began to seek out others who had combat and explosive related TBI.

It was early 2009 and I was trying to understand and validate my Brain Pain. That's when I came across a story on [5]**Lt. Col. Ray Rivas**, an Army Reserve Civil Affairs Officer. After reviewing various articles about him, I realized how similar our stories and symptoms were, and that there were thousands more with the same story. This was someone I could relate to. He, too, had been in injured in two separate blasts, had trouble with headaches, often overwhelmed with emotions, trouble sleeping, problems with speech, balance and memories. Even more important to me, was that we were both in our early fifties when hit. How was he hanging on?

He had a great career, but now stated he had a **"Short circuit of the brain."** What my father so endearingly referred to as *Defective*. He had deployed to Bosnia, Afghanistan and Iraq, as an Officer with a promising career, but because his brain had been damaged, his life and the lives of his family were changed forever.

When I came upon the article, Lt. Col. Rivas had just testified, with the assistance of his wife, **Colleen Rivas**, before the United States Senate Committee on Armed Services Wounded Warrior Policy and Programs. In a short briefing, he attempted to let them know that he was once an intelligent individual, with a bright, active brain and that he was constantly engaged in the world.

In fact, this is some of my inspiration for writing this. I too, once had a bright and active brain. During the writing of this book, I did reach out to his wife Colleen to ensure accuracy. I will use several of her quotes to ensure her words are correct. She told me, "What I do know for a fact though, is that before Ray deployed and sustained his injury, *my husband was perfectly fine.* His memory was intact, both short-term and long-term, and he could function without any difficulty. *There were absolutely no issues before the explosion.* Anyone who knew him would testify to that. Whatever issues developed, had developed as a result of the blast." **Clarity to *Chaos*?**

In front of the [6]Senate Committee, Lt. Col. Rivas delivered a short brief on his experiences and lessons learned: how he didn't

71

remember much of his medevac process, and his first three months at Brooke Army Medical Center, (BAMC); and how he had been assisted by his battle buddies. According to his wife, "BAMC was so totally unprepared for traumatic brain injuries at that point. I don't think they knew what to do with Ray."

What he was most concerned about was how the Service Members' Group Life Insurance Traumatic Injury Protection (TSGLI) Program was failing our returning wounded military personnel. The program is part of the VA Disability Pension and Military Medical Retirement pay. He felt that the warfighter, Guardsman or Reservist injured in combat in a Theater of Operations, wounded by no fault of their own, should not be ***penalized*** for "getting blown up," or "shot," prior to serving 20 active years. In other words, not being able to receive his full retirement benefits.

He and his family were extremely affected by these payment rules, as am I. As a reservist, this was something else we had in common. As I'll talk about later, these payment rules affected me immensely, as well as thousands of others who had served their country and are disabled with combat injuries. It can be so mentally exhausting, to mount a fight for your *well deserved and promised benefits*. Lt. Col. Rivas and his wife Colleen were out there doing just that. If you add surmounting financial concerns with an exhausting mental battle, what do you get? **Our system fueling our *chaos*?**

When it's difficult to think, it's difficult to advocate for yourself. Worrying about your financial future goes back to the basic issues of self worth, esteem and affirmation and survival. Today's military warfighters are the cream of the crop; having spent the majority of their adult lives taking on advanced education and training. Then, after being injured, you're torn down to a life of dependency. Should I have just died a glorious death? ***Earning a living and monetary benefits is at the core of an injured warfighters worries.*** Survival becomes all-consuming during the initial recovery, when it should be the smoothest. It's like a truck pulls out in front of you and you don't have the reaction ability to swerve.

I believe if I could find statistics regarding what weighs most on the minds of Wounded Warriors, **at the top would be their future and how they support themselves and their families**. I'm single and have found it overwhelmingly worrisome. For those with families, it can be crushing. These warfighters don't want to be dependant on any system or be a burden to others; they want to continue to be self reliant and productive members of society and maintain their esteem and self worth.

According to Lt. Col. Rivas' statement, *"This injury has not only ended my Military career, but also my civilian career as an Engineer with the Department of Defense, for whom I worked 18 years and as a Licensed Peace Officer in the state of Texas, where I served as a Reserve Sheriff's Deputy for 8 years with the Comal County Sheriff's Department."*

Here was a warrior with whom I had similar experiences. He was my age and had already been diagnosed with rapidly emerging Alzheimer's disease. If that's not bad enough, did he also have another neurodegenerative disease that could not be detected? According to his wife Colleen, "It was very frustrating for him and us because we witnessed firsthand the excruciating pain he was in and there absolutely nothing we could do. He wanted a definitive diagnosis and he wasn't getting one and I think that is when he felt that he had been forgotten. They took care of his other injuries that needed surgery, but for the brain injury and the pain, **they just medicated him with narcotics**; I think that they even tried brain blocks, but nothing worked. In all fairness though, I will say that at the time, the hospital was in the process of establishing a department to focus on brain injuries, but unfortunately Ray fell between the cracks."

"When the department was finally up and running, Ray was sent for a battery of tests; one of which was a PET scan, *and this scan did show that there was diminished activity in the frontal region of the brain.* Once this was ascertained, they began sending him for outpatient therapy to a place called Health South Riosa, which was a very good facility. I saw a significant amount of improvement after he started going there, but unfortunately, the Army had already started the process to medically retire him. ***The Army was done with him.*** That was when we were told by one of the neurologists that they felt they had done everything they could do for Ray. This particular neurologist believed that Ray was going into **Frontal Temporal Dementia**, not Alzheimer's. Honestly, in my opinion, I don't even think there was anything to back up that diagnosis."

BRAIN PAIN

"When the Army medically retired him, they just called us in to an office one day with no warning and said, *'We can't fix you'* and to look at it as if he were a broken cog in a wheel and that they were going to pull him out and replace him with a new one." Those were the doctor's exact words that day, in addition to looking at me and telling me that I needed to make plans for long-term nursing care because within five years he would need to be placed in a nursing home. I will never forget the look on Ray's face. **I look back now and realize that *was the day he gave up*.** His identity was tied to his career and they took that away from him, in what seemed like an instant. It was a downhill spiral from there." *Clarity* had been his identity, as with me. *Chaos* now took that too.

As I will discuss later, boxers and professional football players have recently been discovered posthumously, with Chronic Traumatic Encephalopathy, or **CTE**. This is a neurodegenerative disease prevalent with individuals with a ***history of repetitive brain trauma***, such as blows to the head, multiple concussions and explosive blasts.

Lt. Col. Rivas had all the symptoms of CTE. Once an engineer, now he had problems doing simple math, driving and getting dressed. I understand it all too well. One minute we're fine and happy go lucky, and in the next, we're slobbering over ourselves in dread. We're invisible until we crack, then the yolk slips out. Those with TBI can easily slip through the cracks. Was he me?

On October 25th, 2004, country music singer **Gary Allan**, legal name Gary Allen Herzberg, found his wife dead, apparently after having shot herself. The reason I remember this, is because this suicide had more to it than just depression. Originally, I read about it in my mother's [7]"People" magazine. Mr. Herzberg's wife, Angela Herzberg, had suffered from extreme and debilitating migraines. I was intrigued because I didn't previously believe in them. It was out of ignorance. I just didn't understand them. No one in my family had them, nor did anyone I knew. So when I read about the lengths one person went to, to rid themselves of such pain, I felt drawn to her story.

Gary and Angela each had three kids of their own. She had been a Flight Attendant when they met on a plane. After moving to Tennessee from California, she began to suffer from allergies. Those allergies would trigger migraines. These migraines were described as so bad that she would black out and be forced to lie down. The migraines would then trigger the depression. She received treatment for the migraines, but not the depression.

The thought that someone was in so much pain that they would choose to leave behind the ones they love, seemed hard to understand. But it happened. *Her story gave me a new understanding of something I couldn't previously understand, a damaged mind.* Now I understand all too clearly how this can happen. I had no idea at the time, how my life would one day be on the same dangerous highway.

As humans, we have the gift of consciousness, self-awareness and free will. These are the actions that make us human and allow us to survive and thrive. The mind is the organ responsible for movement, calculations and predictions. Our brain learns from the mistakes and corrects itself, adjusts and refines until success is achieved. Through our natural competitive drive, we strive to think, communicate and move better than the others around us; we endure to better ourselves. It's survival.

Our brain sees our surroundings and interprets them. This has given us the ability to navigate our surroundings and communicate with other species. **It has also given us the ability to predict**. Starting out with predicting movements, symbols and sounds, while interpreting them, which led to commonalities, which became speech and writing. The brain's unique ability to predict is a complicated methodology of comparisons and contrasts to which our brain reviews past events and predicts how movement or communication can most likely lead to a desired outcome. Once it makes a prediction, it signals to our body to act or move, carrying out the order.

A rifle shooter who attempts an extremely long-range shot is using the body's muscles and is predicting the trajectory of the bullet, based on thousands of calculations. The same thing occurs when a golfer hits a ball, a basketball player throws his ball, a football receiver catches a ball, a boxer responds to a punch, etc. ***Our brain is the great predictor of our abilities***.

I call it "**The Line**." It simply means maintaining the balance of your path, predicting future possibilities, and making the decision to ensure your survival and success. Since I was a kid, I've been riding "the line"; driving, biking, karate, skateboarding, skiing, surfing and pole vaulting, to mention a few. Riding "the line" has long been one of my underlying philosophies that fuel my instincts.

Recently, I was over in Thailand visiting my college buddy Rick. The primary method of getting around there is motorcycles. The methods in which the masses use cycles are daunting. Hundreds of cycles, SUV's and very large tourist buses clog the miniature streets, making for a video game like adrenaline rush.

Not knowing about my philosophy of "the line," Rick spent the first week, as I'm riding with him, relating *his* version of "the line." Predicting, calculating, action versus reaction, consequences, situational awareness, communication, adjusting and re-adjusting, etc. By doing so, his goal was for me to integrate *his* methodology of the line into mine, making it easier for me to ride his line with him. Acknowledging and practicing *"the line,"* allows me to work out my brain. It's brain exercise to me. Rick's thoughts helped put me on track and *exercising my brain* was going to become one of my new tools. During down time, I use Lumosity brain games on my phone to keep engaged. ***Brain training and brain exercise. Working it!***

Don't let *Chaos* steal your moments. *Chaos* still clogs the drain in my brain with indecision and pain, but it's my new standard. My goal is to clear that blockage or to go around it, i.e. **work a round**.

Over the years, I've developed my own Rotor-Rooter system to work around obstacles. More than likely it's different for everybody, but medications are the easy way not to *do the work*. Up to you.

The links in your chain may break, hopefully on the smaller issues, giving you the forewarning of how to handle them during larger crises. You learn how to work around, fixing and strengthening them continuously. It's going to take work. It's one of my new mantras. *"Doing the work?"* It's why I bike almost everyday. My friend Glen calls it "walking off the crazy." I call mine "riding off my *chaos.*" You have to find what works for you. Walk it off, ride it off; whatever works. *But we must "do the work," or the "links" will snap. With us, it's not if, but when?*

The first few years after a brain injury is the adaptation and stabilization period. I started with balance therapy, walking ropes, balancing on the path, and trying to make it to the next phase. Now years later, as a snowboarder, I'm trying to ride "my line" to the bottom of the hill. Working around and learning.

ANTHONY JONES

The hypervigilance of thoughts never stops and it's easy to become overwhelmed. **OVERWHELMED!** When this happens, the anxiety starts and that feeling of dread rolls over me. It grows and grows. But, I've learned to recognize it and manage it, to work around it. Most times I can change up what I'm doing, worst case scenario, I pop a pill.

Managing this includes changing my mindset, continuing therapies, more or less, finding a new routine or standard. It was during this early period that I was extremely hard on myself. My perception was that others saw the *slowness* I felt submerged in. I felt like I was walking around with TBI and PTS written on my forehead. I was my own nemesis; stalked by *Chaos*. It was in my mind – I think?

Once I made it through the sluggishness, around year five, I realized maybe things aren't going to get better, but they weren't getting any worse. I accepted it and I moved on to what I call my *management strategy phase*. I was now riding the line, doing the work and trying to erase that TBI from my forehead. Most importantly, ***exercising my brain*** *was my way of "doing the work" and not letting the cogs rust.*

My biggest complaint is that our government spends most of its funds on bureaucracy, more research and studies, *and it never gets down to the end user, or us,* ***before our links snap****!* 22 vets a day!

It easier and cheaper for the medical system / bureaucracy to hand out prescriptions meds. It's the same with the NFL bureaucracy. Give them some pills or a shot, and get them back out in the game. How many fatalities from overdosing on ***alternative*** treatments like oxygen, weed or acupuncture? *Haven't heard of any.* How many have died from overdosing on pills? I will discuss this later.

As we research deeper and deeper into new treatments to heal the brain, we'll, without a doubt, stumble on high-tech ways to supercharge it. They're already doing it. Cochlear implants for hearing, artificial retinas for eyesight and there's already a brain prosthesis EEG (Electroencephalography) controller that senses the brain waves and can control avatars on a computer. Much like a smart phone today, people will want to have the next greatest capability added onto their brain. That's where all that research money is going. *TBI victims just want to be able to think and we need relief now!*

In Iraq, my nickname was, "**Rocket Man**" because I seemed to always be right in the vicinity of an explosion. Multiple blasts, multiple concussions. My "Spikes" are a constant reminder of my path. I'm drawn to learn as much as possible, advocate and be a voice for what most people don't understand, or simply don't believe. Without an organized mind, our life's experiences are diminished.

As a society, we easily forget. Especially with this "Invisible Wound." Can't see it – don't believe it.

Our society moves to the beat of the next news bite. New treatments are stuck in the research and conversation mode, instead of floating down to the *end users* (TBI & PTS patients), who could mentally and physically benefit. The bureaucracy. As I write this, the Administration is offering up millions of dollars for research and development for new treatments. **Why wasn't this done after Vietnam and prior to going into another war**?

Our government knew we'd have Wounded Warriors returning. As I'll show, there have been plenty of treatments tested and validated by other countries, yet we have to reinvent the wheel, slowing the process of getting that treatment to the end user.

Treatments have to be FDA approved and with multiple controlled studies done, which take years and affect our "quality of life." Wasting ever precious time while we are stuck and in pain. A simple and effective treatment like Acupuncture isn't covered. We, the *end users*, even with our military insurance and VA benefits, can't always afford to go elsewhere and pay for treatments that are actually available. So, we are out there on our own and silently told to, "Suck it up." **This bureaucracy seems designed to wear you out**.

It's been my experience that you're easily forgotten in the system if you don't complain and become someone's pain in the ass. *The squeaky wheel gets the grease.* It shouldn't be that way. We are already angry! *Those who are suppose to heal us, just make us worse by prescribing away our problems.* It's a war of attrition, where our loved ones and us must persevere on our own, because the medical, legal and administrative bureaucracy is wearing us out!

Is there hope? Yes, for the next generations. Just fifty years ago, blood loss (hemorrhage) was the leading killer on the battlefield.

Although it still is, survivability rates have skyrocketed. There's not much doubt that one day soon, we'll come up with some methodology (oxygen, stem cells, medication or electrical stimuli?), that will either speed up the healing or regenerate damaged or broken neural pathways and/or synaptic connections, (i.e. the work around process.)

Just yesterday, *Chaos* stuck a knife in my eye "Mohawk" style, which manifested like a lighting bolt slamming though my head. I was walking down my outside stairs and when it jolted me backwards, vertigo pulling me to the ground as I hit my head against the railing. The blood from my scalp poured into my eyes. The *mosquitoes* were swarming me again, sensing my vulnerability. It was a reminder of how delicate we are. It reminded me I'm **"Defective,"** as Dad would say.

Our brain is who we are, or were? *Chaos* searches out my defects, befriending them. ***Chaos is the firestorm in my brain.***

*On the right is the trailer I was walking into on Oct. 25th, 2007. A 107mm rocket went through the corner hitting the concrete T-Barrier, blasting outward, hitting me. On the left is my roommate **Eric** pointing out the impact crater in the T-Barrier. Eric was inside the trailer and has had his share of headaches too. We made it!*

My father, Lt. Jones, at his gun during the siege of Khe Sanh.

Lt. Col. Ray Rivas at his gun during his tour in Afghanistan.

CHAPTER 6

MORE PILLS?

We'd been out on the weapons range most of the day. It was towards the end of one of our Bodyguard / PSD (Private Security Detail) training courses, where we put everything our students learned during the first few weeks into live fire contact scenarios. In the first years after my injuries, this is what kept me busy. It was now 2010 and I was the Director of Training at CRI Training, a PSD training company here in Las Vegas. The day went pretty well, just long. I was exhausted. I was the first one there and the last one to leave. The courses could be strenuous for the staff as well as the students. **This was usually where I thought;** *I can operate at my former level.* When I got home, I ate something and took my sleep meds. I fell asleep in my easy chair, waking to the TV. I got up, took my sleep meds, set the alarm and went to bed. Several minutes later, I popped up, remembering I needed to take my sleep meds, so I did.

Two hours later a nightmare with a spike, jolted me awake. I got up to take a pain med and discovered I had already taken my nighttime meds, three times. *I screwed up!* **Triple dose***!* Vomiting time. That's exactly what I did. A mixture of mustard, warm water and salt, and a toothbrush down my throat. Doing the Work.

Combat's a breeding ground for injuries, anxiety and medication. Especially afterwards. *Chaos* did not hesitate. At night, the "noise" of daily life diminishes and the pain, tinnitus and hypervigilance of thoughts rise to the surface. Those of us with TBI often have memory issues. I can't count the times I've gotten lost, forgotten something, or believed I had already done something I hadn't. The first year after returning was the hardest. *All this new medication, new routines and therapies became overwhelming.*

With war, there will always be injuries, thus warfighters with pain, thus medications. With war, there will always be anxiety, thus more medications to take the edge off. Morphine was used by the Roman physicians and by medical doctors in the Civil War, then modernized to second and third generation Opioids such as Percocet, Oxycodone and Tramadol, which were used in Iraq and Afghanistan. Similar to the abuse of prescription opiates today, the post-Civil War era saw the materialization of "**Morphinism**," or Morphine addiction. It was the ultimate way of managing pain. With war, you will always have warfighters with sleeping problems, thus alcohol and Ambien or other sleep aids. The names of the drugs have changed, but the reasons they are used have not.

I arrived in Baghdad at the end of August 2007, during "The Surge," and incoming rocket and artillery fire was on-going daily and nightly. The flight inbound was on a C-130 from Kuwait. I had 1000 plus hours in MC-130 Combat Talon and immediately recognized the rapid spiral descent coming down into the Baghdad International Airport. The crew was punching out flares during the descent, to counter heat-seeking missiles. I had done this close to a hundred times in training, but this time it was real and I wasn't part of the crew, but just a passenger. *At first, the anxiety intrigued me.* **As time went by, I sought it out.**

Within a few days I got my first taste of incoming or Indirect Fire (IDF). It had been a beautiful sunset in Baghdad, as I was walking to my trailer. The claxon sounded, and since I was practically alone next to a field, I instinctually jumped into the ditch next to me. Rolling into the ditch I accidentally looked to the sky, where I saw the C-RAM (Counter Rocket And Mortar) mini-gun's snakelike trail of incendiary rounds spiraling upwards. It was memorizing. Much like hundreds of fireworks trailing upwards before exploding. ***"Rocket's red glare."***

The C-RAM is used to locate and destroy incoming rocket and mortar rounds in the air, before they hit the ground. It's radar controlled and shoots out a volley of several hundred rounds that target and destroy the IDF. For a moment it seemed like a beautiful trail of tracer fire against the dark nighttime sky, until they hit two rockets, which exploded in the sky, literally ***"Bombs bursting in air."***

Seconds later, one, and then another landed in the field next to me, thunderously exploding about fifty feet away, sending dirt and gravel accelerating past, covering me with dirt, and filling the air with a sandy mist. *It left me with a helpless feeling of dread.* There's no fighting back, no direction to throw your anger. I had brought extra body armor inserts with me from home and that night I laid them out between my mattress and the springs; building a small shelter I could roll under at night. I also placed my armored vest next to the bed so I could roll into it. I can't count how many times IDF occurred when I was asleep. My roommate, Eric, and I would just fall off our bunks and pull on the vests until the "all clear." It became the norm. Years later, when I would try and figure out what provoked all the anxiety, I realized, *Oh, yeah! Getting bombed night after night.* Much like my father experienced in Vietnam.

Of course, if you went to a doctor, you could get a prescription for Ambien, but that would go down in your medical records and most people didn't want that, or the stigma of being mentally weaker that would accompany it. **Tylenol PM** is Acetaminophen and diphenhydramine, an over the counter cold and sleep medication. This combination is used to treat the common cold and the flu, and it causes drowsiness. You wanted to be 100% every day, so you did what you had to. Abuse of these was common knowledge and dealt with quietly. Most would be sent home, back to their units. But there were incidents of fighting within the ranks as well as suicides.

On May 11, 2009, [8]**Sgt. John Russell** stole an M-16, walked into the Camp Liberty Combat Stress Clinic in Baghdad, and killed two Army officers and three Army enlisted personnel. Sgt. Russell was on his fifth deployment and receiving counseling and treatment at the clinic for insomnia as well as depression and anxiety. He was five years short of retirement and his job performance and personnel interactions were deteriorating. It wasn't looking as if he'd make it to retirement. His doctors believed he was seeking a medical diagnosis that would allow him to be medically discharged from the Army, thus saving his retirement. *Numerous bad decisions, as well as medications,* ***led him to snap****.*

BRAIN PAIN

When we look back to the Civil War, the fighting occurred in our homeland, affecting both civilians and warfighters. The casualties were overwhelming; over 600,000 dead, and double that, wounded and psychologically in despair. The wounded and dying were handled much like they had been for thousands of years after battle; opium, wine and spirits for pain, then biting on leather as doctors removed limbs and shrapnel. To be able to numb yourself psychologically was a means of mental survival for both physicians and soldiers alike. The primary **"social sedative"** was alcohol. *Whiskey, brandy and other various liquors were on the medical supply inventories of each regiment.*

In World War I, part of the daily ration for a British soldier included an eighth of a pint of rum, and an additional ration given to soldiers prior to advancing on the enemy during trench warfare. The Germans did much more, giving their men a daily ration of a pint of beer, a half pint of wine and a quarter pint of spirits. The drug of choice for the German Army, Air Force and front line troops was without doubt methamphetamines. This was designed intentionally to keep them alert and active for more than several hours at a time.

In Vietnam, Darvon, which was a sedative and favorite of medics, would be given for sedation as well as pain. Technology has evolved in the last forty to fifty years; so many people may not remember Darvon. Today's pharmaceuticals have new names with a vast array of uses. Ambien for sleep, Seroquel, to ease mental hypervigilance (being on guard constantly), and Oxycodone or Percocet for pain, are some of them.

Ironically, during the Vietnam War, the use of drugs and becoming addicted to drugs could be considered a war crime, but was mostly responded to by just dishonorably discharging the, (obviously addicted), offender. Every war in the last two hundred years has had problems with soldiers coming back becoming or already addicted to alcohol, painkillers, narcotics and/or amphetamines. Halfway through the Vietnam War, the government quietly suggested a drug awareness program be put in place. This was done after realizing their failure with the hundreds of thousands of returning soldiers with substance abuse issues, the cost of dishonorably discharging them back into society and the costs to society for criminal and mental health cases.

ANTHONY JONES

In 1971 a program called, [9]"**Operation Awareness**," was put into place at Fort Bragg, North Carolina. In the same year, the DOD issued a mandatory directive that all services adopt an amnesty program. This program was available to any serviceman with substance abuse issues, and allowed him to receive drug rehabilitation and if successful, not suffer criminal charges. The program was developed to allow soldiers to get the help they needed so they could finish their service without a dishonorable discharge, seek civilian employment and become an asset to society, not a burden. I couldn't find out whether the program worked or not, but as the article stated, *at least the Army was trying*.

In Iraq and Afghanistan, warfighters are faced with the high-tempo pace of multiple deployments, combat stress and physical injuries. This leads to a rise in prescription drug and alcohol abuse. Prescription drugs help them get through the deployments and then, upon return, alcohol is added. *Many warfighters fall into this category, as I have*. It's so easy to numb the pain and anxiety with a few drinks. And when they cannot get the prescriptions any more they go to the street.

Because of our watchdog media and numerous Veteran groups, our hierarchy has put in place more programs that are supposed to provide intervention and assistance. The hardest thing is asking for help. It's all too easy to go to the doctors and get a prescription. I've heard too many Veterans say, **"If they're giving them to me, it must be okay**." Many of our warfighters are making it back alive, only to succumb to over medicating. Yes, prescription drugs are the default for many doctors, but *personal responsibility* must be part of the solution.

[10]**Senior Airman Anthony Mena** served two tours in Iraq and returned suffering from anxiety, sleep deprivation and back pain. He was diagnosed with PTS and prescribed a cocktail of medications. He passed away at his home in January of 2009. The toxicologists found eight different medications in his blood, including sedatives, painkillers and antidepressants. The toxicologist reported that the combination and interaction of drugs was the cause of death.

[11]Marine **Corporal Andrew White**, who served in Iraq, died in February of 2008, at the age of 23. His death was the result of over-prescribed medications for his PTS, including Clonazepam, Seroquel

and Paxil. [12]**Sgt. Eric Layne** was a National Guardsman who served in Iraq and returned alive, but with a severe case of PTS. He passed away in his home in January of 2008, after having returned from a VA in-patient treatment program. He was on a **cocktail** of prescription medications, including Paxil, Klonopin, Seroquel and others.

This list goes on and on. Once again, I must reiterate that these young warfighters will often say that if the medications are prescribed to them, they must be okay. I had a lifetime of experience behind me, but these young men and women, full of youthful hormones, are facing their demons fresh out into the world. I remember my youth and how alcohol was a social standard. Add this into their med-cocktail mix and the spiral falls into the depths of hell.

Most drugs are tested as a single treatment, not as one ingredient in the combination of medications. Many warfighters are taking and mixing several medications together. *This is commonly known as a Med-Cocktail.* Examples would be an anti-convulsant to help with TBI from an explosion, and an anti-psychotic to assist with the PTS, nightmares and with sleeping. I'm doing this all the time.

[13]*Each day, 44 people in the United States die from overdose of prescription drugs – the majority are opioids.*

[14]An estimated more than one million US veterans take **prescription opioids** for pain, and nearly half of them use the drugs chronically. This report found that alcohol and drug dependence are strongly associated with homelessness as well as with mental health conditions – including post-traumatic stress syndrome and depression – that affect 40 percent of Iraq and Afghanistan veterans in VA care. Drugs or alcohol are involved in one of three Army suicides, and the *VA estimates that 22 veterans commit suicide each day.* When you can't get the pills anymore, you go to the streets, Heroin.

[15]Four in five new heroin users started out misusing prescription painkillers. As a consequence, the rate of heroin overdose deaths nearly quadrupled from 2000 to 2013. My worry came when, last year, the DEA reclassified Tramadol, a synthetic opioid, as a controlled substance. My pain relief had been coming, primarily, from Tramadol. Last spring, I had shoulder surgery and was given

Oxycodone for pain. At the end of the 30-day prescription, I called my doctor and tried to get another. I then realized I shouldn't be doing it any more and canceled that request. That told me that I needed to get myself off of it.

Tramadol had been part of my medication strategy for the last five years. Once, sometimes twice, occasionally three times a day on a very bad day. It helped minimized the brain pain. I started out on Percocets, then Oxycodone, but those made me feel high and drunk or dizzy. They were too strong. I couldn't operate. With Tramadol I could operate normally. But, after years of being on it and then starting Botox shots around my head for the pain, I tried to quit. Three times in the last two years I tried to quit. I couldn't. This told me I might have a problem. Just to think about that makes me feel as if I've failed at something.

Me addicted? No way! But, there were crazy withdrawal pains and each time I just couldn't stop. No doctors had told me to stop; I had just decided that my new Botox regiment, as well as physical exercise was better than continuing on with more pills. Additionally, the DEA had just reclassified it as a controlled substance, along with a warning from the VA that it could be habit forming. *Yep, it sure was.*

What am I afraid of – not waking up. A good friend of mine, **Tommy Glanville**, didn't wake up. Oxycodone. He accidentally misjudged how many to take for his pain.

Before Iraq, I wasn't on any medication stronger than aspirin or fish oil supplements. Post deployment, that's all changed and I've become a Veteran of the post-war prescription medication era. A few months ago I went for a vacation in Thailand to visit my buddy Rick. Purposely, I didn't bring the Tramadol. I was there for thirty days and *quit cold turkey*. I kept busy playing music, re-writing this book, going to the gym, the beach and biking.

Over the years, I've taken notes and done my research, mostly for me to understand and remember. To comprehend these drugs more I wanted to break them down into some categories that can be discussed in relation to TBI and PTS. This issue is at the daily forefront of my life, as I've been on many of the listed medications for the last several years.

TBI and PTS are the most common injuries coming out of the war in Afghanistan and Iraq. Antipsychotic drugs will help with the

PTS, and the anticonvulsant drugs will help those with TBI. I am not a medical doctor and this is only based on my experience, of which I've now had plenty. *Do your research – do your work!*

These are the categories:

Anti-psychotics: PTS - Seroquel, Risperidone, Ziprasidone, Abilify and Risperdal. Antipsychotic drugs are a psychiatric medication used to manage various psychoses, including disordered thought and hallucinations. They are also used to treat schizophrenia and bipolar disorder. New uses for third-generation variations such as Seroquel have been used for a calming effect of the mind. Antipsychotic drugs in the military have risen over 200% since 2001.

These third-generation drugs are often used for treating mild to moderate depression and PTS. These sleep aids also are used for reducing nightmares. Seroquel was one of the first medications prescribed to me, off label, for sleep. The dreams were too vivid and it made my nightmares more realistic, so I stopped it.

Anti-depressants: PTS - Pamelor, Zoloft, Mirtazapine, Paxil, Celexa, Trazodone, Bupropion and Lexipro. Antidepressants are drugs used for the treatment of depression and other conditions such as anxiety disorders, neuropathic pain and attention deficit hyperactivity disorder to name a few. Antidepressant drug use in the military has increased 40% since 2001.

These are commonly prescribed for PTS. I was given Pamelor first, with no results, except that my eyesight worsened. Zoloft was also prescribed to me with little effect except for restlessness. I was also on Bupropion and Lexipro for a while with no noticeable positive results.

Anti-anxiety: PTS - Xanax, Valium, Cymbalta, Librium, Prozac, Lexipro, Antivan, Klonopin and Prazosin. Antianxiety drugs, also known as tranquilizers, are designed to relieve anxiety by slowing down the central nervous system. They have a calming and relaxing effect. Antianxiety drugs in the military have risen over 150% since 2001.

These are mostly prescribed for PTS and Insomnia. I've got to say here that Xanax is one of the most addictive, negative-side effect drugs ever prescribed. It's way too easy to get used too. Having said that, I still use it when the anxiety begins to overwhelm me. Also, Prazosin helps calm the nightly hypervigilance of my mind and calms my nightmares, making sleep easier and better.

Anti-insomnia / Sedatives: PTS - Ambien, Halcyon, Lunesta, Sonata, Phenobarbital, Seconal, Klonopin, Seconal, Valium, Temazepam and Promethazine. A sedative is another form of tranquilizer that induces sedation by reducing excitement of the brain.

My brain's always excited! Pretty obvious. Used to induce sleep and reduce anxiety. I've used Ambien for the insomnia, but never stay on it too long. It produces a deep sleep, but only for a few hours and I've also found myself sleep-eating on it. If I need to go down quick, I'll use this. I've also used Lunesta and Temazepam, both with similar positive results. Every year I switch from one to another, with my doctors overseeing it.

Anticonvulsants: TBI - Gabapentin, Lyrica, Topamax, Clonazapam, Lamotrigine, Depakote, Naproxen and Neurontin. Anticonvulsant drugs are also known as anti-epileptic drugs. They're primarily used in the treatment of epileptic seizures and in the treatment of neuropathic pain and mood stabilization. Anticonvulsant drugs in the military have risen 70% since 2001, as the levels of exposure to explosions from Improvised Explosive Devices and rocket attacks has increased. These were formerly known as anti-epileptic drugs, designed to calm hyperactivity in the brain. These are well known for helping migraine headaches and neuropathic pain, and commonly used for Traumatic Brain Injuries.

In my case I started out on Topamax, nicknamed *Dope-a-max*, which seemed to help some, yet made me slower mentally. Then for the next few years I went to Gabapentin, which stabilized my neuropathic Brain Pain only slightly. Next, we switched to Lyrica, which seemed to work better for me, but after a couple of years, the nerves in my legs and arms always seemed restless and tingling, so I stopped and then so did the restlessness. Two years ago I switched to Lamotrigine, which is working well for me, along with a regiment of Botox injections.

Pain: TBI - Tramadol, Acetaminophen, Percocet, Oxycodone and Lortab. A Traumatic Brain Injury can cause intense pain as well as affect the quality of life of the patient. Finding a pain management solution will be at the forefront of the individual's list. Patients will have to find the right mix of medication and ***alternative*** treatments.

I've been prescribed all the above, finally bringing it down to Tramadol, which worked for me. As I previously stated, I'm mostly off this now, but it's still an emergency option. Primarily, I'll try and use Naproxen instead.

[16]**SSgt. Tom Vande Burgt** was also a National Guardsman, who had served in Iraq and returned with PTS. He was on a medication cocktail of Klonopin, Celexa and Seroquel. When his wife questioned the high dosages and combination usage, he was taken off his meds abruptly. It was then discovered that there were no medical records of them being dispensed. With the help of new doctors, he eventually went off the drugs and his symptoms subsided. By the championing of his caregiver/advocate, he lived to tell his story. ***Advocates!***

I've been through most of these medications and found some work better for me than others. I also don't like feeling a loss of control or "high" feeling. I wanted something that would temper the pain, but still allow me to operate and function. I've been able to say no and accept the trade-off of some pain with minimal medication, but this is usually not the norm, which makes these drugs easily abused. *I'd rather live with pain, than die from misused meds.*

As you will see, I've also gone with many Natural/Holistic interventions, Eastern Medicine, rather than just prescription medications, e.g., Hyperbaric Oxygen Therapy, meditation, acupuncture, visualization, deep breathing, yoga, equine therapy, etc. ***It's all too easy to put a pill in your mouth, but "doing the work" should include these alternatives.***

I tried **Botox** the second year back, without success. Then as I started this book, my neurologist suggested we try again with a newer modernized version, every three months. It took four sessions, 1 year, before I noticed it working. The process is simple and fairly painless, if you don't have a problem with needles. These are the smaller needles and it feels like tiny pin pricks. A doctor who has been specially trained does the procedure. They'll usually have me flex certain facial and jaw muscles to find the correct spots and it's all over in less than fifteen minutes. When I started this procedure it was only covered by my military insurance, but recently I discovered the VA is now covering it as well. Forty injections around my scalp, neck and shoulders. It puts a damper on the intensity of the spikes. *That's something, so I'll take it!*

I get these shots every 3 months. It takes a couple of weeks for the relief to kick in and reduces my Brain Pain about thirty percent for the next six weeks, and then it wears off.

In the past six months, I've added a modernized version of acupuncture called "**Battlefield Acupuncture**," or several tiny needles inside a tiny band-aid, placed around and inside the ear. Acupuncture has worked for me before, but it's hard to get from my medical providers. The first time I had this done I received immediate pain relief. Today, as the Botox wears off at the two-month point, I get the *Acupuncture* to get through the month until I can get my Botox shots again. This, along with the emergency use of Tramadol, is my long-term ***management strategy***.

This prescription drug business or Big Pharma is a multi-billion-dollar industry, that doctors and lobbyists encourage, using the common theme; "the benefits can outweigh the risks." When there is no immediate answer to the problem, prescriptions are the quick fix and we accept it all too fast. *I can't sleep and I've got to go down, shit, I'm popping an Ambien.* I'm so guilty of this too.

Off label usage is at an all time high. This means, (*off label*) a drug hasn't been approved by the FDA for a particular malady, but patient feedback has shown it has possibilities of success. One example would be Seroquel, which is one the VA's top drugs in use today. It's an antidepressant, but the first time it was prescribed to me was for insomnia and my headache. Neurologists and Psychiatrists don't have any good medications for TBI and PTS, so they try to relieve the pain by a little bit of this and a little bit of that. *Their intent is well meaning, but hey, it's your life.*

Part of my lifetime of experience included the loss of a good friend to medications. ***Tommy Glanville***, mentioned earlier, was not only a good friend of mine, but a world class MMA fighter. On occasion, he worked for me as a bodyguard with my security company. As a fighter, he trained hard and often to get the job done. He trained and fought all over the world. For a tough fighter, he was also caring and loyal to those he loved. Throughout the years he had incurred numerous injuries and was prescribed various medications accordingly.

One night after working out, due to an accidental mix-up of those medications, he stopped breathing while asleep. It was Oxycodone. When you see and feel the loss of a loved one, it stays with you forever. It has stayed with me as I navigate my medications protocol. As you've read, more than once, I've mixed up mine. I am **exceedingly cautious** now, to the point of *accepting more pain* rather than possibly putting one too many pills in my mouth. A lesson painfully learned. *I want to wake up!*

Do the research. Every time you are issued a medication you're also entitled to a drug specifications sheet. It's usually given to you automatically the first few times you get the drug and then you can ask for it anytime afterwards. With today's online information and forums it's simple. I started by categorizing each drug that I'm prescribed, what it's for, why I'm taking it, when it should be taken and the negative interactions they can have. I also review my medications for long-term usage, trying to not stay on any particular medication longer than 12-18 months. Every year, I review each medication with my doctors, then find another similar to it and switch. I also test my *kidney and liver functions* to monitor toxicity levels.

Where patient advocates and/or family can help, is by reviewing and ensuring your medications are being dispensed appropriately and that you are being monitored for combination cross-contamination and side effects. Advocates!

I'm single. I don't have a spouse or care giver, so I have to be extra vigilant with color codes, yellow stickies and my own protocols to back up my decisions. I've screwed it up before, so I've constantly got to make it harder for me to screw it up next time. You've got to remember that all medications affect everyone differently. Yes, there's a standard reaction to most medications, but based on your body type, size and your brain, the actual reactions will differ. That's why some medications work better on some people, and other medications don't. This being said, adding alcohol is Russian roulette, yet we play it all the time. Patron anyone? *Chaos* has friends everywhere.

Numerous studies have also shown the efficacy of Hyperbaric Oxygen Therapy, Medical Marijuana, Acupuncture and Progesterone treatments as *alternative treatments.* For years, I've had to rely on just medications, because that's all my medical system would give me. This is the fight of my life and preparing myself is part of doing the work. I've researched these and have actually taken action, with positive results, with regards to Hyperbaric Oxygen Therapy and Acupuncture. A few years ago, I purchased my own Hyperbaric Oxygen chamber, hoping to stem a long-term neurodegenerative disease. I've devoted a chapter to it later in this book.

Supplements are a perfect example of an *alternative treatment*. My experience has led me to three supplements. *Fish Oil* or *Omega 3, B complex 50* and *L – Theanine*. [17]"Omega-3 fatty acids (fish oil) are important for brain health and repair. That makes it useful at treating the symptoms of most conditions involving brain function and that holds true with PTS as well." More recently, as I learn more, I've added B complex 50 and L – Theanine. B Vitamins work together to convert food into energy and they are necessary for healthy development and maintenance of the *brain* and *nervous system*. The complex is a supplementation of eight primary B vitamins in doses that optimize intake with little risk. L – Theanine is used to keep your Hypothalamus strong and is an amino acid found in green tea. The Hypothalamus activates two systems: the sympathetic nervous system and the adrenal-cortical system to produce the **fight-or-flight** response. It has been known to be damaged by impact events (concussions, as in my case). It can also assist to mitigate any *anxiety issues* such as post traumatic stress. Basically, it works in the brain to block anxiety and stress.

Medical Marijuana has been shown to act as a neuroprotectant in healing the brain, according to a recent [18]Israeli study. Israel and dozens of other countries are already using marijuana to treat Traumatic Brian Injuries. As the legalities become clearer to navigate, this is another possibility for me. I am looking more and more into this and once the legal and medical protocols are determined, I'll be the first in line at the door seeking a new opportunity for more pain relief. This is a much safer alternative to the many pharmaceuticals being prescribed to our warfighters.

Recently, I learned of another hopeful possibility known as **Progesterone** treatment for Traumatic Brain Injuries, done by researchers at [19]Emory University School of Medicine. Progesterone too, has been touted to have neuroprotectant qualities. Both males and females have Progesterone, and our brains are full of

Progesterone receptors, believed instrumental in early brain development. Since no new treatments for TBI have been approved in over 25 years, there seems to be a glimmer of hope on the horizon. *Yes, better late than not.*

New research is showing that [20]**MDNA**, commonly know as "Ecstasy", assisted psychotherapy can be an effective treatment for many with PTS who have not responded to traditional therapies. MDNA is known as the "Love drug", and it increases the levels of well being hormones serotonin, oxytocin and prolactin being released into the body. Its also one of the most popular street drugs out there. It has shown success in many of the more complicated cases, but it has also been shown to be as addicting as opioids. It's known to cause an increase in heart rate, blood pressure and body temperture, so it's only an option for the healthier candidates. Although it's had a 60-70% success rate in clinical trails, they were highly restrictive and controlled. I've looked into this and suggest you do the same. I'm not a fan because I've never seen someone die on marijuana, yet I have seen people die on opioids and ecstasy. All of these medications start in a contolled enviorment and its not until later when those pills are sitting on your shelf, that the abuse begins. *You do the research.*

Acupuncture is another natural treatment that has actually worked for me. After only an hour of treatment, my pain level went from a five to a two. My VA doctors then told me I could not receive any more referrals due to TBI not being a "chronic muscular pain." That was short lived.

Sure, I was pissed when I couldn't get more acupuncture, because it worked. But, dwelling on it isn't going to get rid of my pain. It's only going to make me madder. But, in my case making me madder just made me more determined. After 4 years of not being able to get the VA to give me more Acupuncture, I convinced my local VA hospital doctors to put me back on the regiment and am now getting the acupuncture I need! *Remember, the squeaky wheel gets the grease!* It took years of squeaking, but I'm now, finally getting my relief. *It shouldn't have to be like this.*

Doctors are human. Sometimes shortcuts are taken. They're under pressure too. Giving you this med may be easier and faster than getting you that acupuncture appointment. By getting pissed, you're just inviting more *chaos* in. You decide how much *chaos* you let into your life. We're all still learning here, especially when it comes to TBI and PTS. War breeds *"**Lessons Learned**."*

If they're giving you drugs, it's up to you as to whether it makes sense to take them. It's not going to make it better by blaming someone who's trying to fix you. *They may have it right, they may not, but I want to believe they're trying. It makes no sense to blame the system if you're not willing to "do the work" yourself.*

But, then again, **many** of us are NOT willing to do the work. Why? *Woe is me. I have a sad story. I'm a disabled veteran. I served my country. Someone else should do it for me. Why do I have to do it? Shit, just send me my check.*

Don't get me wrong; I'm not that guy that's going to blast the Veterans Administration. We went to war thinking it might be over quickly, like Desert Storm was in 1991, but it wasn't. Then around 2006 the medical system was becoming overwhelmed and was ill prepared for the amount of wounded warriors needing care. Then, as those same wounded warriors, such as myself, were getting medically retired and receiving VA benefits, the forgotten group of Vietnam Veterans saw this and wanted what was duly theirs. As they applied for their *rightfully earned* benefits, this and the continued incoming number of wounded warriors began overwhelming the VA system. The VA has been good to me and overall; I am thankful and grateful for them.

War will always be hell, and medications will always be the short-term fix. Medications help with our pain and anxiety, but they also skew our decision-making abilities. Your decisions should be as informed as possible. Your decisions and choices will either strengthen or weaken the links in your chain.

Chaos and his nefarious friends are equal opportunity killers. *Chaos* will seize the opportunity. Give it an opening, *Chaos* will slip in.

Our lives are precious, so listen to others but *act* for yourself.

The winter of 2015, snowboarding. Being active and outdoors helps me stay "Engaged, challenged and purposeful!"

Camping and mountain biking became an alternative to the many medications I was prescribed. Doing the work also means doing less prescribed medications.

CHAPTER 7

THE SYSTEM

At the top of the list of worries for Wounded Warriors is their *financial future*. In that same way, so can be loss of the "trust" that they placed in the government. Prior to my deployment I was financially comfortable, making six figures. Now home, that changed. Originally, my plans after my Iraq deployment were to focus on my security company, Core Group, hopefully taking it to the next level. Now, I wasn't able to do that. My company fell into disarray, and I felt like I was fighting the government to get my pay benefits. *I was feeling betrayed by the system.* Did Lt. Col. Rivas also feel betrayed? Finances and our retirement pay were the same issues that Lt. Col. Rivas was trying to illuminate congress about during his testimony. It's our world of *chaos*, and you can expect to be forgotten. You need to fight. Arm yourself with a trusted advocate, because you left the rest of your armor *"over there."*

At Khe Sanh, the combat was so intense; lots of things got lost and pushed aside, as the struggle to survive was pushed to the forefront. Dad had learned from his experiences of being hit, medevac'd, then going through the medical evaluation process. Dad's advice was basically, **"Document Everything."** Documentation would be the key, and finding advocacy, the standard.

I was in my late 20s, a young Captain, flying with the Eighth Special Operations Squadron at Hurlburt Field, Florida, or Fort Walton Beach. I was literally living my dream, serving my country and living across the street from the white beaches and warm blue waters of the Gulf of Florida. I had a condominium near the beach and would often run the couple miles down to the end of the road turn around and run back on the beach side. I would always see this young guy, about my age, who seemed to not work, acting odd, just walking by himself or fishing on the beach. He lived in a condo high rise right on the beach. From time to time I would see him at the store, or a local restaurant and he always acted erratic, much like a homeless person who talks to themselves and sees right through you. But he wasn't homeless, he had a condo on the beach, dressed nice, yet he didn't drive and walked everywhere. No one in our crew knew his story, whether he had won the lottery, or was just an eccentric savant.

One day, returning on the beach side of my run, he was at the water's edge, fishing. I stopped and introduced myself, since we had seen each other so many times. I told him I was in the Air Force and stationed over at Hurlburt Field. His face lit up, smiling, stuttering out that he too had been in the military. In fact, he was an Army Lieutenant, a retired Tanker Commander. Come to find out, he had been inside a tank when it was hit by a practice round and had some sort of **brain injury**, and had been medically retired from the Army. *This would be my first encounter with the "**Invisible Wound**."*

We remained local acquaintances, sometimes he'd remember me, sometimes he wouldn't, but I've always remembered him. His erratic behavior, talking to himself, walking in circles and not being able to maintain a normal conversation, stayed with me. I met his parents once in the parking lot. They were always around just checking on him, but he was adamant that he lived on his own. His dad was retired military as well, and his son's advocate.

If you're in the military, from the moment you're injured, non-combat or combat, you become part of the Disability Evaluation System (DES). Whether it's your civilian medical plan, Worker's Compensation, Social Security Disability, and Medicare, or as in my case, the military's Disability Evaluation System, protocols are in place because they are lessons learned from experience. *They also sometimes seem as if they were designed to wear you down.* **My advocates**, starting from my return to the States, as well as my family and friends, made all the difference in the world. When I was unable to think clearly for myself, I leaned on them.

After lots of denial, I had to realize my brain was not right. It just wasn't. I knew myself and the pain and misconstrued thoughts were rampant. Something was wrong and it wasn't getting better. *Outwardly I looked fine, normal.* **The Invisible Wound.**

Initially, I would lie, telling the doctors what they wanted to hear, to stay in-country for as long as I could. Looking back, had I not heeded my dad's advice, things would be dramatically different. Time after time, the doctors were overloaded, paperwork got lost and I was forgotten and left on my own.

When I left the ER, after my second blast, there were no pain meds, just bandages, a sling, a T-shirt, "sign here" and you're released. I had to call a friend at the Embassy for a pair of pants, T-shirt and ride to the helicopter pad. Shit, I was walking/talking. Who cared? I was too lost in the delight of being alive to care. Later that afternoon when the adrenaline wore off, the pain hit home and only through the help of my roommate Eric, did I get through it. *Remember, he had been hit in the same Oct. 25th incident.*

Later, I went to the doctor because I couldn't sleep. It was a pretty persistent problem for me and I had tried everything - over the counter meds, melatonin and exercise. The doctor gave me 800 mg of Ibuprofen for the headaches. Nothing for the sleep. So, I went back to doing what I had to, **Tylenol PM**. The nightmares became a nightly occurrence, with a occasional blend of reality. On many occasions, I'd have a nightmare, wake up, then realize the alarms were really going off and real incoming fire was landing. *Those were probably some of the most surreal experiences in my life.*

I didn't feel I needed to see Mental Health, but was ordered to as part of the protocol for blast trauma patients. Never in my life had I been to counseling. My walls were up pretty high. My anger could easily be brought to the surface by any of their questions. During my second interview, when asked about whether I had had any trauma in my childhood, I retorted, "What's my childhood got to do with this? *I was friggin blown up!*" Then walked out. That's how my introduction to Mental Health Professionals went. Years later, and hundreds of hours in, therapy is now just part of my management strategy.

During this time my **irritability** and **anger** surfaced quickly, with me snapping at subordinates and others. It was out of character for me. Or so I think. I remember snapping at a young Captain, Chad Bieber, who worked for me. It felt really wrong. I later apologized to him, but the incident left me with deep questions regarding what was going on in my head. *My brain had lost the ability to process and sort before speaking.*

Another time when we were extremely low on manpower, a volunteer from Kuwait, TSgt. Geri Davis, was coming up to help us out. I was trying to get a place for her to stay, when a young lieutenant, in charge of the temporary quarters, told me he couldn't help, I was not his priority and he was done here. I went off, wanting to reach across the counter and grab him by the throat.

Luckily I didn't. At first I started turning red, then began to hyperventilate, then took a step back and walked over to the unit Sgt. Major and asked him to get that lieutenant in line and I'd be back in an hour. I was and he did. The incident still stands out, because I became livid so quickly. *It was beyond road rage level.* Normally, I could have taken a breath, pointed out his disrespect and diplomatically taken care of the situation.

Finally, two months later, on December 28th, I was flown to Balad, Iraq, for brain and eye scans. After seeing several doctors, more scans and x-rays, they determined I needed to be sent to Germany. In Germany after more tests, it was determined to send me back stateside to Wilford Hall, San Antonio, and the Air Force Medical Warrior Transition Unit.

I was placed on a last minute flight, a 17-hour direct. It was one I will never forget. You see, there were three warfighters that had been hit in an IED attack, with burns over the majority of their bodies. They were all in induced comas. They were being sent to Brooke Army Medical Burn Center, just north of San Antonio and I was along for the ride. What I remember most about that flight was how well the doctors and flight nurses handled them. I realized my pain and struggle was miniscule compared to the challenges and obstacles these warfighters had ahead of them.

We arrived on American soil the 1st of January 2008. After landing, I was driven over to Wilford Hall Medical Center, at Lackland Air Force Base, just south of San Antonio. There, I was checked in and given a list of appointments.

ANTHONY JONES

The Air Force Wounded Warrior Program wasn't quite set up yet. At the time it was called Palace HART - Helping Airman Recover Together. Things were changing and the Air Force Wounded Warrior Program was undergoing the appropriate upsizing to match the newer requirement "The Surge" had placed on the system. Once the new Air Force Wounded Warrior (AFW2) program stood up, the assistance and support was nothing short of excellent.

The year earlier, in 2006, the Army had undergone a major scandal regarding allegations of neglect, unsatisfactory treatment, and general poor conditions of wounded warriors at the Walter Reed Army Medical Center, in Washington DC. This changed the system for the better. The war had over burdened our current medical system. Someone should have thought of that prior to going to war.

I took the list of appointments and made sure I showed up, which meant for me, making a weekly journal of things that needed to be checked off and living from yellow stickies. The first appointments were for the [21]**Defense and Veterans Brain Injury Center, DVBIC**, at Wilford Hall. According to the paperwork they gave me and their web site, the DVBIC is part of the US Military Health system. Specifically, it is the TBI operational component of the Defense Centers of Excellence for Psychological Health and Traumatic Brain Injury. Their mission is to serve active duty military, their beneficiaries, and Veterans with traumatic brain injuries through state-of-the-art clinical care, innovative clinical research initiatives, educational programs and support for force health protection services.

Because I was a blast victim, they needed me to undergo a battery of extensive testing. Three days worth. It wasn't mandatory, but on a volunteer basis. They say that at the micro-level, DVBIC treats warfighters and veterans with mild, moderate or severe TBI, and helps them from the moment of injury to their return to duty or reintegration into the community. Sounds really impressive, right? *I never heard from them again.*

All this money goes into the education and awareness aspects of this injury, but we at the end user level hardly ever see, or more importantly, feel the benefits of what they mandate. We are often in too much pain, too lethargic, too procrastinative to self-advocate and scream out for help, so we end up just folding back into our cocoon.

BRAIN PAIN

Organizations like the DVBIC, who help TBI and/or PTS victims should reach out to us, not the other way around. Our combat injuries are documented. They know who we are and where we are. We've been in their computer research database since we presented to them. How difficult would it be to put together a list of TBI recipients and organize a monthly newsletter for them, letting us know of the ongoing news, trends, treatments and therapies that could help us improve the quality of our lives? **To me, the DVBIC has failed us.**

There were only a handful of Air Force Wounded Warriors there at the time, and the hospital assigned us a patient advocate, **Darla Sekimoto**, Licensed Master Social Worker, or LMSW. She was a Godsend. She was, without a doubt, the most important asset in my Wounded Warrior transitioning process. As a TBI patient, I could not think clearly enough to help myself, so having an advocate to guide me through the maze, eased the stress and helped more than I can say. She ensured I made all of my appointments, followed up with my physicians and with me. *She became my memory.*

The bottom line is that as you navigate this system, or any medical system, you must learn to deal with them with **patience**; not always easy for someone with TBI and PTS. A lack of patience can quickly lead to an alienation of your support system.

Darla also had the VA Disability and Compensation representatives come in to interview, sign me up, and review the evaluation process, which became instrumental in my getting into the system, instead of becoming one on the thousands backlogged, as we've heard about in the news.

After I was released to the medical facility back home in Las Vegas, at Nellis AFB, I started work back at my old office, the 99th Air Base Wing Exercise and Plans office. I was working for **Bob Jones** and **Ernie Giovanni**. I had worked with them prior to my deployment. Bob and Ernie knew me well and knew my performance level before Iraq. I was one of their go-to guys to get things done, and they saw my performance as I worked full time at the office and completed Air Command and Staff College. After my return, they started to see the difference and how the sudden onsets of "spikes" were affecting me. The support I received from them as well as my boss back at Fort Belvior, JPRA Commander **Col. Brendan Clare**, was exceptional and I greatly appreciated that.

ANTHONY JONES

Admitting to yourself there is something *defective* going on inside your head is an on-going process. It's so easy to think you're back on track and things are getting better. TBI and PTS can last a lifetime. Having a support system throughout can be so emotionally uplifting. That summer I signed up for and attended the VA PTS program. *Once again, trying to nip it in the bud.*

In September of that year, I was placed on the **Temporary Duty Retirement List (TDRL).** This meant I was officially entering the Disability Evaluation System. *Much like the Social Security Disability System, the military's Disability Evaluation System is a process designed to review military personnel who are injured or ill and cannot perform their duties.* This process is designed to ensure a smooth transition back to civilian life, or to retirement pay and the appropriate medical care. The process is slow and tedious, but proven. *It consists of maintaining an on-going evaluation, your treatment plans, and your records, keeping a paperwork trail of the process, much like preparing a law case.* Unfortunately, that's how you need to look at it.

Doctors must first file a report stating the disability that causes the patient to be unable to perform their job, or meet the requirement of worldwide deployability. It's also designed to determine if it's temporary or permanent. The majority of warfighters going through the DES *do not* have combat injuries, but rather normal duty or non-duty related injuries or disabilities occurring during their enlistment. It's the same as when filing for workman's compensation.

The TDRL is a list of warfighters found to be unfit for military duty (by reason of disability) that has not stabilized to permit an assessment of a permanent disability rating. This process can take from six months to 5 years while they observe the patient. Mine lasted three years. During this time, you must observe all the doctors orders, following their protocols to the letter. *In most cases that means being ordered to take the pills they tell you to.*

The warfighter is evaluated for this period, and then if there is no improvement, the case is recommended to the Medical Evaluation Board (MEB) for review. The patient is then given a rating for their disabilities. The Medical Evaluation Board consists of three physicians, in some cases, like PTS, a psychiatrist is included. The officers review the case and decide on one of two recommended actions: A return to Duty (RTD), which is just that; or a referral to the Informal Physical Evaluation Board (IPEB), due to a potentially unfitting condition for duty.

The US Military Disability System operates under disability laws (Title 10, USC, Chapter 61, Retire or Separation for Physical Disability), which were enacted to establish a means of removing members from active duty who can no longer perform their duties due to a physical disability. The intent of these laws is to maintain a fit and vital military force.

This is similar to civilian Workman's Compensation Programs since the determination is job specific. The Air Force, or appropriate service's, Physical Evaluation Board (PEB) must determine if a member's physical defect or condition renders the member unfit for duty. Once referred to the PEB, the Military has the legal and moral obligation to give each member a full and fair hearing before separating or retiring them. In my case, my medical officers referred me. The PEBs use the guidance provided in the Veterans Administration's (VA) **Schedule for Rating Disabilities** when assigning disability compensable ratings. A 30 percent rating is the minimum rating, which would result in disability retirement for members with less than 20 years active service.

For the first few years, while I was going through the medical evaluation and VA evaluation process, I kept busy training and working on my security business. I also took courses through the VA Vocational Rehabilitation (VocRehab) process. Keeping busy was and still is essential. For me, the only goal was short range, trying to move through and not regress. Working part-time allowed me to have *purpose* as well as continuing to *challenge and exercise my brain*. **Routines** became important because of my short-term memory problems. Things like just going to the gym, working out, reading the paper, making my bed and cleaning the house, although miniscule, were purposeful.

After three years, the MEB offered me a rating for the TBI and PTS. Initially, I was ready to accept it, but after my father (who advocates for me) reviewed it, we decided to not accept it and ask for a hearing before the PEB. **Documentation was the key**. I hired a lawyer who specializes in this area to review the case files my father and I had put together. His name is **Jason Perry** and his law practice is devoted to Military Disability Law. Once Jason reviewed my files, I felt confident going to the hearing with the representation the Air Force provided me.

My Air Force-appointed attorney made some notes and adjustments to my files, which I updated and corrected. He went before the board with these in hand, and afterwards the board gave me what we believed to be a fair rating.

Although methodologies and protocols for TBI and PTS treatments vary and may not be perfect, in the military, some are at least in place. At a minimum, all military TBI patients should have continued **advocates**. The very concept of having a brain injury screams out, "It's hard for me to think clearly!"

*They should also be placed into a **database** where a local advocate is up to date on who they are, what their on-going maladies are, and the latest research, treatments and protocols, as well as what holistic remedies are available.* There's a record of every combat incident that involves troops in contact. There's a record of every injury sustained in combat. And we can't follow up on these? **DVBIC?** Oh yeah, when will that newsletter of current TBI treatment trends and available medical options be coming out?

We live in a society where I can Google how to learn anything, and where phones can track your movement, where data mining companies know everything about you. *How is it* that medical records, specifically diagnosed TBI and PTS patients', can't be categorized, and organized into a database? *How is it* that the latest data on what has worked, what has not worked and what may work, is not passed on to the patient struggling with these injuries? *How is it* that in a society that lives on detailed marketing lists, we can't seem to put together an phone/email list of the warfighters and caregivers, to maintain a long term follow-up relationship?

When you're injured in the line of duty for your country, the military promises that their medical system will care for you. What's the level of care they promised? *Is it just enough, or is it the best possible?* I wouldn't be writing this if it were the best.

Like the civilian workman's compensation program, *fraud* is happening. **Yes, I said that!** There are two sides to every story. Most have earned it, but many are gaming the system.

BRAIN PAIN

Those gaming the system clog the system for the others. One I know of hurt himself on his motorcycle showing off then went back to his base and claimed he fell during physical training. Another was drunk off base, got into a fight and was knocked down a stairwell. He had his buddies carry him back to the barracks. Both are getting their checks. The allure of that military disability check is all too tempting.

Fraudsters! Those gaming the system are also to "blame" for the lack of proper attention to those who deserve it. Those headlines aren't quite the sound byte that the "VA is killing our troops," and the "VA is in disarray" are. Two sides to every story. *Overall, the VA has been good to me.*

Earlier I mentioned a friend of mine. **Dave Messer**, a Special Forces Vietnam Veteran. He's one of my best friends. In 1970 Dave was a young Sergeant in the Army doing a tour in Vietnam. Dave was exposed to numerous grenade blasts, IED blasts, firefights and death. He made it out alive and left with a Bronze Star marked with "V" device for Valor.

Dave went through ups and downs. He got his masters degree, became a pilot and started a family. *Depression* and *Chaos* chased him down.

Dave was discarded by the system, being medically retired at the lowest percentage, or rating. The **"System"** in place at the time didn't know what to do with him. Dave's marriage failed and he was left to raise his son on his own. For the last fifteen years, he's lived at the poverty level, fraught with depression.

After my injury Dave and I became closer. We understood each other. For years, Dave had gotten the runaround by the VA. Last year his case was finally reviewed and his rating increased to what he'd deserved all along. *He's taken back control of his life.* In the last three years he's slowly working to better himself and re-ignite his zeal for life. I'm proud of Dave for *doing the work*. He's taking the many steps to a bigger and brighter future.

Jimmy Hughes is another friend that I'm proud of. We've been friends for years and he works with me as an instructor and operator with my security company. He's a Vietnam combat veteran and Army Ranger who survived combat, earning 2 Bronze Stars marked with "V" device for Valor and a Purple Heart. For years he's dealt with his own personal struggles and also the VA "System," initially receiving a minimal rating. Recently, after much prodding by myself and another veteran, he went through a re-evaluation and was awarded a much higher rating. He continued to do the work and lives a purposeful life with his wife, Sharon.

When you're lost in the "system," with a damaged brain, you don't have the strength or will to fight. Without friends, family or an understanding advocate, you're left to your own resolve.

Yes, caregivers are doing their best and for the most part we should trust in the medical establishment and maintain patience. But, because clarity of thought does not come naturally to us, we must have ***continued advocacy*** on our side. My advocates, from Darla Sekimoto, to my family and my best friend, Richie, have made all the difference in the world.

Expect to be forgotten. Arm yourself with a trusted advocate, because you left the rest of your weapons "over there."

Admiral Gorman, Special Forces Officer Captain Dave Messer and myself, Ocean Venture 84. A Vietnam combat veteran, Dave was discarded by the Medical 'system' but is doing the work and getting back to a fuller life.

Me and my Air Force Wounded Warrior program patient advocate Darla Sekimoto, at Wilford Hall Medical Center in Texas. Thanks!

My Homecoming with mom and dad after my return from Wilford Hall Medical Center. I was in the "System" now.

CHAPTER 8

PTS

"Chaos has many faces"

Chaos tastes your pain and after savoring, it goes for your spirit, your passions, and then sets its sight on your soul. *Chaos presents itself with many faces.*

As a 12-year-old boy, I can clearly recall my dad's nightmares, barking out orders that curdled our blood; with a deathly sense of urgency, and heavy breathing, as if he just finished a marathon. Then waking and quietly recovering in his own sweat. My little brother and I had our own room and slept on bunk beds. When those nightmares happened, I'd roll off the bed and sit on the floor leaning up against his bunk, reassuring him that it was all okay. My sister would come into our room and we'd all huddle together. I understood that this was the result of the war, but didn't understand the depth of Dad's despair. Years later when the incoming fire was real, exploding all around, I'd roll off my bed again, this time grasping my vest and weapon. ***It isn't about what's wrong with you; it's about what's happened to you.***

For years, after he returned from Khe Sanh, Dad had horrible nightmares. He was a survivor as were we. We were the children of Marines, of warriors, and became stronger for it. Yes, he had anger issues, but never physically took it out on us. He is, and always has been, able to control it, yet the anger was always just underneath the surface, ready to explode outwards. *Defective*. His word to describe this. Mine is *Chaos*. My *Chaos* is different. Your *Chaos* is different. *Chaos* manipulates into its host, stealing the best of them. It manifests into darkness and despair.

Much like Migraines, I've never believed in depression nor did I understand mental illness. I had studied mental health issues in college, knew the theories behind them, but the truth be told, I just couldn't grasp it. To me, you were weak, delicate and frail.

For the majority of us, our only reference point is from a working brain, so understanding mental health deficiencies is not easy. If you see signs of depression in yourself, you may deny it. I was a high functioning Type-A personality and thought that depression was a form of weakness and frailty. I clearly admit I was one of those individuals who believed people who were going through depression were either just feeble or delicate.

[22]"We all know what the *"fight or flight"* response feels like. We know what it feels like to be on alert. And, we know what it feels like to have bad memories. However, with most of us, those feeling are fleeting. They are there in isolated moments then fade away. But, imagine if they didn't go away. What if you always felt stuck in "fight or flight" mode, were always on alert, and always plagued by a particularly bad memory? What would that be like? For people suffering from post-traumatic stress, that 'what if' is their reality."

When we look at someone with TBI and PTS, we don't see the damage. If you have a damaged kidney, knee, arm, leg, spine, etc. the doctors see it and formulate a plan of recovery. *When your brain is Defective there's no tangible wound that can be seen.* Until it happened to me, I couldn't see it either.

I have absolutely no doubt that my TBI's led to my PTS. There are numerous studies that show that blast injuries exacerbate PTS. These blast waves cause damage to the brain, as I discussed earlier, making us more susceptible to PTS. A recent medical study by JAMA Neurology not only verified this, but also concluded that our symptoms (in a 5 year study) are *worsening*.

"[23]"Among the 94 participants (87 men [93%] and 7 women [7%]; mean [SD] age, 34 [8] years), global disability, satisfaction with life, neurobehavioral symptom severity, psychiatric symptom severity, and sleep impairment were significantly worse in patients with concussive blast TBI compared with combat-deployed controls, whereas performance on cognitive measures was no different between groups at the 5-year evaluation. Logistic regression on the dichotomized Extended Glasgow Outcome Scale (GOS-E) at 5 years as a measure of overall disability identified brain injury diagnosis, pre-injury intelligence, motor strength, verbal fluency, and neurobehavioral symptom severity at 1 year as risk factors for a poor outcome at 5 years, with an area under the curve of 0.92 indicating excellent prediction strength. Thirty-six of 50 patients with concussive blast TBI (72%) had a decline in the GOS-E from the 1- to 5-year evaluations, in contrast with only 5 of 44 combat-deployed controls (11%). *Worsening of symptoms in concussive blast TBI was also observed on measures of posttraumatic stress disorder and depression. Service members with concussive blast TBI experienced evolution, not resolution, of symptoms from the 1- to 5-year outcomes.*

CONCLUSIONS AND RELEVANCE. Considerable decline was observed in military service members with concussive blast TBI when comparing 1- and 5-year clinical outcomes. These results advocate for *new treatment strategies* to combat the long-term and extremely costly effect of these wartime injuries."

Remember that during combat operations you "suck it up" for the sake of the mission. Getting a "time out" often isn't an option. Also, a large portion of TBI's go unreported, whereas the warfighter just man's up and moves through. It took years for the NFL to come up with and enforce "Concussion Protocols." Military medics are just now being trained in similar combat blast protocols.

There is another adversary threatening our warfighters. Much like multiple repetitive hits during practice and training of both young and old football players are leading to long-term brain disease, the same is being realized by the military. Blast intensive weapons and repetitive explosions during *training* missions are exposing warfighters to unseen and unquantified brain injuries. Dad was an artilleryman in the Marines, having been through hundreds, if not thousands, of mini-explosions during his youth, both in training and combat. The fact that he can barely hear is proof that those loud sounds affected his body. Those same loud sounds came with huge concussive waves. We know that blast exposures cause brain damage. We believe small repetitive blast exposures may be asymptomatic, but can lead to long-term neurodegenerative disease. We need a way of quantifying these blast exposures.

There are now *blast overpressure sensors* for warfighters which the warfighter wears in his helmet and on his body armor, which can give a quantitative analysis of the force of any blast wave that the recipient experiences.

"[24]**BlackBox Biometrics**" is one of these companies building proactive equipment to help detect and quantify brain blast wave experiences, allowing for the immediate acknowledgement and medical recognition of an injury. According to their website, "BlackBox Biometrics develops and deploys technology solutions to reduce the risk of neurodegenerative disease and long term injury. I've personally seen indisputable scientific evidence of this and yet the U.S. Military continues to drag its feet on presenting many of these proactive solutions. *Our veterans need an overhaul of our blast monitoring and treatment programs*!

One day my father came over to my condo to help me out with my computer. He plays golf three to four times a week and I mountain bike in the mornings. When we were both finished with these morning activities, he met me at about 10. I could tell there was something else on his mind, and asked him about it. He told me that he and Mom had gotten into a fight about her always defending me. Since we both live in Las Vegas, we're very close and I spend most Sundays with my parents, for family dinners. He then blurted out, *"You've got to stop blaming your injury for things and deal with it - I never blamed mine!"*

It felt like a punch to the gut! I'm a grown man and my knees weakened. I sucked it up though, because I knew it would be treading on thin ice to argue with him. We'd been here many times. I backed off and thought to myself; "He's lived through hell, provided food and a roof over our heads, and been the backbone of this family, so - he's earned his opinion." *Chaos* was rising up; bubbling and overflowing onto my spirit. He never once blamed his injuries, nor did I, *or so I thought*? War is hell, before, during and after.

On more than one occasion, when the subject of Vietnam comes up, he minimizes it. By his own admission, he's "put that part of his life away in a box." It was like fighting snakes, trying to get him to open up and talk about this subject for the book. He's a Marine and he's sucked it up. I was the son of a Marine and therefore should follow his lead. *Here was my hero basically telling me to "**Man Up**."* I thought I had been, but when the Spikes suddenly manifest, it's like an explosion in my brain. I don't have control over the tourette-like profanities I spout, or the tapping of my head. It's an unseen injury, invisible and misunderstood.

You can't see it, therefore does it exist? Was I, *"Woe is me?"*

For the first year after my return from Baghdad, I thought he believed me and understood my Brain Pain. Two arguments later assured me he didn't. He related to and understood the PTS and nightmares but he hadn't experienced the headaches or Brain Pain and he was *blown up four times*. I needed to acknowledge to myself that I would have to accept the disconnect between us on the Brain Pain, if I was going to nip this animosity in the bud.

I'm sure he sees himself in me, in my injury, and the pain and struggles he silently endured. As well as the emotions he pushed to the back. He's the badass of badasses. Surely his son's a badass too? Or is he broken? *Defective? My dad's a fixer and he tries to fix everything*. That's what he's good at and it's saved his life, and those of others, more than once. He sees that *something* in me is broken or defective and struggles with how to help me. *As would any father, **he wants to fix me**, but there's nothing in his toolbox that can fix this.*

***Mom** was the homemaker* and Dad, the provider. She wasn't prepared for the man who returned from Khe Sanh. She had no idea what he had been through and how he was dealing with it. There were no family support seminars, booklets or counseling for wives of the deployed, explaining what to expect. She had no idea where the distance, anger and nightmares were coming from.

Since Khe Sanh, Dad's always had the nightmares and irritability. *Defective.* Throughout his career in the Marines and his later career in the Border Patrol, keeping engaged and challenged, kept them tempered, but they never left. He found other missions and was "doing the work," without placing that moniker on his process. Much like I enjoy snowboarding and mountain biking, dad enjoys *golf*. He's been playing golf since his twenties. To this day he can still shoot in the seventies. Yet, over the last few years, due to his retirement and slower pace, his nightmares have gotten worse, and many times he inadvertently acted out the violence in his sleep.

Many of the lessons I've learned have been from my parents. One of the exceptional lessons I learned from my mother only surfaced once I returned from Iraq. She had been doing this one to my father all my life, but I never really noticed it. The way she did it was so simple, *transitions*, it was seamless. Most people would simply call it *"changing the subject,"* but I know she was doing much more than that. I grew up with a dad who was caring, loving and a comedian most of the time, but he could, in an instant, change and snap, veins pushing out of his head; especially after Vietnam. He could scare the shit out of you. Forget pedaling fast, you'd be blown off the bike!

Mom was able to sense just *before* things would get heated and she would turn the direction of the conversation very subtly, easing the tension and calming things down. *Transitions.* I call it, *"Pattern Interrupt."* Once I turned into a person who could also go from calm to dangerously irate in a split second, I saw it so clearly. It has been one of the greatest tools I have, dealing with TBI and PTS. I can't count the number of times it's saved me from exploding in anger or from a violent rage.

It starts with an unexpected "**wrong**." Whether it is or isn't, all I can see is a wrong/threat. I lose my peripherals as my focus on the "wrong" tightens. My intensity and focus squeezes laser tight, as my orientation to the world around me dissipates. *Chaos* and friends steal my normal thoughts and fuel my focus on anger. As the anger builds, I instantly justify the wrong/threat as real, and then transition into an aggressive counter attack mode. The waning darkness turns to black. All in a matter of seconds. Mentally, I need to recognize when *Chaos* has entered the room and then realize it's not me doing this. *Easier said than done.* I find myself searching for my peripherals, trying to re-orientate. Fighting my way back to reality to stop the defensive attack I'm about to commit on the perceived "wrong-doer."

Once, "over there," I jabbed my pen into my thigh to get back. I needed the "Pattern Interrupt" to change my thoughts to something else, to calm down. The pain brought me back in an instant. We all have to find what works for us. Sometimes it's as easy as changing the radio station, the pattern, or sometimes I have to inflict physical pain. According to my friend and therapist, Dr. Galante, [25]This is called, *"cognitive restructuring,"* in Cognitive Behavioral Therapy (CBT). It is about changing one's thinking in order to change/modify the negative emotional response to a more realistic or positive response.

September 11, 2007, my journey to the dark side of an unbalanced brain began. So did the stalking by *Chaos*. They began that night, after the first explosion. I had seen blood many times before, mine as well as others, but blood in combat made it all too real. Now, I can't get the blood out of my mind, reviewing it over and over.

In country, after finally going to sleep, I'd relive the explosions in my dreams, waking me up exhausted and sweating. This became the norm. We had to have our sleep, in order to do our job, so when it happened, I'd walk it off outside, then try to get back to sleep. Sleep was so important that my roommate, Eric, and I, had an unspoken protocol during the nighttime incoming fire. Whoever heard the siren's blasts or explosions first, would yell out to the other, ensuring a response, as we hit the floor and rolled into our armor. To this day, I'll still fall to the floor. Much like when my father would have his nightmares. And yes, I still have my vest and weapon next to my bed, waiting. *Why?*

PTS wasn't fully recognized as a human malady until after the Civil War, 150 years ago. Reasons include: the rise of modern science and psychology; the use of advanced artillery with better explosive affects; and the advent of various forms of disability compensation, where lawyers and advocates looked into long term care and at the costs of these injuries.

Post Traumatic Stress has been called by many names. It's not surprising that the majority of names were spawned after large conflicts and wars. The Germans and French called it ***"Homesickness."*** After the Civil War, it was called, ***"Soldiers Heart*** or ***Irritable Heart,"*** due to increased heartbeats with anxiety. After World War I, it was called, ***"Shell Shock*** and ***Battle Fatigue,"*** because of the intense amount of artillery used. The latter is probably the most well known of the terms. After World War II, the military was classifying all of these cases as "transitory" or "acute," meaning temporary, therefore not "chronic." They, for reasons unknown, assumed that "normal" veterans would have short-term difficulties after returning from combat, and that there were no physical injuries to the brain. *If you can't see it, it doesn't exist.*

After World War II and the Korean War, PTS was called, *"Operational Exhaustion, Combat Exhaustion* and *Combat Fatigue."* After Vietnam, it had changed to, *"Stress Response Syndrome."*

[26]The Veterans Administration (VA), declared that if the problem lasted more than six months after the soldier returned home, it was an obvious pre-existing condition, thus had nothing to do with their combat experiences and thus non-compensable in the form of disability compensation, i.e. not covered. *Yes, our government did that to our warfighters.*

Between 1980 and 1992, after the Gulf War, it was reclassified as, *"Anxiety Disorder,"* and clinical guidelines began to acknowledge that it could be chronic, or long lasting. What seems so clear to us now, took so long and ruined so many lives. The huge debate earlier on was, was it physical or psychological? The term, "Shell Shock," itself, brings to mind the idea that the brain has been shaken up and physically damaged. But the lack of any physical visible bodily injuries or damage, sustain it being put into a psychological category.

That was true until **Dr. Omalu**, the forensic pathologist, discovered the darkened Tau proteins now known as CTE. There was now a way of physically determining this invisible wound. Unfortunately, this can only be done post mortem.

I mentioned earlier that *CTE was found in 4 of 4 deceased US military combat veterans* exposed to blasts in combat after their brains were examined at the Boston facility. The first concussion crisis was sports related; the next will be our warfighters. All of them were diagnosed with PTS as well.

Generally, TBI is physical, PTS is emotional. TBI presents immediately, PTS presentation is delayed. PTS, more often than not, requires long-term assistance. TBI generally improves quickly, but can last a lifetime and lead to the earlier onset of a neurodegenerative disease. If you've endured life-threatening trauma, it's psychological. I'm no scientist but it seems pretty simple to me. *If you've been exposed to an explosion or head injury, it's both TBI and PTS. Acknowledge this and treat them.*

When I was DPRC and responsible for reviewing and disseminating the brief (mentioned earlier) to my staff, the first thing I noticed was that it was called, *"Post Combat Stress"* not PTS. It then went on to discuss the long-term effects of combat and operational exposure, as well as the symptoms.

Physical: Fatigue, chest pain, weakness, sleep problems, nightmares, breathing difficulty, muscle tremors, profuse sweating, pounding heart and headaches.

Behavioral: Withdrawn, restlessness, emotional outbursts, suspicion and paranoia, loss of interest, increased alcohol consumption and substance abuse.

Emotional: Anxiety or panic, guilt, fear, irritability, depression, intense anger, agitation and apprehension. Those exposed to front line combat, especially sustained combat were more at risk. Wow! Only recently, has this been acknowledged.

[27]Statistics regarding PTS from the VA showed that 11-20% of Veterans who served in Operation Iraqi Freedom and Operation Enduring Freedom, 10% of Desert Storm Veterans, and 30% of Vietnam Veterans have been, or will be affected by PTS. *More than likely, these are low estimates.* Only time will tell.

The common theme throughout the military, now and then, is that most warfighters are resilient. They will and can work through their issues. Hundreds of years of war has shown this. We forget easily and lose touch with the warfighters as they transition back to civilian life. **The warfighters don't lose track, it's their life story**. *Due to money and compensation, support is easily forgotten, as is the survivor.*

In the briefing, we then discussed those who have difficulties adjusting from combat to a safe zone, or back home. It mentioned how they may have nightmares and flashbacks. When I read this, I honestly wondered about how a flashback occurs. Nightmares, I understood, and like all of us, grew up having them, from time to time. *Flashbacks* were another thing. Transporting into another realm of reality, instantly? Months later, back in the states, it would happen to me.

Walking out of Wilford Hall Medical Center, in Texas, I was headed to my car. Things were clear and I was feeling normal. Suddenly, I heard a, *"Boom!"* and hit the ground, then started low crawling into a space between two cars. Looking up I saw a plume of smoke, and then could smell the cordite of the explosion. My heart was pounding, thinking it was real, and that I was back in Baghdad. I immediately focused on my mantra, *"Move through,"* took to my knees, grabbed the vehicle's fender, and figured out what to do next. The only real thing was the smoke, and the older couple walking by. The woman was looking at me as if I was a carjacker, but the man looked at me, with an almost understanding gaze. His eyes captured mine, bringing me back to reality. He stood there holding the stare until I started to rise. He then nodded his head and silently walked off. Our minds are a beautiful organ with one ultimate goal, to survive. This had to be what people experienced as "flashbacks."

I've always been a social person, a happy-go-lucky person, but now social interactions made little sense. There was no urgency in life, and everywhere all I could see were people who had forgotten what was going on over there. People who idolized reality stars who became famous for a leaked sex tape, or some athlete who just signed a deal for a new line of shoes.

I called it the **"Bling"** affect. It seemed as if our society was caught up in fashion, cars and reality TV. I was still stuck on go mode and everyone else around me was on cruise control, having mostly forgot there is still warfighting overseas. The only ones that understand this are other warfighters who've experienced it. We share that bond. Doing our job under the most stressful of environments, and doing it to the best of our abilities is what we train to do. We either are or have battle buddies and wingmen when things get tough. But, when things are routine and slow, our focus wanders.

*Today, I'm a **peer mentor** with the Wounded Warrior Program.* I mentor others who are now finding themselves in positions I've been through. I've counseled countless hours and always find myself not only sharing my lessons learned, but re-learning some of these same lessons. We're "battle buddies and wingmen," fighting *Chaos* together.

The majority of those injured or wounded in action are front line ground troops, usually in the early twenties, and under thirty. The brain does the majority of its development in the first twenty years. At that age, are they mentally prepared to handle the rigors of brain damage and the extreme traumatic stress? *These younger warfighters,* *who are full of **testosterone/hormones**, have brains that are just finishing their development.* Younger warfighters are not only dealing with a lack of maturity, but enormous levels of hormones as well. They are the ones that will show the deterioration ten, twenty years from now.

There's a darkness that surrounds someone with PTS. It comes on quickly and can permeate our souls. You try to not think or dwell on it, and do everything possible to try and put it out of your mind, into that box, but with the *hypervigilance of thought*, you can be easily reduced to numbing yourself with alcohol or drugs. I've been there - still doing it. Trying to numb the pain, only to double it. When the meds don't do it, or don't seem like they're kicking in fast enough, you might kick start them with a shot, then a beer, then another until the pain's gone. I was in my 50s when I was hit, both times. I had significant amount of life experience and maturity under my belt, which allowed me to control it. Or rationalize that I was controlling it. Even with all my life experience, I've taken my share of cabs home.

My dad's nightmares and angry outbursts were more than likely undiagnosed symptoms of multiple concussions and PTS. **Defective**. He controls them and didn't let them control him. Dad was in his mid 30s during his first combat tour. I was in my early 50s. We both had experience on our side. That being said, *Chaos* stole my passion. As you've read, I lived my life as full and complete as I could. I was a Special Operations Electronic Warfare Officer, Air Liaison Officer, Personnel Recovery Officer, Bodyguard, as well as Mr. Las Vegas. I lived life with zeal. I enjoyed life and used to be passionate about everything I did. ***Then it was gone***. Existence became dark and monotonous. Admitting there was a problem was the first step, then seeking and accepting help, the next. Seeing how the war affected my father was instrumental in my quest to *"nip it in the bud."*

*For most of my life, I can't remember understanding **anxiety***. It's dark and full of dread, that heavy and lethargic weight on your shoulders. By textbook, anxiety is that time period your intuition alerts you that something's wrong, real or perceived. What's that noise around the corner? Fear is when your intuition is confirmed. Shit, that's a mountain lion! Where there's anxiety there's fear. Fear's a feeling in response to an actual or perceived threat, brought on by our natural survival instinct. It's that wave of dread, electrically moving though you as the danger closes in.

What I do know though, is that *Chaos* is a nefarious chameleon, changing it's appearance (fear, anxiety) to meet its needs, not yours. For many, the deeper issue is, we begin to **seek it**! *We actually look for that crisis where we can respond, where we get that next adrenaline fix*! We want to be awesome again, not home drinking beer on the couch, watching cable, and getting fat. After coming home, (fear, anxiety) *Chaos* was sitting on my shoulder, like the bad voice, telling you to beware of what's around the next corner. It never used to be there, but now it was, and in order to brush it off, I needed to admit it was there.

One of my instructors, *Roman Garcia*, who is a former Army Combat Infantryman, sent me a meme about PTS that has stuck in my mind to this day. In the photo it shows a US Warrior engaging the enemy with a machine gun. The caption underneath it says, *"PTSD - What happens when you get home and realize you will never be this awesome again!"*

This is all too true for so many combat veterans. [28]"War/combat is a great seducer; it is for many, the best of times and the worst of times. A time when they feel most vital and alive, but also a time that separates them from their own soul." The adrenaline high is all too addictive, but you've got to be able to replace that high with a new mission, new direction and other new passions. Easier said than done.

Being a logical person, I've always dealt with fear from two standpoints, training and statistical. *I believe that fear is an inability to move through a moment because of lack of preparation and training*. This is a belief of all warfighters. Training gives you the ability to move through the moment with the least amount of fear. That's why in the military; everyone trains over and over.

As aircrewman, we flew over and over, simulating combat with a real enemy. But you'd also go through survival and medical training, in case of a crash or being shot down. That's preparation. If you are prepared when the "**Moment**" occurs, there's a greater likelihood that your training will kick in, allowing you to do what needs to be done. If you're not prepared when that "moment" comes, then fear will hold you back, wasting valuable time.

From a statistical standpoint, I look to the simple concept of riding a roller coaster or bungee jumping. Thousands and thousands of hours have gone into the research and development to make these somewhat safe for the general public. The statistics are pretty high that you're going to survive, so most will take a leap of faith.

Emotion is a cornerstone of what makes us human. If you accept this, you should understand why TBI and PTS, or any damage to the brain, would affect us with depression and lethargy. There are many different types of emotions: fear, sadness, anger, surprise, disgust and happiness, to mention the most common. Our sensitivity to these emotions can thrust them into overdrive. These emotional challenges can affect our morality. The constant *hypervigilance of thought* can run our mind into despondency.

The constant battle between good and evil, anger and love, can either dull or enhance our feelings. Hasty or uninformed decisions can then lead to a downward spiral, resulting in depression and hopelessness. Without our hopes and dreams, we're left naked and unprotected.

As a Marine's son, I didn't see Dad's PTS as depression, but as his mind's way of working through his combat memories. He had struggled with nightmares, yet I never saw him depressed. For me, the depression came when the **Brain Pain became practically unbearable** and *I realized it wasn't going away. Chaos* bored deep into my brain and had decided to stay. It was sucking the life from me. Lethargy/depression was my new reality. For the first few years, I lived life on a roller coaster. ***Ups and downs, highs and lows.*** New medications, back to old medications, side affects, new therapies, new diets and different workouts. Sometimes, I would feel as if I was back on a positive path. I'd go strong for a week, sometimes two, then crash hard in lethargy and depression. The crash was always inevitable, but I would forget it was coming.

Every hour of every day, the Brain Pain is there. Some days are better than others. What I have noticed over the years is that I fall into a rhythm, forgetting for a moment; thinking I am the person I used to be. A person who has the ability to multi-task on multiple levels. A person who has clarity. ***I want it back so much.*** I'll even torture myself with pain to momentarily catch a glimpse of it. Just as I catch that glimpse of clarity, the machine begins to break down again.   It starts with irritability, then to feelings of being *overwhelmed*, despair and then my emotions become askew. Finally I shut down, reminded of the dark, lethargic and miserable reality.

I had to admit to myself that I couldn't keep getting on the same roller coaster, over and over. There would be peaks then there would be troughs. *I had to find a middle road.*

I have had to learn a new kind of balance in my life. Along with this balance, I've learned to pace myself. Finally, I've come to realize that I am not that good at the hundred-yard dash anymore, but if I pace myself, I can still run a pretty good mile. To help me pace myself, I'll journal my goals for the year and then break it down to months and days. It not only keeps my mind busy, but also helps with recall.

Noting all my daily, weekly, monthly accomplishments allows me to pace myself out on paper first. *Like writing this book. But I am not the same person I used to be.*

Writing this has put me back into many bouts of depression, mostly during re-writes.   Trying to re-visit the many memories, and eloquently express myself as well as accepting the inevitable critiques hasn't been easy.   At one point, I was ready to shelve what I had and be content that I had been working through my healing process.

But this is bigger than just me. I truly believe my story can help others, so I moved through and got it done. Ten years ago this would've been a six-month project, completed. Now, I'm three years into it. I knew this project would take a toll on me and that I would have good days and bad days, so pacing myself was essential, starting out one page a day, then four to five pages a week.

An unproductive body and mind is fuel for depression. Falling into lethargy only worsens your situation. Keeping busy challenges your mind and body. Golf was the game of choice for Dad. It kept him engaged and challenged and outdoors exercising.

Since I was a kid, I've never left the house without making my bed. I'm still the same way. Keeping busy kick starts the mind. Getting things done around the house is a great start. Then getting out. Working with a sense of accomplishment, exercise, volunteering, etc. I mountain bike, hunt, train, golf, snowboard - just enjoying the life I've been blessed with. Today, I'm riding my line. Ins and outs, ups and downs, to the end of the trail and beyond!

It hasn't always been that way. Darkness and depression, or *Chaos* would hold me back. There was no one moment of clarity where I told myself to get up off my ass. There was an accumulation of hundreds of moments that reminded me I needed to *get off my ass*. It's part of doing the work. The risk is worth it. ***We're fighting for our lives***!

My dad's been back from war for almost fifty years. The memories dwell deep and he's still fighting his nightly battles with the Vietcong. *Defective*. **It may not go away, but it can be managed**.

For me, keeping busy and exercising my mind and body is instrumental in my plan of recovery. *Keep engaged and purposeful and don't let your challenges overhaul you*!

On October 25th, 2012, the 5th anniversary of my alive day, I had to get out. My head was my own worst enemy that day. I went mountain biking in the morning, and then found myself at the golf range hitting balls. I was listening to music from my cell phone when a familiar song came on. It was one that was anchored in my memory from Iraq. Also one, which I had first heard years earlier in flight school. The song took me right back.

I could feel the anxiety as the song ended. I set the club down and took a seat, lost in thought, and then, as the song transitioned to the next, I heard *my* voice coming from the speaker. It was me laughing and saying, ***"Hey. Awesome day, hope you're enjoying it!"*** *My younger self, talking to my older self.*

Caught off guard, I swelled with emotions. I soon realized that a year earlier, I had converted my mix tapes from the 80s to digital MP3's. I used to be that guy who would make mix tapes for all his friends. It was my voice introducing the tape, from 1981. *A blast from the past, reminding me to get on with living.*

Screw *Chaos*! I've got a glimpse of clarity and I'm riding my line through. Easier said than done? ***I can't change what happened to me, but I can change what's wrong***.

Defective – Maybe not?

BRAIN PAIN

Me and my horse 'Buddy.' (Photo courtesy Karen Swigart)

CHAPTER 9

Horse Therapy

"Buddy"

This first time I met Buddy, a beautiful golden-beige, 13-year-old Buckskin Gelding, he walked over and greeted me by snorting right in my face. Then he pitched his head up and down until I began to stroke his forehead. Equine therapy was completely new to me. The first time I groomed him, it took way longer than expected. Almost forty-five minutes. Stroke and brush, rear to front then the other side. Switch brushes, and then do the same. Then untangle his mane and tail and brush some more. Wax on, wax off. Then try and get him to raise up each leg to clean out his hooves. I remember leaving there that first day, thinking to myself, is this for me or did Buddy just get a forty-five minute massage for free? But from that first day, *I never left there without a smile.*

It was 2009 and the start of me once again participating and engaging in life, but I was years away from realizing it.

For High School graduation, my dad brought me a faded red *1966 Ford Falcon.* It was about as ugly as a week old rotten tomato in 100 degree heat. It needed body work, a paint job, stereo, interior work, engine work and wheels. Even so, attached to it was a sense of love and freedom. For years I'd been helping Dad work on cars and now I had my own and I started working on it. All my life I had been the "grab" kid; grab that for me, grab this for me. From as early as I can remember, I was handing him wrenches as he explained how and why he was replacing an alternator or bleeding the brakes. Now it was my turn. Dad sold his boat to buy me this car. It was a gift that would turn out to be instrumental in my life. It was the beginning of me venturing out on my own and applying the lessons I had learned. Dad had always been the "*fix it*" guy, and now I was doing the same, while finding my own way.

Now, this car ended up being many things to me, but most of all, it helped get me through college. Not from driving back and forth, but from the skills I learned while restoring it. I used those skills in other jobs, to work my way through college. I learned *hustling* from Dad. He'd make extra money buying cars, fixing them, and then reselling them. I'd end up doing the same through college. *I also learned that anything worthwhile, you have to work for*. **It was the genesis of "doing the work."**

I learned to do bodywork and paint with my Falcon. It was my first canvas. At the time I didn't know anything about bodywork and paint, but I learned. Since I didn't have the money to get the bodywork, paint and custom paint done, I bought a book, read it, and proceeded to do it all myself. I did all the bodywork, fixing the dents and rust, we then went through an iteration of stripes and colors, allowing me to experiment and practice. By the end, it had a sweet stance, new wheels, shiny interior and interesting to say the least, custom paint job. I was driving around in my own advertisement and other people started to hire me to do *their* cars and vans. *Sometimes the gift isn't about the gift itself; it's what you do with it.*

My next project was a 1959 Volkswagen panel van. My dad and I rebuilt the engine, fixed the brakes and added custom tires and wheels. I also fixed all the rust and primed and painted it, the first time blue with silver flames, the last time black with silver ghost stripes. It was my first custom interior as well. I gutted it, added shag carpet on the floor and ceiling, wood paneling on the sides, custom bubble portholes on the sides, a refrigerator and sink, and a stereo in the dash. It also carried all of ours band's gear to and from our gigs. It was the epitome of a seventies badass van. I had several more vans during college. Parents of my girlfriends hated to see me coming. That boy with the van. Back then; if you had a van, you had to have custom paint. I discovered I knew how to draw back in high school.

If I could see it, I could sketch it. These skills and my determination facilitated incredibly well, in improving my financial situation. In other words, "I was making bank," for a college kid.

A lot of my custom paint jobs included flames, murals and airbrushed artwork, which was popular. Much like Harley and Hot Rods festivals are popular now, van festivals were popular then, hence the sayings, "Keep on trucking." We'd convoy to the festivals, 20-30 vans deep. Once there, I'd set up shop with a sign, get out the compressor and a case of beer and go to work.

Most of my customers would show me a piece of art or an album cover and want that on their vehicle. I'd quote them a price; we'd haggle, and then get to work. I recreated lots of album covers and murals by the artist Frank Frazetta. Conan Style pieces. I also had a team. I'd pay the neighborhood kids to sand and tape, then I'd pencil out the art on the side panels, get my background colors laid, then go to work airbrushing the scene. Afterwards, I'd lay down a coat of clear, let it dry and collect $500, for two days work. Back in the late 70s, I was doing pretty well. I'd spend a little, but most would go into the bank for tuition and books. My dad helped out as much as possible and my now married sister and her husband kept a roof over my head for a couple of years. So, once again, Team Jones was adapting and my plan had come together.

That Ford Falcon was **the catalyst** for me making it through college and onto my career path. Now Buddy and Equine therapy would be **the catalyst** for me to start "doing the work" in my recovery.

In 2008, after my release from Wilford Hall Medical Center in Texas, I returned to Las Vegas. I was assigned to a local psychologist at the Nellis Air Force Base Mental Health Facility. It was there that I met Dr. Valerie Galante. She is a Ph.D., Licensed Clinical Health Psychologist and published author. Dr. Galante was now the seventh or eighth psychologist I had seen. As I mentioned earlier, I never fully understood the various mental health issues. Unfortunately, I, as many others do, saw it as an regrettable weakness. My point of view was, "That's what friends are for." Talking about issues with close friends, who already knew me, allowed me to springboard problems off of them and work through some things.

BRAIN PAIN

I was initially resistant to therapy, as I had been with every other psychologist, but I presented myself as open. It was another box I had to check. Dr. Galante was understanding and intelligent. After working with her for a few months, she told me she was on the Board of Directors for a non-profit called, **"Spirit Therapies."** It was a center that offered Equine/Horse therapy for veterans.

I had never been much of an animal person, and definitely never horse person. In college, I was thrown from a horse twice. It was an experience that left me with no desire to pursue horse riding. Counseling was already more than I wanted to be doing. Dr. Galante never pressured, which gave me time to bring down my walls and allow myself to be open to it. Spirit Therapy had started a new program called, **"Horses Healing Heroes."** It was launched on September 11, 2009, two years out from my first alive day.

It was there I met Laurie Willmott, the owner. Laurie's father and brother were both veterans and her husband is a retired Las Vegas Metropolitan Corrections Officer. Her father, Harold Carpenter, was a staff sergeant in the Army Air Corps, who served in World War II. Her brother, Steven Carpenter, also served in the Air Force during the Vietnam War. Her family members were part of the inspiration and motivation behind Horses Healing Heroes. To Laurie, it's her way of giving back.

Numerous studies have shed light on how military veterans with PTS are finding help with equine therapy. When Laurie started the program there were only a few of them around the United States, but today there are hundreds. She was able to convince me to be open to it. Part of my resolve with getting through my initial discomfort was the promise to myself to do the work, to nip this in the bud. I remembered how my father struggled with his nightmares and I didn't want that to define *my* future.

There is plenty of science behind human-animal interaction. The relationship (love) affects us hormonally. It kicks in the **Oxytocin** in our bodies. Oxytocin is a powerful hormone, which acts as a neurotransmitter for the brain. It's also called the bonding hormone because it plays a powerful role in bonding. It's the one released when we kiss or hug, and the hormone that bonds all mammals to their babies. *The "Love" Hormone*. Oxytocin and the human-animal interaction effects largely overlap. Animal assisted therapies have been shown to be beneficial for social and interpersonal actions, anxiety and high blood pressure, reduction of stress, increased trustworthiness, reduced aggression, enhanced empathy and improve learning, to mention a few.

Equine Assisted Psychotherapy, or EAP, is a form of psychotherapy, focused on helping people overcome emotional and physical trauma by working with horses. EAP has been used to treat a wide range of mental health and basic human development issues including attention deficit disorders, behavioral disorders, substance abuse, child abuse and post traumatic stress. Although it's not clear when this therapy was first used, it can be traced back to the ancient days of Greece. Back then, horses were primarily used as a mode of transportation, but it's well documented that they were also used in the emotional assistance of individuals with disabilities.

The **Professional Association of Therapeutic Horsemanship** or PATH, is renowned and accredited with the methodologies and protocols for horse therapy, which are the standards within the industry. Their focus is more on the mental-health aspects of the human-horse relationship and interaction. They provide certification within the industry and work closely with the *Wounded Warrior Project (WWP)*. For the first three to four years, Laurie funded the operation herself, only recently receiving PATH accreditation and being accepted into the Wounded Warrior Project family.

At Spirit Therapies, their first and primary charter was to assist with children with learning disabilities, mental challenges and autism. The goal of horse therapy is to provide interventions that would not be possible through interaction with other humans. The animal interacts with humans in ways that increase mutual trust between the two. Horses are not easily manipulated or bullied. They don't trust naturally but if respected they, in return, respect.

Being prey animals, horses are also herd animals. Herd animals live by a hierarchy of rules, a family system. They must communicate with each other with **body language.** They read each other and they read us. They are naturally curious and can mirror our human behavior. Horses not only read the subtle changes in our body language, but also feel our emotions, both negative and positive, and can sense our basic intentions of harm or safety. With humans, close to 60% of our communication with each other is done through body language.

On my first trip to Spirit Therapies I was introduced to several of the horses. *As I mingled and interacted with them, **Buddy** showed interest in me.* I've been working with him ever since. For the first several months, every Friday, I was introduced to the grooming routine and as I mentioned before, I wasn't really getting it. The free massage thing. My walls were up pretty high. Not getting it, but always laughing about it.

Grooming is the initial basic social interaction between the horse and human. Similar to the way we have seen many primates do for each other. It's part of the process. You're placed in the ring, an open working area, with your horse. There is always a safety instructor there. The first thing you do is place the halter on. Although a simple thing, it took a while for me to get it right. Then you must tie the rope with a particular knot to the fencing. Now the grooming begins. You're given a kit of grooming tools, and then you get to work. You start with a hard rubber brush; brushing in a circular pattern, front to back and left to right, then move to a hard bristle brush, doing the same thing. Next, you move to a soft bristled brush, then to the horse's tail and mane and lastly his feet. It took me a while to get the foot thing down, but now I can get them done pretty fast. His pedicure, I call it.

Although, it seemed like I was doing all the work, grooming and cleaning him, the daily debrief with Laurie, going over our interaction, often revealed the real trust building between Buddy and me. We were building a bond with each other. The horse, being a prey animal, has a primary instinct for flight. My instinct is the exact opposite, to fight. *Together, we found a **middle road**.* It's actually beautiful to see these honest interactions. *Like us, horses just want to survive.*

Most of my sessions at Spirit Therapies last an hour, some less, some more. But the majority of my sessions include working Buddy, or what they call "lunging." I've ridden him several times, but I find myself getting more from it by interacting on the ground. There is definitely a connection with Buddy that allows me to look at my daily life and see things more clearly. Every interaction had mistakes and successes. Buddy will react to how I'm feeling as I enter the ring. If

I'm irritable, he'll notice and be standoffish until I start to relax. On more than one occasion, I've found myself being worked by him. As I'm lunging him around the ring, I'll notice that instead of me directing him, he's maneuvering himself to direct me.

A great instructor can make the difference between a good or bad experience. Laurie, being a certified therapist, is not only there for safety, but also as an observer. She can see our interaction from the outside, and during our debriefs, will define the challenges and obstacles she's observed and how to work toward positive change. The challenges of the horse-human interaction often mirror things going on in my life, allowing me to step back, take a breath and move through with new insight. For instance, if I'm over-tasking myself, Buddy will notice my aggravation and stress and he'll pull back until I calm down. *Pattern Interrupt.* Whether or not the goal of each session is achieved, the insight gained on how we moved through the interaction together is the reward.

Working with horses also helps foster communication and problem solving. Just about every time I work Buddy, I'm communicating with him as he is with me. The way he turns his ears lets me know the direction he's listening to. Same with his eyes. In recent years, there have been times where I'm lunging three horses at the same time, having to problem solve their positioning in the ring, communicating their direction and keeping them working together. The workout helps build confidence. The animals reward us with their body language approval. Their tail wagging and nods equal smiles. The social interaction within a safe environment is a whole lot of fun, putting smiles on faces that have not seen them in a while.

This therapy also offers instant insight. Because horses are honest, they offer instant feedback, shedding light on the veteran's thoughts and feelings before he or the therapist are conscious of them. Negative feedback from the animal is often repeated until noticed and corrected. This is why I say Buddy is often *working me*, instead of me *working him*. This can also be beneficial for the therapist observing, helping to understand the veteran's interpretation of his environment and his interaction with that environment.

Animals are honest and pure, providing a non-judgmental environment for the veteran. Pre-injury, I was a very social person, but after my return, I thought everyone I came into contact with could see my mental deficiencies and judge me for them. *Working with Buddy allowed me to strengthen my interaction skills, boosting my confidence in a pure and trusting environment.* There's no risk of rejection, criticism or judgment, only truth and connection.

I had a hard time with trust after I returned from Iraq. There's a certain safe feeling you get when you finally place your trust in another and vise versa. Although Buddy is a pretty big horse, he knows me and I know him. He trusts me and I trust him. Buddy was a big playful teenager but we knew each other's boundaries and adhered to the unwritten rules of engagement. We respect each other. We also understand the boundaries of assertiveness and aggressiveness. **Most importantly, it's a form of healing *that doesn't come from a pill!***

It's hard to get warfighters to make that first step; to do the work, to get out there and be open to the process. Once they do, then the positive energy seems to come out and a lot of our negative feelings are left at the gate. We've had many returning wounded warriors, who came to Spirit Therapies and enjoyed the experience, only to fall back into the simplicity of medications and alcohol, easily discovering excuses to not do the work. There have been many days that I could have easily come up with a reason not to go, but there has never been a day that I've left *without a smile.*

Spirit Therapy not only deals with wounded warriors, but their family members as well. Millions of children in the United States have had a parent deployed to a war zone. As I mentioned earlier in my chapter about "*Brats,*" the children of warfighters often face their own battles here at home. My mom, sister, brother and I had been through the stress of possibly losing, not only our loved one, but the one who provided for our well being. It could sometimes be overwhelming.

Having grown up the son of a father at war and a mother who was our only support system, horse therapy would've been a great activity to participate in as a family. Today, an increasing number of military spouses and children are forced to deal with their own isolation and lack of support, while their spouses are deployed. With today's Global War on Terrorism (GWOT) military families are enduring not only multiple deployments, but shorter time between deployments and sometimes longer deployments. These parental deployments can lead to depression and isolation, as well as poor academic performance in children, as in my case. During my father's second deployment I started hanging out with the wrong crowd. It was only through mentoring by my English teacher, that I found a way to get back on track.

The plethora of emotions that family members go through with parents returning from war with TBI and PTS can be numerous. From the fear of losing their loved ones, to the joy of having them return alive, to the frustration and disappointments of their actions when they return. In my case, it was always being afraid of that military green car pulling up with the Marines in their dress uniforms.

For families, horse therapy is a form of emotional "pattern interrupt," in a safe and trusting environment. It fosters communication between parents and children. It's a friendly environment, where doing the work doesn't always feel like doing the work. You're focused on the moment. For me, doing the work also means exercising. Horse therapy is not only a mental exercise, but a physical one as well. Just about every time Buddy and I workout, we both break a sweat. Lunging, turning and practicing the various commands can be strenuous. It's both a physical and mental exercise.

A major part of my TBI management strategy is exercising my brain. **The entire horse therapy process is one big "Solution Generating Machine."** It's filled with hundreds of choices; thousands of calculations and predictions for movements are being made. The consequences of these are immediate. It's not just the horse that's part of the interaction, but the instructor/observer, who can see it from another perspective, allowing for an introspective debriefing. Whether the workout goals are reached or not doesn't really matter because its all part of the problem solving and brain exercise.

One of the other wounded warriors that participates in the program is **Danny**, an Army veteran. Danny returned from Vietnam socially dysfunctional and very angry. Much like many of us, he didn't like crowds and lived his life in seclusion, staying away from others, with no toleration for them. When he was young he had been around horses quite a bit, training to be a jockey. He had been away from horses for over 40 years before coming to Spirit Therapies and being re-introduced to them.

BRAIN PAIN

Danny's VA therapist recommended Spirit Therapies. After being around horses for most of his younger life, working with them again brought him back to a place of relaxation. As he described it, "It took a large weight off my shoulders." Working with horses helped his social interactions, patience and tolerance. He also volunteers, helping with the children, enjoying their interaction. Danny is "doing the work."

Kim is another Army wounded warrior who returned from Iraq with the anxiety and guilt many of us have. Kim is one of the funniest guys I know and if you were to meet him on the street, you'd think he was just another funny guy who happened to be a veteran. Outwardly, he's confident and funny, but throughout the years he's been fighting a battle with the demons that followed him back home. He's fighting to get the work done just like me. That is how we became friends. Doing the work is easier said than done. *Chaos* is insidious, nefarious and patient. It can re-engage you at your most vulnerable moments.

A few years ago, I met a wounded warrior with a service dog at an airport. The dog was lying at his feet and when I approached, he sat up, alerting his owner and putting himself in between the warfighter and me. The dog was kind, yet firm and on guard. It was incredible!

Service dogs are trained for up to six months and not all dogs graduate to Service. They are usually one to two years old at the time of placement, energetic and require a significant amount of attention, as animals normally do. But these dogs can sense anxiety, alerting their owner prior to fear settling in. *Pattern Interrupt.* The more the wounded warrior can control his anxiety, the more he can adjust to the slower-paced civilian life. The earlier they can be warned of high anxiety moments, the sooner they can catch themselves before their emotions get away from them and *Chaos* slips in.

These programs not only help the warfighter, *but help **decrease** the overall cost to our healthcare system and society,* by keeping our wounded warriors as productive members of society. Service dogs can also help children deal with the stressors of parents being deployed. They can provide social support to children, offering a calming presence, as well as helping the children deal with and communicate their fears, anger and anxieties.

ANTHONY JONES

Human-animal interaction therapies are not cures for TBI are PTS, but they are instrumental tools in overcoming the various anxieties that are new to the warfighter and their families. Animals provide unconditional trust, acceptance and bonding, helping us move through our anxiety and stress.

I did the work for almost seven years, not always understanding why, many times not wanting to go. Buddy reminded me to get going and search out alternatives for working through the brain pain and fighting *Chaos*. **Buddy** passed away in the spring of 2014, after the initial writing of this book. I've never been much of an animal or pet person, but that has changed. For those of you with animals, you can understand the pain of losing a beloved animal friend. He was young; only thirteen and it was unexpected. Colic. His last gift to me was the gift of sadness.

I felt the loss. I cared. Something I hadn't done in a long time. He gave me more than I realized and helped me more than I can say. The program has been a consistent source of my recovery and never once, did I leave without a smile. *We* did the work.

It all started here for me. Working with Buddy and Laurie. Getting out, interacting with others, becoming engaged in the world, finding the courage to get back on the ski slopes, get out to the mountains, camping and biking, picking up my guitar and getting my jam back; *the catalyst* to get me going again – just like my Ford Falcon was in college.

I realized, through writing this book, I wasn't going to become a suicide statistic. 22 a day.

"Someone I loved once gave me a box full of darkness. It took me years to understand that this too, was a gift." — Mary Oliver.

135

Me and 'Buddy.' (Photo courtesy Karen Swigart)

'Buddy' running me around the ring. (Photo courtesy Karen Swigart)

CHAPTER 10

HYPERBARIC OXYGEN THERAPY

When I was flying with the 8th Special Operations Squadron, prior to take off, while going through the checklist, we'd put on our helmet and oxygen mask and go to 100%. *100% oxygen*, forcefully and coolly rolling into your lungs was just the trick after a late night out. *I'm just saying.* We were young and on the road a lot. The rules were always, "Twelve hours bottle to throttle, topped off with 100% oxygen!" It's as common as biscuits and gravy in Georgia. It was a trick to get our brain back on track and up to speed. Today, there's 5-hour energy drinks, back then it was 100% oxygen. *Oxygen is one of our body's most essential nutrients and is essential for life and healing.*

Every year, as part of our flight physical, we would enter a Hypobaric Altitude Chamber and experience the induced pressure of high-altitude, as well as the increased lack of oxygen. We would then take off our mask, going off oxygen, to experience and recognize the symptoms of hypoxia, or *lack of oxygen*. The chamber taught you what it felt like if you lost cabin pressure, thus oxygen. The deprivation of oxygen to the brain would result in incorrect thoughts, then actions, then loss of conscience.

Other types of chambers known as Hyperbaric Oxygen Chambers are used for the opposite, treating decompression sickness, known as the bends or divers disease. This is caused by divers coming to the surface too quickly and bubbles forming in their body as depressurization occurs, causing joint pain, skeletal pain and neurological disorders.

In the spring of 2010, one of my students in our Tactical Driving course told me about **Hyperbaric Oxygen Therapy** or HBOT, for war veterans with TBI. He also told me about two US Air Force Airman injured by a roadside IED blast in Iraq, who had been helped by HBOT. He went on about the research and success of **Dr. Paul Harch**, of Louisiana State University School of Medicine. He told me HBOT was approved by the FDA for other maladies such as open leg wounds and was also being used with thousands of autistic children. At first, I assumed he had watched one too many You Tube videos, and immediately thought of Michael Jackson. But then, I found out my student had a PhD, and was entrenched deeply in the industry. Always searching for a way to ease the Brain Pain and to bypass a future of possible Alzheimer's, I started looking into it.

HBOT works by breathing pure oxygen, under pressure, which speeds it through the bloodstream, reducing edema, activating senescent neurons, down-regulating inflammation, promoting growth of neural pathways, stopping swelling/reperfusion injury (damaged tissue due to lack of oxygen), restarts stunned cellular metabolism, stimulates white blood cells, regrows blood vessels and activates stem cells eight times faster than normal. This is not new, it has been used for the treatment of brain injuries for over 100 years.

HBOT is approved by the medical community and the [29]FDA, to treat over 14 different conditions, including diabetic open foot/leg wounds, soft tissue injuries, acute skin burns, carbon monoxide poisoning, crush injuries, decompression sickness, severe anemia, intracranial abscesses and compromised skin grafts and flaps. It provides oxygen, you breathe under pressure, to deep tissues inside the body. *But, not yet for TBI's.*

Over the last twelve years, one third of the HBOT billed by hospitals has been for diabetic foot/leg ulcers, which has led to the rapid proliferation of large multiplace chambers throughout the medical community. **Yet, as with acupuncture, wounded warriors can't get a referral!**

The oxygen helps the healing and re-growth of damage at the cellular level. Breathing pressurized oxygen is known to boost the effects of some antibiotics, stimulate white blood cells and promote healing. The reason it's primarily used for diabetic foot wounds is because one, it works, and two, it's cheaper than amputation and long-term disability compensation.

What's the difference between a non-healing open foot/leg wound and a non-healing brain injury? The damage in the brain cannot be seen at the cellular level, thus is assumed not to be there. *Remember the story of my eye injury?* My **Ophthalmologist** told me that the blast pressure burst the capillaries in my eye and that's why I have a yellow spot in my vision. **If the capillaries in my eyes had burst, then the same most likely happened throughout the soft tissue of my brain.**

[30]**Dr. Gaylan Rockswold**, a neurosurgeon, has treated TBI patients with Hyperbaric Oxygen Therapy since the early 80s and found this therapy reduced the death rate in serious TBI cases from 33% to 17%. He is just one of many scientists to recognize this conclusion.

After a TBI, whether explosive or trauma related, the brain cells often die due to lack of oxygen. The hypothesis often believed is that many of these cells and neural pathways can be revived with HBOT. In 1990, a study by [31]**Dr. Richard Neubauer** found that neurons can be reactivated up to 10 and 14 years after the initial trauma. [32]Another 1975 critical trial of almost 100 patients with TBI in the midbrain found that HBOT decreased mortality rate by 40%.

If HBOT can assist with repairing injuries such as carbon monoxide poisoning, crush injuries, skin burns and severe anemia, it would be natural to think it can help with other injuries throughout the body. Studies have shown that additional pressurized oxygen re-energizes dead or damaged brain cells, and neural pathways. Repairing the cells and invigorating these pathways can improve the patient's concentration, memory and focus. Many of the cells injured aren't dead, just damaged, like a bruise. Why not try? *Oh yeah; equipment, infrastructure and manpower.* **The COST.**

A growing number of troops with TBI are turning to HBOT to help better their lives, and I am one of them. Not because my military medical system offered me help with this, but because **I took action** and purchased my own. $20,000. ***Yeah, I'm upset!***

Other military members with blast injuries had already been successfully treated with HBOT prior to my injury in 2007. If it weren't for one of my students, I wouldn't have known about it.

The DOD has spent ***tens of millions*** of dollars doing research, only to come to the conclusion that HBOT is not a provable science. Yet, ten times as many studies, nationally and internationally, show just the opposite. The *latest* research study funded by the [33]US Department of Defense and the military medical system showed that there was no significant effect on post-concussive symptoms. In the study, "Bioethecists" stated that this treatment doesn't pass the test. A "Bioethecist" is a individual with an advanced degree, who is concerned with the ethical questions that arise in the relationship among life sciences, medicine, politics, law, and philosophy.

What's a "**Bioethecist**" doing splashing news bytes around on a medical protocol? Justification of their opinion by media? There's no ethical question here. It's a brain injury that needs treatment! [34]These "Bioethecists" are everywhere, commenting on everything from abortion, euthanasia, to HBOT and governmental health policies. "Bioethics provided the means by which officials can justify *'rationalizing'* the care of persons to fit the cost-cutting goals of government and, not coincidentally, to promote the needs of business." *These guys are basically* ***lobbyists*** *for hire.*

[35]"The researchers were told by the ***majority*** of participants that they felt better, that their traumatic brain injury or PTSD symptoms improved, but the researchers hypothesized that these *'improvements'* were placebo effects." It significantly downplayed the actual improvements of many of the participants, although there are dozens more studies from countries all over the world, touting the opposite. *Russia, China, Israel, to name a few…*

The COST? *Of course it's the cost!* According to [36]Dr. Harch, "The federal government's reluctance to accept HBOT as a legitimate treatment form for PTS and TBI comes down to money. 'I firmly believe that's No. 1,' he says. 'We charge $200 an hour at our clinic. The Medicare rate is about $275 an hour. This is billed in hospitals at $2,000 an hour. DoD has thrown out a figure that you need $500,000 lifetime to treat a brain-injured veteran for these symptoms and problems. First of all, there's no evidence for that. Secondly, if you even took the 80-treatment protocol that I developed, that's $160,000 at the billed hospital rate.'"

If the government studies showed that HBOT is a viable science and works, the cost they would incur putting it into place, could be in the hundreds of millions, not to mention the bureaucracy infrastructure costs.

Once again, the warfighter has been shuffled to the back of the line, and the promise of the *"best medical care"* has been ignored. This treatment has been proven to work when done immediately after the injury or within the first year.

Military researchers say they don't want to rush the HBOT, but warfighters don't have the advantage of waiting. A warfighter with a damaged brain is living day-to-day, carrying their personal *"Chain,"* fighting their own personal **Chaos**. Military researchers talk about proving the efficacy through peer reviewed scientific processes, but the Veteran whose Brain Pain is overwhelming his human operating system, is trying to navigate his life. *As I'll discuss, those with immediate access and insertion into the HBOT protocols, have had the best results.* **The longer you wait, the less successful the results**.

Back to my concept of "nipping this in the bud." In the fall of 2010, I purchased my own chamber. The cost was nearly $20,000. I could've bought a more stylish SUV, new furniture, 20 new guitars, 3 new Rolex's, but my brain was more important. I made the purchase to give myself every chance of maintaining my brain health, *hopefully stalling any future deterioration of dementia, Alzheimer's and neurodegenerative disease.*

According to the [37]Mayo Clinic, a primary treatment protocol for *cluster headaches* (which I have been previously diagnosed with) is to briefly inhale 100% oxygen. This has been proven to provide dramatic relief for those who use it. It's a safe and effective, as well as inexpensive, protocol for treating these types of headaches. It was only during my research that I came upon this. *None of my neurologists have ever mentioned this to me*, and when I brought it up, I was told I couldn't get it, unless I went to the ER. Shit, I see elderly people all over Las Vegas walking around with their oxygen tanks. *Come on!*

BRAIN PAIN

Preliminary results from a [38] **National Brain Injury Rescue and Rehabilitation Project** showed that of over 1000 patients with TBI, treated with HBOT, *all participants improved, and no patients worsened.* Most showed *substantial* improvements. They concluded that the earlier the patient is treated, the better the result. They also concluded that HBOT reduced the patient's need for additional meds, and that the PTS often associated with TBI improves as well.

My chamber is around 9 feet long and 40 inches tall. I removed the bed from my spare bedroom and placed it there. It has an aluminum tubular frame as well as a soft cushion floor, which allows you to lie down comfortably inside it. Mine is built extra sturdy, having double walls, meaning there's an interior tube, which seals, and a second exterior tube with multiple nylon bands sewn around it for additional strength. This additional strengthening allows for higher pressure. It's filled with the compressor that's attached to the outside wall, as well as an oxygen concentrator that delivers the oxygen under pressure. It's has multiple gauges, relief valves and safety features to prevent over pressurization. It's designed to be operated, entering and exiting, by one person. Although I've done that to ensure that it works, it feels much safer having another person there for added assistance.

Initially my experience with small closed-in spaces led me to feelings of claustrophobia, but when you have $20,000 invested, you find a way to overcome it. *A one-hour protocol inside the chamber is commonly called a "**dive**."* My first dive lasted about 10 minutes, or about three songs on my iPod. I gradually went to 4-5-6 songs lasting 20 to 30 minutes. Like most new situations after trauma you go slowly, building and adding to your comfort zone. Now, an hour long dive goes by quickly.

Lately I've been using my iPad and headphones, listening to binaural beats and meditating. **Binaural beats** are played through headphones with one frequency going into one ear and another frequency going into the other. They mix in your head creating a center frequency, much like Buddhist chanting. *It drowns out the constant ringing of my tinnitus* and allows for a much more restful state, increasing my ability to *meditate*, which decreases my anxiety. I've been lucky to have friends, like my buddies *Richie Emanuele,*

Quest Borras, and other Veterans *Jimmy Hughes*, *Oscar Castenada* and *Rayshaun Washington*, to help me in and out of the chamber.

Dr. Paul Harch is a groundbreaker and long-term advocate for Hyperbaric Oxygen Therapy. His 2010 [39]Louisiana State University School of Medicine IRB-approved study of **15 blast-injured veterans** showed a significant improvement in patients treated with HBOT. Patients showed an average IQ jump of 15 points in 30 days, 40% improvement rate in post-concussion syndrome symptoms, 30% reduction in PTS symptoms and 51% decrease in depression. Yet a similar study done by the Department of Defense showed no significant improvement. **WTF?**

Earlier I mentioned that our DOD had spent *tens of millions* of dollars doing HBOT research, only to come to the conclusion that it doesn't work; yet the researchers on the most recent study, were told by the *majority* of participants, that they felt better and that their traumatic brain injury and/or PTSD symptoms improved. *First*, when dozens of peer-reviewed studies already existed, why do we need to waste more money on more research? *Second*, those tens of millions of dollars could have bought several hundred HBOT chambers like mine. They could have been given to the wounded warfighters, along with training, to immediately begin assisting them in their healing.

Once again, you can't see our "Invisible Wounds" so they don't warrant some of the expensive medical equipment intervention, *as do amputees*, who need prosthetic limbs, wheelchairs and handicap vehicles. *Weren't we promised the best care available?*

The US Olympic team has treated numerous sports injuries and concussions, as well as the US military's Special Operations Commands who have used HBOT to treat knee replacements, fractures, and concussions, as well as hundreds of professional athletes, including professional football players, MMA fighters, soccer players, rugby players and professional wrestlers. [40]Air Force research demonstrated that fractures heal 30% faster and stronger under HBOT. There are also hundreds of Plastic Surgeons across the country using HBOT post-surgery to speed the healing process. A Department of Defense study said HBOT didn't work, yet our *Special Operations Command is using it!* **Why weren't we told about HBOT? Money?** *Am I repeating myself again?*

BRAIN PAIN

When you're put into a chamber, the doctors don't tell you that they're targeting a specific wound, such as a diabetic foot wound or severe anemia, because they can't target specific injuries. They're treating the whole body and compressing more oxygen into your bloodstream. *More oxygen, equals more nutrients to all areas.*

The **standard protocol** for a TBI regimen is 40 treatments, or **"dives"** at 1.5 atmospheres of pressure, equivalent to an hour of diving underwater at 33 feet of depth. The pressure causes oxygen to saturate tissues seven to twelve times that of normal breathing.

In my case, I believe my brain is trying to heal the neural pathways, *or create workarounds*, creating new pathways, making new connections, while letting older ones heal. My chamber gives me a better chance of keeping good oxygen flowing deep throughout my body and *stemming a possible future with CTE*.

[41]On August 21st of 2005, US Army **Brig. Gen. Patt Maney** was blown up by an Improvised Explosive Device (IED). The blast left him with a transient loss of consciousness, and several seconds' anterograde memory loss (loss of the ability to create new memories after the event). Other symptoms he had were headaches, short-term memory loss and fatigue. He was medically evacuated to Walter Reed in Washington, DC, where his cognitive deficits were noted as low normal. He was medically retired in April of 2007.

General Maney was not only a military General Officer, but a Florida County Judge, as well. This injury left him unable to balance a checkbook, understand the storyline of a TV show, read a paragraph in the newspaper as well as remember what he had just read. This was very similar to my experience my first year back. I understand these feelings all too well.

With his wife as his advocate, she discovered HBOT through **Dr. Albert Zant Jr.** According to Gen. Maney, "We were initially told about HBOT by Dr. Zant, who then consulted with the PM&R physician at Walter Reed and with the, then hospital commander – both wonderful physicians who were willing to try something different. The hospital commander had to contact Tricare to have the treatment at GWU Hospital authorized."

He began the Dr. Harch protocol at George Washington University one-year post his incident/injury. There he had 80 dives at 1.5 atm, of one-hour, with blocks of 40 each. He showed noticeable improvement at 18 dives. At 25 dives he was much more sociable and had less fatigue. After 80 dives there was a significant improvement in his cognition and he was able to return to duty in the summer of 2007, as a Judge in Okaloosa County, Florida.

At six months post HBOT, he suffered a partial regression. He had ten additional dives by Dr. Albert Zant Jr. and showed improved cognition. He continues as a full time Judge. He maintains a full caseload and also started the "Veterans Docket"/later Veterans Court, which was the first Veterans Treatment Court in Florida.

As a Wounded Warrior, his experience "Has left me sensitive and sympathetic to the plight of some 200,000 wounded warriors with Traumatic Brain Injury, and their families and their communities and veterans in general." The State law was named for him; SB 138, the "T. Patt Maney Veterans' Treatment Intervention Act."

This was in 2007, just prior to my injury. *Why wasn't the success of General Maney's case broadcast out to those who could assist other blast victims?* The media? This success could have been passed down to the tens of thousands of TBI wounded warriors that followed him, yet they weren't.

I contacted General Maney for this book and he told me, "*I have tried to disseminate the information but the DOD and VA medical establishments **were and are resistant**. With several other volunteers, I've met and written to members of Congress, Surgeons General of each of the services at different times and with VA officials. For many of the meetings I was accompanied by a former Secretary of the Army.*" He was doing everything possible (with a brain injury), to advocate for this cause.

This was a General Officer attempting to get the word out and it seems as even he was mostly dismissed. Trying to advocate with an on-going brain injury can in itself be exhausting, yet he tried, and still advocates to this day. *What do you have to do? Write a book?*

If it were not for his advocates, he may have never found this treatment. His was a remarkable, post-injury recovery. If I had even suspected this could have been an option, I would have sought out the same treatments on my own. How many of thousands, yes, tens of thousands of young men and women were left behind? That's the deal! *That's why I'm pissed.*

BRAIN PAIN

Here's another one. In January of 2008, two [42]**United States Air Force Airman** from the 720th Special Tactics Group, Hurlburt Field, Florida, were injured by a roadside IED blast in Iraq. Although both survived with no physical wounds, both suffered from TBI concussive injuries. Soon afterwards they both developed insomnia, headaches, irritability, memory difficulties and other cognitive issues, typically what I call Brain Pain.

Prior to their deployment, they were tested with the Automated Neuropsychological Assessment Metrics or ANAM. This is a computer-based testing tool designed to observe the speed and accuracy of the person's attention, memory, and thinking ability. It's conducted prior to an individual's deployment and is used to identify and monitor an individual who is involved in a brain-related injury. This allows a before-and-after analysis of any TBI's. Six months after being injured, the two airmen were tested again and the scores were notably decreased, showing marked deficiencies in memory and thinking ability.

Once again, these two Airmen were also able to get treated with HBOT. Someone knew something? The Special Operations community knew something. These successes _were documented_. **_Were they buried?_**

They were treated with hyperbaric oxygen with 100% oxygen, at 1.5 atm absolute. Both had between 40 and 80 dives, one hour in length, which soon resulted in the improvement of both Airman. Both had continuous symptoms of TBI, which did not improve for almost 7 months and were on track to be medically discharged. With HBOT, substantial improvement was made within the first two weeks. Headaches and insomnia improved quickly, while irritability, cognitive defects, and memory problems improved more slowly. Follow-up testing at 9 and 12 months post-injury showed continued improvement in all areas. **_Both airmen were returned to duty_**, saving the government an estimated $2.6 million each in lifetime disability cost. Most importantly, their Brain Pain was gone.

Gen. Maney was injured in August of 2005. These two Airmen in 2008. No one ever mentioned HBOT to me as an option. This not only affects me but also **_upwards of a quarter million combat blast injuries_**, as well as the millions of civilians who are living with TBI.

The cost here must be too high. Again, it seems as if the easiest and cheapest methodology is to medicate the patient *with pills*, send them to counseling, medically discharge or retire them and/or leave them to their own resolve.

[43]**Dr. Shai Efrati** and **Prof. Eshel Ben-Jacob** of Tel Aviv University's Sagol School of Neuroscience believe they have proven that it is possible to repair brains and improve the quality of life for TBI victims, even years after the occurrence of the injury. This brand-new Israeli study was done on 56 participants, who suffered mild Traumatic Brain Injury within five years and were no longer improving. All still had headaches, concentration problems, irritability problems as well as other cognitive impairments. In their article published in *PLoS ONE*, Dr. Efrati, Prof. Ben Jacob, and their collaborators present evidence that Hyperbaric Oxygen Therapy (HBOT) improved chronically impaired brain functions and improved the life of mild TBI patients. These new findings not only corroborate findings made by Dr. Paul Harch and Dr. Richard Neubauer, but also challenge the often-dismissive stand taken by the American FDA and the Centers for Disease Control and Prevention.

According to the Israeli study, "The participants were randomly divided into two groups. One received two months of HBOT, while the other, the control group, was not treated at all. The latter group then received two months of treatment following the first control period. The treatments, administered at the Institute of Hyperbaric Medicine at Assaf Harofeh Medical Center, headed by Dr. Efrati, consisted of 40 one-hour sessions, administered five times a week over two months, in a high pressure chamber, breathing 100% oxygen and experiencing a pressure of 1.5 atmospheres, the pressure experienced when diving under water to a depth of 5 meters. The patients' brain functions and quality of life were then assessed by computerized evaluations and compared with Single Photon Emission Computed Tomography (SPECT) scans.

The HBOT sessions led to significant improvements in tests of cognitive function and quality of life. No significant improvements occurred by the end of the period of non-treatment in the control group. Analysis of brain imaging showed significantly increased neuronal activity after a two-month period of HBOT treatment compared to the control periods of non-treatment."

BRAIN PAIN

Each veteran with TBI/PTS can cost approximately $60,000 per year by way of lost tax revenue, disability compensation, incarceration costs and substance abuse cost. The societal costs will most likely include homelessness, welfare, long-term care facilities and nursing homes. After reviewing these monetary statistics, it seems obvious we could save millions and millions of dollars if those identified, were initially treated with Hyperbaric Oxygen as soon as possible after their injury. They could soon return to productive lives instead of becoming dependent upon the disability system, as well as mental health facilities. *Pay now or pay later?*

When the patient is a military member and injured they are normally placed on light duty or a casual status. This means they have time on their hands. *Inexpensive portable HBOT chambers, like mine, could easily, inexpensively and effectively be placed in every forward deployed Combat Support Mobile Hospital, every wounded warrior transition unit, as well as almost every base or VA in the United States.* The injured member could then be ordered to report for treatment, just as they would an hour-long physical therapy session, and receive a one-hour per day, pressurized dive over a 30 to 40 day period. Makes sense to me.

[44]According to the "Report to Congress on the Use of Hyperbaric Oxygen for Medical Care and Research in Response to HR 3326, the Department of Defense (DoD) Appropriations Act for Fiscal Year 2010" the DoD does not recognize traumatic brain injury as an approved medical indication due to lack of medical evidence. With the exception of single person hyperbaric chambers with operational units, DoD has few hyperbaric chambers at its military hospitals. To support its hyperbaric research program, the DoD had to lease four hyperbaric chambers specifically for new studies. Come on!

I wonder if you took all the salaries of researchers, as well as grant money and more, added them up, and threw that at the problem, how much could we get done sooner than later? A Hospital medical grade hyperbaric chamber will cost upwards more than $100-200,000. A top-of-the-line portable like mine can cost $15-25,000. A private clinic will provide a one-hour session for an average of $200 and a hospital will charge upwards of $2000 for the same service. HBOT is recognized by Medicare and approved by the FDA for 14 different conditions, not TBI or PTS. **Israel, China and Russia all approve this treatment for over 80 different conditions, including TBI.**

There are 34 major military hospitals in the United States, as well as eight overseas. This does not include the basic medical facilities overseas and on every military base or those deployed with the US Navy. There are also over 1,800 Veterans Administration medical facilities worldwide. The DoD had to lease four hyperbaric chambers to complete their research. This tells me that since there is no infrastructure already set up with hyperbaric chambers throughout the military medical community, that the cost for hundreds of medical grade chambers will be somehow be found to be too costly.

Yet, in every major city, the majority of civilian hospitals (due to treatments for diabetic foot wounds) are already set up with these chambers, but our insurance and the VA covers only FDA approved conditions. *Give me a referral!*

At a minimum, portable HBOT chambers should be located at every Combat Support Hospital (CSH) deployed to a hostile area. The cost is minimal, $15-$25,000 and it requires minimal space, a 10 x 8' area. *This can be used immediately on any blast victims while they're recuperating from their injuries.* If there had been one at Camp Victory in Baghdad, I would have been there everyday, including it in part of my routine, like going to the gym.

We may have to start small, but we have to start. If we had spent just a part of the bureaucratic research money on employment of these portable units, *TBI patients would now be reaping the rewards*, and at a minimum, feel the *confidence* that their government, who has used our might to flex it's political muscle, has not forgotten them and is doing everything possible to treat their injuries.

When we go to war we "plan" on blowing things up. In turn, we know our enemy will do the same. Kill or be killed. Just like our logistic lines must resupply those tank rounds, plane bombs or mortar rounds, we have to realize that a "**plan**" must be in place to maintain a healthy and *intelligent* fighting force.

We must "**plan**" for their return and the care they will need to reintegrate back into society and become thriving members once more. We did not learn that lesson after World Wars I & II, Korea and Vietnam, and we must learn it now. *We owe our combat veterans.*

BRAIN PAIN

Out of every war our medical communities learn valuable lessons in life savings protocols. When it comes to blood loss, pneumothorax, airway obstructions, eye and ear injuries, infections and amputations, these wars have produced dramatic increases in survivability. *These lessons have helped millions of civilians as a result.*

We need to put into practice some of the newest and most advanced protocols for TBI's, giving our veterans *every* possibility of a future without neurodegenerative diseases.

We see our "Invisible Wounds" daily.

Oxygen is essential to our survival and soon we'll realize how essential it is to our healing. I hope that in the next war, HBOT chambers will be forward deployed to the Combat Support Hospitals in the field.

I've spent hundreds of hours in my chamber, firmly believing HBOT has helped. ***It is now part of my long-term management strategy.***

My spare bedroom containing my Hyperbaric Oxygen Therapy chamber. I'm being pro-active!

CHAPTER 11

HOW'S IT GOING?

A few years back I was visiting with one of my best friends and his family. I remember it well because of the insidious way *Chaos* attacks me. We were having dinner out on their deck and the conversation was moving along smoothly until the topic turned to the Bible. My friends are Christian, as am I, but we had differing opinions on the specifics of religion. This subject can quickly become passionate and heated, as it did. As the discussion continued, it went from one on one, to two on one, then three on one, etc. I, being the one, was becoming **mentally overwhelmed**. *Chaos* saw the opening and slipped through a crack. It slipped into my mind and clogged up my gears. They were making their arguments and I couldn't find mine. *Not being able to retort or access my memories, my anger swelled.* My mind went blank, exploding in pain, finally causing me to walk away and retreat inside, to regroup. "*Access Dyslexia.*" Embracing my new standard is part of doing the work. I still needed to learn this.

Having an opinion, making an argument for that position with an intent to persuade and/or manipulate others over to your side of an argument is one of the most basic of communication skills we use to survive. I'm sure the person who invented the wheel had to persuade the others that it would work. Not being able to communicate my thoughts or even find my position leaves me feeling naked and unprotected.

BRAIN PAIN

During this time, my friends, compassionately, would ask, **"How's it going?"** It was a question I was asked over and over and over. It was one I took more seriously than it was meant. It's just a form of greeting, but for me it was always hard to answer. *Every time I heard it, I had to instantly complete a re-evaluation of my injuries and my state of mind, spinning me into hypervigilance and dread.* I would have to figure out what lie would fit this situation and person. No one really wanted to be brought down with the anxiety and reality of my truth.

Just prior to four years out from my injuries, I came to realize that I wasn't getting any better, but I wasn't getting any worse. The truth was, that there hadn't been much improvement. I was still tapping my head and squinting in pain when spikes occurred. It's uncomfortable to say you're doing well, and then minutes later bark out uncontrolled, in pain.

Ultimately, with good friends, there comes another question. Remember when we did this or that? **Remember? Remember? I don't. I DON'T**! Then, that look on their faces, of why don't you remember? Are you losing it? After years of having answered these questions, it forced me into the ultimate personal inventory. I have realized that life has a plan for us. Sometimes it's a change of *our* plans. Embracing this meant working around my challenges. Embracing this meant the necessity for my **management strategy**.

I still worried about long-term dementia and CTE, but I needed to push out of my stalemate. I had always been very passionate about whatever I was doing. Post injury, I lost my passion and zeal for life. My life consisted of a roller coaster of emotions and frustration. I'd work hard, thinking I was better, back up to the standard of my old abilities to multi-task. *Then, in private I'd go dark, lethargic and fall into depression.* It was an on-going roller coaster of ups and downs, ups and downs. I was constantly pedaling, trying to outrun *Chaos*.

Social engagements made me anxious, due to the interaction and communication necessary. You know you're supposed to feel happiness, excitement and compassion for your loved ones, but for me, those feelings just weren't there. To compensate I would find myself becoming a **actor**, forcing out emotions and feelings I thought the situation required. It would become exhausting.

Just like when I was a child, moving from town to town, meeting new friends and trying to fit in, I was "doing the job." I was acting, reading people and adapting to their expectations. I had lost the emotional connection to others and compensated for that by trying to be better than I was. *Trying to fit the bill*. "How's it going - Oh, I'm doing great, thanks." Bullshit.

Dad had retired for the second time. He had accumulated over ten thousand hours in the Cub and Hughes 500 helicopter, survived one crash and several close calls. Throughout his careers, the Marines and the Border Patrol, he had literally cheated death more times than I can keep up with. He and Mom had earned their retirement and settled on moving to Las Vegas. There were shopping malls, medical facilities and most importantly, for Dad, golf courses.

Dad had always dealt with the **nightmares** *from Vietnam*, but now retirement and the slower pace brought them back to the surface. His quick temper and sudden anger hadn't dwindled, but by this time we knew how to put a fire extinguisher on it. Most times.

In 1998, I returned full time to Las Vegas. My good friend Duff Kaster got me an interview with the House of Blues and I became one of the opening managers for a private club atop the Mandalay Bay Hotel and Casino, called the **House of Blues Foundation Room**. It's on top of the Hotel, on the 61st floor. It was literally the best view in town. I used to be Mr. Las Vegas. I knew everyone; entertainers, show maitre'd's, club and restaurant owners. My phone was constantly ringing. *I was single and a social butterfly*.

It was a pretty exciting time. Having never worked in the Hospitality/Service industry, or the high-end luxury experience, this gave me a greater understanding of humility, which was a bonus. The "**Room**," as we called it, was decorated with the Far East/Indian motif. There was a 2000-pound marble Buddha greeting you as you got off the elevators. Not only was there an exclusive restaurant, lounge and media area; there were also several private rooms where you could have dinner and/or lounge with cocktails. Although the majority of our clients were local businessmen, casino personalities and entrepreneurs, we had more than our share of celebrities, actors and musicians. We were the first of the "*Super Clubs*" in Las Vegas; exclusive, elegant and elite. It was a networking dream.

BRAIN PAIN

Working in the service industry, you would barter in favors. It could be as simple as front of the line entrance to a club, to back stage passes to a concert. That's called the *"Vegas Hook Up."* The majority of service industry workers aren't well paid, and this was just another part of the compensation package. Las Vegas is a small town and you never knew when your venue would need a favor from another venue. Since Las Vegas is all about the customer experience, your customer might have dinner at another restaurant, but then need late night access to your venue. Everyone just took care of each other, with the ultimate winners being the customers.

Before the slogan, "What happens in Vegas, stays in Vegas," became popular, our venue had already kept the secrets of numerous celebrities. From the infamous, (having to kick out Anna Nicole Smith,) to the famous, (enjoying guitarist, "Slash," making drinks behind the bar.) There was never a boring moment.

The Foundation Room was where I first met the "**client**." That's what I'll call him because he is a former client and I am a stickler for confidentiality. He was a multi-billionaire of the technology industry. He often used the Foundation Room to entertain his family and clients. We met through his assistants and bodyguards, as well as the many events they held at the Room. After working together quite a lot, his handlers asked me to join their team. They needed someone to handle advances, protection and eavesdropping detection as they traveled. *I joined their team, starting my security company.*

The House of Blues was a fantastic organization to work for, but the lifestyle was getting to me. There's a reason it's called, "Sin City," and anyone who knows me, knows I work hard and I play hard. The balance I had learned early in my career was becoming *askew*, or off track. The fun meter was pegged and *I needed to feel more purposeful.*

The client's pace was intense to say the least. We traveled around the country and overseas constantly. Going to trade shows and meetings around the world as well as traveling for vacations and leisure, I would usually go ahead as part of the advance team, setting up prior to their arrivals. I confirmed pre-arranged hotels, dinners, entertainment and transportation. I would also sweep all the conference rooms for listening devices and hidden cameras.

ANTHONY JONES

At this company's level, ***corporate espionage*** was just a daily concern of the business. Company secrets needed to be protected and that was part of my job. My military background in electronic warfare gave me a solid base. To up my game, I went to a top corporate school (R.E.I.) in Electronic Eavesdropping Detection, to modernize myself on the latest technologies. I also attended a leading Personal Protection Security Contractor/Specialty school. This was prior to the rapid growth of Security Contractors and Bodyguards, like Blackwater, that followed 9/11.

Working for a high net worth individual has its ups and downs. On the upside, you're using your skill sets to protect your client, his business assets and his family, while living on an adrenaline-fueled edge. On the downside, that same adrenaline-fueled edge has a price. I could write a whole book on the client and the life style of the rich and famous, but that's not the story here.

*The lesson I learned in this situation was that money can't buy you happiness or **integrity**.* In fact, there's a darker side that goes along with having and acquiring billions. When you have that kind of money, it seems as if everyone is trying to get a piece of it, and with that, character, morals and values are put to the test. Little by little, the purposefulness ***I sought for my life was slipping away into trepidation and darkness***.

One night, when confronted with the cost of my character, I left. I'm not going to say what happened, but it was serious enough that it questioned my integrity. ***It was my integrity check.*** It was a reminder to stay the course of righteousness. I decided that the price to momentarily discard my morals and values, everything most important to me, was too high. This was my Soul Defining Moment. No longer was I going to be Mr. Las Vegas, my soul had another purpose.

Our generation will always remember where they were the morning of **September 11, 2001**. I had been out very late that Monday night, having just returned from a business trip to Los Angeles. I woke from my sleep to multiple phone calls from my dad. When I finally answered he told me to turn on the TV because we were being attacked. He told me we were going to war. It didn't make sense until I turned on the television. We had been at peace since Desert Storm but now we had been attacked on our soil. As I watched the towers get hit, the Pentagon get hit and flight 93 go down, the somber reality was that yes, we were going to war.

Like the majority of Americans I wanted to do something. I was still in the Reserves and wanted to contribute. My buddy **Randy Moulton** was now the Commander of the Joint Personnel Recovery Agency (JPRA) back in Virginia and was able to find me a Reserve position there.

Was this the path to getting my soul back on track? Was this the table I wanted a seat at? During the initial incursion into Afghanistan in 2003, my cousin **Ben Jones** (Dads brother's son), who was with the Third Special Forces Group, was shot in the leg during a firefight. We'd grown up together. He recovered and was awarded the Silver Star, 2 Bronze Stars with the "V" device for Valor, and a Purple Heart. This was a terse reminder that terrorism affects everyone, in one way or another. I was more determined than ever to make a contribution.

After I began writing this, my younger brother Marcos came to visit. It was during this visit, that he asked my favorite question. *"How's it going?"* But, this time I told him the truth, venting. As we discussed it I came to realize that like a roller coaster, I was going through various ups and downs, like waves in the ocean. My emotions and abilities would roll upwards to the high point of the peak, then fall downwards into the depths of the trough. Through this discussion, I came to realize, I needed to find the *middle ground*. Admit it, and then move through. *Peaks and troughs.*

On the "peak" side, I needed to stop believing I could operate at the high levels of mental engagement, which I had always done. On the "trough" side, I needed to *not* allow myself to fall into dread and depression. Admit it, and then move through. *Easier said than done.* I needed to avoid the peaks and troughs, to navigate my new intellectual and emotional standards with less intense highs and lows, enjoying the middle ground. I needed to pace myself.

During the summer of 2010, I went to Hawaii with a group of friends and took one of my screenplays with me. Writing was already part of me. In the mid nineties, my friend **Steve "Moses" Moloney**, introduced me to writing. We completed our first screenplay together. All told, I had written 4 screenplays prior to deploying, but with passion gone, they stayed on my shelf. I wanted to catch a glimpse of what my writing was like and how my mind worked back then when I wrote it. I hadn't read it since the last re-write in 2003. I was looking for a project to keep me busy. I read it one afternoon at the pool. Afterwards, I thought to myself, "Not too bad. Maybe some small touch ups. It's worth updating." I never did.

Years later, (March 30th 2012), I was at dinner with my good friend, **Michelle Gaw**, and during our conversation, I had an *epiphany* on why I couldn't touch the screenplay. It was a military story. Part of me was inside it. That thinking process would just bring on more memories, leading to more Spikes, Mohawks and Teslas. More *Chaos*. But also *in that moment*, I decided to start this project, to write this book.

Understanding the problem is the path to the solution. That understanding of how my nemesis *Chaos* worked was the seed I sewed to begin this book. Face and fight my enemy, *Chaos*! Time to get back on the horse. *To keep busy*. Not giving *Chaos* a chance to fester in my depression. Small steps maybe, but steps, nonetheless.

Since it was winter, I also decided to get back on the mountain, literally and figuratively. Skiing first, with more to come. Since everything stemmed from my head injury, the first thing I did was go out and *find a helmet*. More importantly, I was keeping busy and "doing the work." *Small steps can add up to a long walk.*

That winter I spent several days trying to get my ski legs back. Once my legs were back, I decided to push myself even further and learn to snowboard. Not knowing a thing about it, I bought the gear first, so I couldn't back out. I researched the how-to part, and then booked a morning private lesson. My instructor was a great kid, who explained the basics of balance, weight transfer and braking. He told me the average for non-boarders was about three days of falling, and then on the fourth, I should have it. He was right.

I bounced and tumbled for three days before I made it down. Success that day equaled a smile. To this day, I'm snowboarding. Riding my "**Line.**" It's not only a great physical exercise, but **brain exercise** as well. It's another form of balance therapy. From the moment I get off the chair at the top of the hill, there are hundreds of predictions and decisions to make.

I've been a surfer and skateboarder since my teens. I started skateboarding with my best friends from high school, **Don Bieger** and

BRAIN PAIN

Wes Edwards. We had traveled the country, surfing the beaches and skateboarding any parks we could find.

My whole life I've been a runner, but the constant bouncing agitates my brain. Searching for another avenue for cardio, I found mountain biking through the Wounded Warrior Program. I had never had an interest in biking, but I needed a summer time activity to embrace. What would it hurt?

Next, I searched pawnshops and found a decent bike. Next, I purchased the safety tools and car carrier. Much like the snowboard equipment, once I spent the money, I'd have no excuses. Starting slowly, I began riding different trails and parks throughout Las Vegas. It got me out of the house on my bad days and mentally challenged me, thus working out my body and brain. The beauty of the outdoors bought on more smiles as well.

One of the positive things was that I was constantly having to focus on what I was doing, constantly making new decisions. *Riding my line.* Moving forward, turning left or right, or stopping, were all forms of movement my mind was working through. This turned into another form of balance therapy, as well as taking me out of my head and putting me into the moment.

Last year I took mountain biking to a whole new level. I biked almost every day, riding miles in various parks throughout Las Vegas, changing up terrain as well as scenery. On weekends I took longer trails. There are some world-class mountain bike trails in Boulder City as well as in the local Wetlands Park. For the first few miles, you can be totally engrossed in the wetlands and marshlands, with the birds and fowl, then suddenly you're in the middle of the desert, and then you're up against the mountains in the rocks. Then you turn around, head back and do it again. The fresh air and gorgeous scenery makes the exercise worth the work. *Once again, it got me out of the house, challenged and exercised my brain, as well as provided the smiles.*

Snowboarding and mountain biking remind me that I'm still engaged and problem solving. ***I'm riding my line.*** Like the first time I pole vaulted over fifteen feet, everything clicked, I was in the zone, moving through, visualizing the outcome, seeing ahead of myself, predicting my challenges and adjusting to ride through them, keeping ahead of the moments to come. I'm practicing to predict, by finding and riding my lines. I'm riding *Chaos*; he's not riding me.

Since I was about 11 years old I've played the guitar, playing in several bands throughout high school and college. I have a collection of guitars. My most precious one is the 1971 Fender Bronco my parents gave me. Prior to deploying to Iraq, I was working on my guitars all the time. I customized them all; stripped each to the wood, refinished and ensured all electronics were brought up to the original year specifications.

Music was the essence of my youth and playing the guitar allowed me unique expression. It got me through some of my toughest times as a teen. There was always passion and joy attached to my music.

Post-injury, I lost the desire to play. Since returning I've rarely played my guitar, just not being able to get into it. Six of my guitars are hanging on the walls, like artwork. My Fender Bronco guitar, a gift from my parents, sits, ready and waiting, in front of me in my living room. The amp's a Fender G-Dec, so I can plug in the SD card and play along with an MP3 song. I was trying to make it as easy as possible. I bought it two years ago and it's just sitting there. I thought if I bought everything I needed I'd have no excuses. Not this time.

*This last page was written on August 3, 2013. After writing and reading it back, I decided to stop. As I shut down the computer, I looked up and there was my guitar, sitting at the ready, staring back at me. I thought to myself, "You've been putting all these thoughts down on paper so, **walk the talk!** Get off your ass and play something!" So I did.*

After playing a couple of familiar songs, to warm up, I said to myself, "Let's do this - let's learn a song you've never played." I went through a few songs and settled on, "If I'd Been The One," by 38 Special; classic southern rock. A couple hours later, I learned the first new song in over thirty years. As I played along, I was smiling again. ***The catharsis of emotion overwhelmed me.*** Finding my smiles. *Living and enjoying my life!*

BRAIN PAIN

Putting this on paper is a way of searching deep into my psyche, and the reward is smiles. Since that night, playing my guitar has become almost an everyday form of therapy now. I've learned dozens of new songs and my fingers, for the first time in thirty years, have calluses. I often forget chord transitions and finger placement, but it's challenging and exercises my brain, as well puts a smile on my face. It also raises the noise level, which tempers the pain.

A few years ago, my friend Rick pushed me back on to the stage, allowing me to sing some songs with his band. It was a completely awesome and comforting adrenaline rush, with "friendly anxieties." More recently, I played my guitar and sang on stage with him for almost two hours! Now, there's an answer for, "How's it going?"

Music Therapy could be a whole chapter or book in itself. I wish I had started it earlier, but it's never too late. It's as much a form of emotional therapy as my Equine Therapy, and that's saying a lot. Music therapy has turned out to be a powerful and resilient caulk, filling the gaps in the cracks, further insulation from *Chaos*.

A couple of years ago one of my good friends, **Eric Fleischmann**, who's a local fireman here in Las Vegas, slipped and fell on his head, incurring a concussion. His wife, *Stephanie* called and told me what happened. When I heard, I went over to see if there was anything I could help with, and to let him know what I had gone through in the first few months after my concussion. When we talked, I could see many of the symptoms I incurred. A few weeks later, he decided to go hunting in the middle of Nevada, on his own.

He's always been an outdoorsman, but due to his recent TBI, his wife didn't feel very comfortable with this idea. I understood. I packed up my SUV and headed north. I found him later that evening and we ended up having a great time. What's interesting is that I went up there to help him, but he ended up helping me. He re-introduced me to the **outdoors**.

Camping and getting out into the wild puts me in an uncomfortable, yet beautiful place. Getting deep into the wilderness, hunting for food and building your shelter, refreshes your perspective on life. It's getting back to the basics. Practicing basic skills; like starting fire, finding water, building shelter, can be so very rewarding and so very humbling. It also challenges me with various forms of problem solving.

ANTHONY JONES

Problem solving is what makes the high level special military operators so special. The ability to think quickly and problem solve, under duress, can be life or death.

We should live our lives, feeling just a bit of angst and dread. These feelings kick start my involvement, making life all the more exhilarating. Practicing new skills puts me out of my element, forcing me to do the work, exercising the neural pathways in my brain. Constantly making new predictions and choices challenges me.

*The **Brain Pain** is always there, but these new activities act as noise, drowning the pain with natural serotonin and adrenaline.* Life is hard enough, working through the day-to-day challenges, but when you can't think clearly, it becomes overwhelming. All my life, my standard was operating and multitasking with a healthy and good brain. Now, post injury, my standard has changed. Peaks, troughs and finding the middle ground.

Getting started is something you do over and over. You find yourself fighting your way out of depression, and adjusting. Internally, I needed to re-evaluate what was important to me. Otherwise, the peaks and troughs would continue. Something deep had to change for me. I needed to re-address my beliefs and values. These had always been based on family, friends, career, integrity and ambition. Maturity and my slow recovery changed this. Maturity had given me plenty of life experience to call on as the recovery process continued, and my injuries forced me to put more thought into everything I did. My beliefs and values are at the core of my decisions. At the top are still family, friends and integrity, but health and fitness, accomplishments and spirituality have been added.

Each of us live according to our own set of beliefs and values that subliminally direct our actions. If these beliefs and values are true to our core, then our resulting actions are pure. Self esteem, joy and happiness then follow. Clarifying my core beliefs and values, allowed me to discover a new direction. For me, this meant taking a deep hard look at where I spent the majority of my time and asking if that time spent was meeting my needs. ***This became my new management strategy***.

Although the Brain Pain was still there, I needed to find methods of working around it.

BRAIN PAIN

Maintaining my health, both physical and mental, was pushed right to the top of the list. This meant spending more time on physical activities as well as mental activities. Snowboarding, mountain biking, camping, as well as playing my guitar met this requirement. Deciding to write this, is a mental activity that led to the deep discovery of who I was, who I am and most importantly, who I want to be. *I was given a second chance at life and I'm determined to make it worthwhile*.

By prioritizing my activities, I get the most bang for my buck, getting much more accomplished. I had been doing this already for years, with sticky notes. My way of optimizing my time. I would use them to remind myself things I needed to do. What's changed in the last two years is that I now prioritize that list to ensure I accomplish what's most important to me first. While preventing the procrastination that goes hand in hand with TBI and PTS, I try not to sweat the small stuff. In other words, I put pen to paper to reinforce my memory. The multiple actions of processing the thought, physically writing it down while prioritizing it, and reviewing it strengthens the likelihood I'll get it done. *My work around*.

Since I wasn't the same person I used to be, I had to be okay with that. I definitely wasn't Mr. Las Vegas anymore either. Accepting who I am now is part of my recovery. I've been through plenty of denial, thinking I was getting better and multitasking through various projects. But each time I'd become *overwhelmed*, then I'd crash into depression. Becoming okay with this, my new standard strengthens my resolve to find the middle path through life's peaks and troughs. I am basically throwing away my old methodologies of navigating life, and putting new ones in place, working around my challenges. I am also strengthening my "**Mental Health Chain**" and filling the cracks, keeping *Chaos* at bay.

A sturdy chain can weaken in an instant. Any link is vulnerable to snapping at any time. Maintenance is key. Working the body and mind together and listening to the feedback they give you. *In my case, it's my triggers.* Identifying and recognizing these triggers helps me to navigate the peaks and troughs. I've been able to find my comfort zone and not be overwhelmed. This means leaving the known and venturing towards the new.

Like when I was a kid, "doing the job," I am adapting again. But when you think about it, isn't that what we all do to survive, adapt?

As I said, Life has a plan for all of us. Sometimes it's a change of *our* plans. The Beatles said it perfectly; *"Life is what happens to you while you're busy making other plans."*

We can adapt, maintain our balance and stay the course. Everything I've just said is nothing unless you act on it. The last few years of my new management strategy phase have been all about action. **"Walk your talk!"** Embracing our new standard is part of "doing the work." Growth and adaptation means to work around your challenges. Find your smiles.

I still may not remember a story from "back in the day," but when someone asks, "How's it going?" I now quickly retort with ***"Walking, talking and happy to be here!"***

Getting my jam back. Playing my guitar back in 1975, and this year, 2016, on stage. Music therapy could be a whole chapter in itself. It has exercised my mind and finger coordination as well as singing. It's great to be back playing. ***Finding my natural 'Endorphin' boost!***

BRAIN PAIN

That's me on the left and my buddy Bill McCoy. This was our aircraft, the Special Operations Combat Talon or MC-130.

In Iraq, my nickname was, "Rocket Man" because I seemed to always be in the vicinity of an explosion. Here I'm being presented with the 'Order of the Purple Target' medallion from my boss, Colonel Eduardo Gutierrez. It's taken from the movie 'Patriot Games' for being hit too many times. **It says 'Shoot Me.'**

CHAPTER 12

WARRIOR PRIDE

The strength of America's National and International Policies comes from our Military. The cost of our Republic, our democracy and our freedom is paid for with our Military as currency. We should always maintain and revere the value of this currency. Wounded warfighters are not damaged goods or *Defective*. *You can't control the cards you're dealt, but you can control the game you sit down at and you're strategy.*

In the Appalachian mountain communities, there's a way of life called, "*Mountain Pride*." It's a core system of self-reliance and unwillingness to accept handouts from the government. These are down to earth, hard working people with care-for-themselves kind of values that hold their pride in their souls. It's a hard-core version of self-reliance, an amalgamation of stubbornness and autonomy. The concept that you must provide for yourself, always, and never turn to the State for help.

These people learned their lessons from their ancestors. Their forefathers turned the wild into homes and communities. They rely on each other, band together and make it through the hard times, as well as celebrate the good. *This pride of self-reliance is a belief in taking care of themselves, their families and friends.* It's a conviction and belief, being an Airman and raised the son of a Marine, I believe in as well.

BRAIN PAIN

My father came from a similar large, poor but proud, country family. My mother also came from a poor family but had a loving brother and sisters who looked out for her. Both survivors came together to instill this same pride in their children. Hard work and self-reliance has always been our way of life. The people we rely on are each other. Warriors are by and large the same way, especially wounded warriors. I call it, "**Warrior Pride**."

As warfighters, we understand the choices we made that got us where we are, and we are usually the last to ask for assistance. *Although, we do expect what we're promised.* In my father's case, it's always been a "man up" kind of attitude, move through and move on. When he was hit and went through his medical board hearing, there was no Warrior Transition Unit or Wounded Warrior Program. There was no family counseling. You just sucked it up.

Many years ago our government recognized the need to strengthen and preserve our fighting force and those veterans who served their country during its time of need. The **Department of Veterans Affairs** is the second largest department, after the Department of Defense. The original concept was conceived after the Revolutionary War, and then another version was authorized by the Government in 1834. After the Civil War, State homes for Veterans were established, and assistance for those Veterans of the Indian Wars, Spanish American War and the Mexican Border conflict. Another newer system, that included disability compensation, medical care and rehabilitation programs, was put in place as we entered into World War I. In 1930, Congress consolidated the multiple organizations throughout the country, assisting war veterans, and established what we now know as the VA.

The civilian world also spawned their own organizations. Some of the larger ones include the **Disabled American Veterans**, which was established after World War I, in 1921. Their main charter was to help protect the welfare of injured and disabled war veterans. The **Paralyzed Veterans of America** was established in 1946, after World War II. As their name suggests, they worked to assist war veterans with spinal cord injuries. One that most people recognize is the **United Service Organizations**, or USO, which supports active duty and veterans with Morale and Welfare programs and services.

ANTHONY JONES

At Wilford Hall in San Antonio, I was assigned to the Hospital Medical Center and my Intelligence unit. I was given a checklist and on that checklist was my patient advocate, assigned through the **Air Force Wounded Warrior Program**. *Her name was **Darla Sekimoto** and she became instrumental in my transition.* Had she not been there, it would have been impossible to navigate the numerous appointments and treatments. She had my back.

Looking back, I was actually just another brain-injured Airman, having a difficult time cognitively. Darla became my go-to person and mental co-processor, as she made sure I made all my appointments, helped with all the basic questions, and redundantly ensured I understood what was being done and why it was being done. Also, my local unit Commander, **Col. Kinder**, as well as my JPRA Commander, **Col. Clare**, were constantly on the phone, ensuring I was getting the necessary care. Both Col. Kinder and Col. Clare came down personally to ensure everything was on track.

Growing up, as a kid in the 70's, I remember rummaging through one of my dad's wooden *Marine green footlockers*, and finding a field manual. I don't remember what it was called, but I spent the next hour reading through it, and looking at the drawings of numerous killing devices, some booby traps, some IED's, that were made of punji sticks, grenades, mortars and artillery rounds, and were used by the Viet Cong against our troops.

How do you kill people? You put holes in their hearts or put an explosion so close to them, that multiple vital paths or arteries of human blood, neuro-cognitive pathways, nutrients and oxygen are interrupted and/or destroyed. We've gotten several hundred percent better at saving the lives of those with blood loss, but Brain Pain due to explosive blasts has been essentially left to civilian medical institutions. Doesn't make sense.

We know from past wars, a large percentage of the wounded are going to have blast, and more specifically, brain injuries. That's the fundamental function of artillery, rockets, mortars and grenades. Any enemy we fight will improvise and use our guerrilla tactics against us. Since the Civil War we, and our enemies, have been using explosive-based munitions to kill or slow the enemy. We have massive amounts of explosive munitions to bombard the enemy and we know they will use the same technology against us, especially in an underground insurgency. Since the Vietnam War our battlefield survival rates have increased dramatically, but so have the *complications* in caring for those survivors. Our government should spend the same amount of time, money and energy that we spend saving those lives out on the battlefield, for long term care and quality of life issues. This is what civilian organization and non-profits are forced into to doing. Where was the "**plan**" for this?

My job as DPRC was to ensure everything was done, training and briefing, to ensure our guys safe return. The patch on my shoulder carried the POW MIA flag with the iconic ethos of, "You are not forgotten." *When we go to war, we know from past lessons, that we will have dead and wounded, but that our survivability rates will increase and long term care will be needed.* Maintaining a strong fighting force, a follow-up health care system and long-term care system is crucial to America's strength. How many times have we come out of a war, only to decrease our military's size and benefits, while bureaucratic managers are doled out healthy bonuses?

Those same *leaders* know they'll be long gone before the dust settles. The intentions, with the establishment of the Department of Veterans Affairs, were on track, yet were behind the power curve from the start. There's no doubt they knew, our politicians just placed this priority on the back burner, to deal with it later. The VA is not "all it can be." As I explained earlier, there are many reasons for this.

How long did it take to get the VA up to speed? Is the VA up to speed now? Unfortunately, no. It's still not there because somewhere along the line **no one planned for this**. The VA is overwhelmed and overloaded; just ask anyone who works there.

Blame also lies elsewhere, with many veterans themselves. There are tens of thousands of *"fraudsters"* stealing and clogging the VA's time and services that rightfully belong to real combat and disabled veterans. I've heard so many stories from others that have either seen or know of cases of fraud, as do I. Even if investigated and discovered, that's still taking precious time away from those who deserve it. *Do you know someone?*

There are also *dozens of organizations* that have misused, even stolen donations. The seduction of power and money has crept into some of the largest and most prominent organizations around. As the wars wind down, they need to keep growing, to pay for their salaries, to justify their existence. As I write this, several of these are under investigation. The organizations grow, yet the "need" dwindles. But, as a positive, the majority of these organizations are helping and are engaged and assisting our wounded in need.

Our warrior ethos of, "*Leave no one behind*," was forgotten by our *leadership*. Remember, the scandal with the Wounded Warrior Transition Unit at Walter Reed in 2006? If you don't, wounded soldiers were left in very unsanitary conditions and ignored.

If our system lived up to its promises, we would not need private organizations and non-profits. Just like the law of supply and demand, if that demand is not being provided, it will have to be filled privately.

In our case, the demand is over 50,000 physically OIF/OEF wounded warriors; another 70,000 approved VA PTS claims; another estimated 200,000 with PTS; at a minimum, 200,000 with combat related blast TBI's; as well as over 240,000 Vietnam veterans already in the VA system, who need assistance with long term care and quality of life issues.

With that said, this *demand* is being filled by the numerous private organizations and non-profits. Were it not for private citizens, there would be no Wounded Warrior Project or Spirit Therapies. Thankfully to millions of private citizens, these organizations and non-profits have risen up to assist.

My initial experience with the **Wounded Warrior Project** was during my arrival in 2008, at Landstuhl, Germany, and the Warrior Transition Unit there. Shorts, socks and toiletries went a long way to ease the most basic of needs. The following is from their website: [45]"The history of the Wounded Warrior Project, (WWP), began when several veterans and friends, moved by stories of the first wounded warfighters returning home from Afghanistan and Iraq, took action to help others in need. What started as a program to provide comfort items to wounded warfighters has grown into a complete rehabilitative effort to assist warfighters as they recover and transition back to civilian life. Tens of thousands of wounded warriors and caregivers receive support each year through WWP programs. *"Nurture the mind and body."* Becoming whole again is what all wounded warriors want. At least, as whole as possible.

BRAIN PAIN

In the spring of 2012, I received an offer to attend a "**Project Odyssey**" from the Wounded Warrior Project. I shot back a short email reply that I was interested in attending, and forgot it. Prior to this, I believed there were others more deserving of these opportunities than I. But, in the back of my mind I knew I needed a break in my patterns and to change things up, so maybe this would be good. I was pleased when a week later I received an acceptance email.

"Project Odyssey." The name derives from Homer's poem about overcoming adversity and finding the way home. The program is designed to help warfighters overcome combat stress through outdoor, rehabilitative retreats. It encourages connection with peers, staff and nature. The *outdoors* and *peers* parts were what excited me about it. Not having any experience with these types of programs, I thought it would be a bunch of combat veterans going biking, zip lining and rafting. I was in for an introspective awakening. The staff was experienced, professional, mission oriented. The counselors had specific objectives and goals for us. Still, it was 5 days in Lake Tahoe.

Post OIF I'd become a journal writer. It helped me remember everyone I met, as well as the new things I learned. I ended each day journaling, trying to put the day into two words or concepts. Two ideas that summarized the feelings evoked through our daily interactions. There were 14 participants, 12 Wounded Warriors and two staff personnel. The WWP staffers were, **Mike Green**, also a Wounded Warrior and the other, **Suanny Espinosa**, a Warrior Caregiver. All were military Wounded Warriors and Suanny was married to one.

All had been affected by the wounds of war, either themselves or through a military family member. Some had been on similar get-a-ways, others had not. My traveling partner from Vegas was Kim Tanner; an Army retired Staff Sergeant injured in OIF, who had been on similar retreats. He is also one of the participants in horse therapy with me, mentioned earlier. Everyone flew into Reno on a Monday. Some of us arrived earlier than others, so we set up and relaxed as other flights and warfighters arrived. Then, in multiple rentals cars we headed out to the chalet. Yep, I said chalet. Also, no one mentioned rank. We were all equal.

ANTHONY JONES

After checking in, we all got together with a local guide/planner Stephanie, and they hauled us off to an outdoor barbecue at a park next to the river. Afterwards, we went back to the chalet and in-briefed in the conference room. As we sat around the table, we introduced ourselves, playing the name game in hopes that we would start remembering everyone's name. It did help and also broke the ice. Most were like me, by that, I mean quiet.

We all had some form of injury, but we were comrades in arms, and understood where each other came from. Most were Army, but all branches of service were represented. Other than medical waiting rooms, this was the first time I had interacted with other wounded warriors, and it was a good feeling. Mike summed it up by letting us know this was a time to *"slow down, take a step back and get some perspective,"* and he was right. The adventure began.

The next morning, we were all up and enjoying breakfast by 7 am. We regrouped into the vans, then headed off to some mountain trails for a morning of **mountain biking**, (this is where I discovered mountain biking, which, to this day, has turned out to be instrumental in my fighting off *Chaos*.) There we met some professionals who went over the basics with us. Based on our weight and height, the bikes already had our names on them. We broke up into two groups, one for a slower and flatter ride, then the second for those who wanted to push themselves. The competitive side of me moved right over to the second group. As we bursted from the start I realized these were all competitive guys and that meant there'd be more endurance work than nature watching. Early summer in the Tahoe Mountains, a path up and down, in and out of the woods, was turning into work. It was exhausting, but mostly set the baseline for us getting to know each other. *Magic Mike*, the Marine, smoked us all.

After another lunch in the park, we moved into the town for the scavenger hunt. We broke up into two teams and set about hunting for clues, placed by Stephanie and our WWP staffers. We all motivated differently and interacted differently. I've changed the most socially. I've gone from Mr. Las Vegas to not being social at all. It was completely uncomfortable for me, but that was the purpose. After two hours, literally running from business to business searching for clues, we all successfully completed our missions. I honestly don't remember which team won, I didn't include that in my notes, but we did complete the primary mission, which was participant bonding and teamwork. It didn't go perfectly smooth. There were attitudes, irritation, jokes and smiles, but we talked it out and moved through.

After dinner, we went to our nightly team debrief. We began to talk to each other, trust each other, and most importantly hear each other, myself included. We all had injuries, thus we all had no injuries. The slate was clean for us to continue to move through into the next few days. My words for the day were **persistence** and **perseverance**.

Day three, after breakfast we broke up into teams and once again the competition began. We were going kayaking. We headed down to the lake and got our kayaks into the water. I'd been in lots of boats before, but never something this small. With the assistance of our instructors, we practiced the fundamentals and were on our way. We started out on the California side of Lake Tahoe and slowly made our way to the Nevada side. Although the weather was great, the water was cold. It was also clear to 40 feet, at least. Once again, on our return from the Nevada side, we were notified that we were now ready for the kayak race. I can't remember who won, but I do remember the cold water and smiles. More importantly, we were forgetting the normal stress of our lives back home. It was like a real vacation. Time to relax. A time out or **Pattern interrupt**.

Next, in the same afternoon, we were off to a tree top obstacle and zip line course. This was awesome. To get the picture, you have to imagine a bunch of current and former warfighters, staring into a line of trees, with ropes, steps and zip lines. It was beautiful. After our instructors in-briefed us, we were off. Five different tree top courses and two zip lines. Some were easier than others, and some were harder, but once you committed, there was no going back. No one on their own, it was a big team effort. We were all getting more comfortable with each other, and the afternoon turned out to be a complete blast.

On our way back to the chalet, we stopped off in Truckee, California, at a place called, "Burger Me." The burgers and service were awesome. Most of us had some form of WWP apparel and camos on. One by one, people would stop by and ask us about it and we would explain. They would thank us for our service and we would exchange pleasantries. Just as we arrived back at the chalet, a black SUV pulled up. It was a couple we had met at the restaurant. The wife got out and handed us each separate bags of custom gourmet chocolates. They were the "*Pope Family*," and she thanked us again for our service and then told us "she owed someone something," and this was a little something to show their appreciation. We understood. For some reason this hit home. So many people were affected by these wars. Here was a family we didn't know, and will probably never see again, who sincerely understood and appreciated us. Simple selfless acts. That we understood. Later, during the debrief, we talked out how our day went and what we had experienced; some adrenaline topped with selflessness. My words for the day were, *perspective* and *communication*.

The fourth day was going to be a long one and full of surprises. After breakfast and packing multiple sets of clothes, we loaded up the rentals and headed out for the two-hour drive to Auburn, California and the American River, for an afternoon of white water rafting. We arrived, changed into our bathing suits, and played some volleyball before having lunch. Because of what was ahead of us, no one went hard on lunch. Most of us went for the peanut butter and jelly sandwiches. After some instructions, we all loaded up into three rafts and headed out. Each raft had one guide/instructor onboard. The initial first hour down the river was calm and relaxing. Slowly we all felt out our positions, got used to the instructions and got our reactions and communication down.

The first groups of rapids were level II and just enough to get some adrenaline going. Then, going into level III rapids, our last few days of getting to know each other and training together allowed us to work together as a team and move through. Every raft had a man tossed overboard and just as quickly, other team members stepped up to ensure everyone got back in. No man left behind. Many of us missed that *military camaraderie* that we had felt during deployments. This was a welcome reminder.

We were all looking out for each other and that was simply how the Wounded Warrior Project works. Everyone is there to look out for each other and this last rafting experience was just a great metaphor of our week together. Once again, call it, "*Warrior Pride.*"

BRAIN PAIN

After a two-hour drive back to the chalet and some dinner, we headed into our final night's debrief. We had learned new lessons from each other. This personal interaction helped us feel more confident about social interactions back home, at least for me.

It was also a much needed pattern interrupt from our daily lives, allowing us to step out of complacency.

In this short time, we bonded together, with discussions and feedback that was honest and forthcoming, with laudations of the experience and each other. ***These were warfighters that were all doing their own version of 'Doing The Work!'***

There were three phrases of the week that made it into my notes that night: *One*, that it was okay to be a survivor; *two*, that we are still able to contribute; and *three*, that we are not damaged goods or *Defective*.

The many Wounded Warrior programs and veteran assisting non-profits keep wounded warfighters **engaged, challenged** and **busy**, as well as helping them get back to some normalcy of life. Even though I firmly believe our government and the VA should be responsible for the many services civilians are providing, the importance of these civilian programs cannot be understated. They are instrumental in keeping our Wounded Warriors engaged in the world. *"Nurture the mind and body."*

For me, the most important thing I've gotten from them was the opportunity to become a **peer mentor**. My years of experience and growth, through my own turmoil, has allowed me to pass my lessons on to several of my WWP peer mentee's. Mentoring others wounded after me, using my lessons to help them get through their challenges keeps me grounded, as I often find myself repeating many of the tools I discuss in this book. *Paying it forward and giving back.*

Although the general public and some of our leadership have seemed to forget, the millions of Americans that fund these organizations have not forgotten. We are still a strong and vital currency, which will pay forward the cost of our Republic, our democracy and our freedoms.

Former veterans, current active duty, and future veterans - persevere to maintain the strength of America. ***Warrior Pride.***

*This was the **Wounded Warrior Project's** outing called "Project Odyssey" in Lake Tahoe in 2012. It's designed to help warfighters overcome combat stress through outdoor, rehabilitative retreats.*

I was introduced to mountain biking and other outdoors activities through this program as well as some new friends. Job well done!

BRAIN PAIN

CHAPTER 13

SPORTS CONCUSSIONS

As a young man, playing sports was a great way to fit in, test yourself and shine in the eyes of others. I was a Pole Vaulter, having lettered in both High School and College. 117' 6" was the length of my run. I had broken dozens of poles, falling into the padded pit, if I was lucky; to the ground if I wasn't. I hit my head dozens of times; having seen stars most of those. My heroes were world champion gold medalists, pole-vaulter Bob Seagren and decathlete Bruce Jenner. They shined. *They didn't wear helmets.* Dare Devils don't wear helmets. I didn't either. *Chaos* doesn't discriminate. *Give it an opening and it slithers in.* We tend to follow the lead of our icons.

If it's good enough for them, then it's good enough for us? *We tend to idolize our favorite athletes and entertainers, so when they're injured, we see their invincibility and our vulnerabilities are exposed.* According to the [46]CDC there are approximately **1.7 million TBI's** in the United States every year.

TBI's are a contributing factor in over 30% of all injury-related deaths and 75% of TBI's that happen each year are concussions or mild TBI's. The leading causes are falls (35%), motor vehicle accidents (17%), sports injuries and struck by or against object (16%), violence or assaults (10%) bicycles, suicide, unknown and combat (22%).

Each year *52,000 die from TBI*, 275,000 are hospitalized and 1.7 million are treated for related head injuries at the ER. *Three quarters of the sports-related TBI's come from Football, Soccer and Basketball, in that order.*

It was the summer of 2011 when I first read the life story of Former Chicago Bears **Dave Duerson**, 50. He was a former Pro Bowl football player and Super Bowl champion. It was in an article in [47]*"Men's Journal"* magazine. What initially drew me to the story was his suicide, but as I learned more, his story became so much more intriguing.

Dave Duerson graduated from high school with honors; graduated from Notre Dame with a degree in Economics; was a defensive back for the Chicago Bears; Pro Bowl and Super Bowl champion; successful meat processing businessman, he owned three McDonald's; husband and father of four. Most notably, in his later years, he was a Chicago Bears Team Union Advisor and pension board member and likely successor to Gene Upshaw as Director of the NFL Players Association. *Outwardly his accomplishments were numerous, he was smart and successful.*

As a Team Union representative, Dave had helped establish a board to hear disability claims for active players and retirees whose injuries prevented them from holding a job. *Dave then became infamous for consistently denying players and veterans with concussion related brain injury, any disability compensation benefits. Duerson sided with management, telling many injured veterans they could still work and hold a job.* **He was a non-believer, denying their claims.**

Mr. Duerson, in his later years, knew something was terribly wrong. Another thing that struck me in this article was, not only had he fallen into many depressions, dealt with constant bouts of irritability and blurred vision, but he described what he called excruciating *"Starburst Headaches."*

His description of his headache hit me like a BULLDOZER! Since day one, I had referred to my Brain Pain as *"Spikes,"* so the familiarity was all too real. **I knew *exactly* what he went through!**

As the years went by, Dave's decision-making ability was more than likely affected by **CTE**. He had fallen hard. He was forced into bankruptcy and barely able to make his condo association fee payments. His life followed a familiar pattern. *"The Chain."* *His mental health "chain" had disintegrated.*

Towards the end he had become financially ruined and was divorced from his wife, to whom he had become abusive; depression, bad choices, disarray, with no way out. Earlier in *his* life, his perspective on concussions was very different. ***Sounds familiar.***

Dave Duerson committed a meticulously planned suicide, after texting out, "***Get my brain to the NFL's brain bank in Boston.***" He succumbed to the same damage and injury that he had denied his fellow veterans, disability compensation for. Depression, bad choices, emotional disarray, stress and shame, with no way out. *He lost his peripherals, his focus tightened, and the links in his chain snapped.* ***Chaos had killed another host.***

For the first time since my return, someone else described my Brain Pain. It was one of those *"Aha!"* moments. His description of *"Starburst"* hit me in the gut. Could that be me? Dave Duerson wasn't the first to commit suicide due to the numerous effects of TBI and depression, and unfortunately won't be the last. Since the initial writing of my book, several more famous athletes have also succumbed to suicide.

Chaos had stolen the bright scholar and professional athlete. It had slowly eaten away at his mind, thus his decision-making abilities. *From all accounts, he was a great guy in his younger years, but then Chaos took root and stole his brightness and shine.* We see it over and over. Unfortunately, Mr. Duerson saw the truth too late. We WILL see much, much more of this as the years go by. We are now witnessing the **Sports Concussion Crisis**, but in the years to come, because of the many years of war, we will be seeing the **Combat Veteran Concussion Crisis**!

CTE is a neurodegenerative disease of individuals with a history of repetitive brain trauma such as concussions and multiple concussions to the head. *There is no treatment.* CTE has been known to affect *boxers* since the 1920s and more recently; published reports have confirmed the connection between CTE and retired professional football players.

In 2005, it was discovered by [48]**Dr. Bennet I. Omalu**, a pathologist who did the autopsy on football player Mike Webster's brain, attempting to understand and explain how he died.

[49]*Recently published reports have also shown that CTE was found in 4 deceased US military combat veterans exposed to a blast*

or multiple blasts in combat. *This is literally just the tip of the iceberg.*

There's no doubt in my mind, that CTE is affecting me. I'm working hard to not only acknowledge it, but to search for triggers as well as methodologies that keep my brain strong. **I'm Doing the Work.** We need to understand that our brain is a vital operating system, and repeated blows cause damage. The brain is suspended in a very tight space within the skull with little room to move around. It seems obvious that repeated trauma to it could cause irreversible damage.

[50] *In a convenience sample of 202 deceased players of American football from a brain donation program, CTE was neuropathologically diagnosed in 177 players across all levels of play (87%), including 110 of 111 former National Football League players (99%).*

CTE has been found in nearly every former NFL player's brain that has been examined posthumously by autopsy. The changes in the brain can begin immediately or even years later. Symptoms include impaired learning, headaches, memory loss, confusion, irritability, impulse control problems, aggression, depression, and eventually dementia or Alzheimer's. *Sound familiar?*

This is a volatile mix of symptoms and when topped off with a cocktail of medications, recreational drugs and alcohol, the sudden onset of irritability fuels the anger and frustration, then ignites the bomb. The "**Screw it**" attitude, and possibly suicide.

In case after case, TBI and PTS can lead to depression and anxiety, which leads to anger and irritability, which leads to feelings of betrayal, which leads to poor decisions, which lead to a dissolution of family and friends, which leads to poor financial decisions, which leads to personal destitution, which leads to overwhelming frustration, which then leads to their perceived last choice, which is often suicide. *Military veterans, athletes, civilians; Chaos doesn't care.*

Former NFL linebacker, [51]**Junior Seau**, 43, committed suicide by a self-inflicted gunshot wound to the chest. He was one of the greatest linebackers in the NFL, retiring a very wealthy man, having earned more than $50 million over the course of a extremely long 20-year career. But in the years before his death he began to act uncharacteristically, making terrible business decisions, abusing sleeping pills and alcohol. `

Much earlier, in his twenties, he had complained about headaches, dizziness and suffering from insomnia. He was spiraling downward following the same all too familiar patterns. Everyone who knew him knew he was struggling. A year prior to his death, Seau survived a 100-foot plunge in his SUV off a cliff in Southern CA, suspected to be a suicide attempt, hours after being arrested on a domestic violence charge against his girlfriend. Eight months after Junior Seau's death, doctors discovered he also had CTE.

Former Pittsburgh Steelers lineman [52]**Terry long**, 45, committed suicide by drinking antifreeze. He had suffered from depression and there had been other suicide attempts. He also had been indicted on Federal charges that he allegedly burned his business to the ground for the insurance money. He was also separated from his second wife. An all too familiar story; depression leading to bad decisions, leading to emotional disarray with his family, and finally not being able to see a way out. His autopsy showed he, too, had CTE.

Former Eagles defensive back [53]**Andrew Waters**, 44, had spent 12 seasons in the NFL. He also committed suicide and an autopsy revealed he was found to have CTE. Former Atlanta Falcons safety [54]**Ray Easterling**, 62, also committed suicide and an autopsy revealed he had CTE.

As I write this, the autopsy of former Grand Valley College and [55]NFL Ravens Quarterback, **Cullen Finnerty**, 31, revealed that he had mild CTE. It was found to be a contributing factor in his death. Cullen was found dead in Lake County, Michigan, two days after failing to return from a fishing trip. There were no signs of foul play at the scene or on his body. He was found to have painkillers also in his system. This brings to over 35 former NFL players that have been diagnosed posthumously with CTE at the time of this writing.

Last year, more than 5000 former NFL players sued the League over the handling of concussions and denied disability benefits. Recently the [56]NFL reached a **$765 million settlement** with those former players filing suit against them for brain injuries. This is a start. A settlement can provide immediate relief for the former players and their families, as well as fund medical exams and concussion-related compensation. As of this writing, a US District Judge rejected the settlement, *saying it wasn't enough.*

This is not limited to football. Recently 10 former players of the National Hockey League filed a class-action lawsuit with regards to their brain trauma. More recently, it was determined that major league baseball player, [57]**Ryan Freel**, who also committed suicide, had been diagnosed with CTE post mortem.

World Champion Professional Wrestler, [58]**Chris Benoit**, 40, had many of the same symptoms prior to his death. There's not much doubt that he suffered through many undiagnosed concussions throughout his career. He killed his wife and son then committed suicide in a gym. Post mortem, it was discovered he had CTE.

[59]In Jan of 2015, two former professional wrestlers accused the WWE of ignoring concussions and having performers do dangerous stunts that left them with serious brain injuries. The men, **Vito LoGrasso**, 50, and **Evan Singleton**, 22, filed a potential class-action lawsuit in federal court in Philadelphia. Currently, the complainants number is 53.

[60]BMX icon **Dave Mirra**, who died in February 2016, suffered from the type of chronic brain damage that has shown up in the brains of dozens of football players, a University of Toronto neuropathologist has concluded. Multiple neuropathologists confirmed the diagnosis. Mirra is the first action sports athlete to be diagnosed with chronic traumatic encephalopathy (CTE.) He died on Feb. 4 from a self-inflicted gunshot wound.

[61]**Chris Nowinski** was the youngest WWE's Hard-Core Champion in history. He is also Harvard educated and an advocate for education about brain trauma. According to his website, he is also the co-founder of the Sports Legacy Institute, a non-profit dedicated to solving the sports concussion crisis and the *Co-Director of The Center for the Study of Traumatic Encephalopathy*. Chris chose to retire from wrestling in 2003, after a series of concussions and went on a quest, much like mine, to better understand his condition.

An excerpt from his website states; "Chris connected this lack of awareness and denial among athletes, coaches, and even medical professionals to costing him his career and threatening the health and well-being of athletes of all ages. *This led him to write the critically acclaimed book, Head Games: Football's Concussion Crisis,* published in 2006, in an effort to educate parents, coaches, medical professionals and children about this serious public health issue." He's a survivor, advocate and has been down this road that is normally filled with despair and agony. *He chose the health of his brain over the sport he loved.*

For over the last 10 years much of the "cutting edge" work done on the study of head trauma on athletes has been done at the Center for the study of Traumatic Encephalopathy at the **Boston University school of Medicine**. This was where Dave Duerson said he wanted his brain sent, in his last text.

I grew up a skateboarder, surfing and studying karate, filling my need for the adrenaline ride and my desire to push myself to the limits. I loved the concept of extreme sports before it had a name. In college, I pole vaulted, running faster and faster, jumping higher and higher. I would race down the path, plant my pole, produce my bend and let it snap me skywards over the bar. I broke more poles than I can remember, falling into the pit many, many times. Karate was the same way; work hard, train hard, then fight even harder.

Back then I didn't use a helmet. I never wore one, but I made my little brother wear one. Youthful ignorance. But as you push yourself further and further, somewhere there will come a time when you reach your limits and injuries occur. With today's growth in extreme sports we see more and more young participants wearing helmets.

A few months back, I took my friend, **Mike Keefe**, mountain biking. Nothing serious, just some trail riding. I got ahead of myself; trying to take a photo of us riding, and seconds later I hit the ground, hitting my helmet hard. Had I not had it on, it would have been a hospital event. ***Cracked my helmet, but saved my head.*** That's a good thing; today my helmet is my co-pilot. Whether I'm on my snowboard or my mountain bike, it's there.

[62]**Kevin Percy** is a young man who was on the rise in extreme sports stardom, specifically snowboarding. We often revel at the human species' ability to reach new heights and pass new physiological boundaries, often not done before. Kevin Percy was at the top of his sport, when in mere seconds, a tragic fall while snowboarding, left him with a TBI. With the 2010 Olympics in sight, Kevin's athletic ability was at its height, when he crashed during a training run in Park City, Utah.

BRAIN PAIN

His battle had just begun. He was wearing a helmet but hit the hard packed snow face first. He was knocked unconscious; left eye socket broken, and there was bleeding in his head. As many of us with TBI, he struggled with memory loss, vision problems and mood swings. Also like many, he was an elite athlete/operator.

Going from elite to normal is almost impossible to bear. What you once were is no more. *Clarity* **is gone.** Kevin still believed he was an elite athlete and could return to his former physical abilities, as many of us do. *One of the many downsides of concussions is that the second, third, fourth, and so on, can lead to devastating loss of self and memories.* Remember that our conscious ability to think and problem solve, allows us the ability of movement. When our thinking is slowed, so are our physical movements and abilities." Access Dyslexia." In other words, our disrupted thinking process diminishes our motor skills. *Our prediction process breaks*.

What I relate to most is Kevin Pearcy's courage to say **NO** to himself; much like Chris Nowinski. Those of us with brain injuries must realize that another hit or concussion can leave us disabled, worse than we already are and much closer to memory loss, dementia and Alzheimer's. The toll is not only about us, but those we surround ourselves with. They too, will pay a price. A couple years after Kevin's injury he hoped to start training again.

Then, he and his family reviewed the possibilities of him hurting himself again and what that could mean. He bravely decided to retire. I admire his courage. *This courage shows others that life and family are more important than one's shining abilities.* New doors can now open to all of life's other possibilities. Iconic athletes are the role models our youth look up to. Strength comes in many forms.

It took me years to get on with my life. Three years after my brain injury, I had a custom helmet made and began my new protected sports journey, mountain biking and snowboarding. No longer the jumper and hurdler I once was, I am content with just cruising. Riding my line, practicing and preparing for the bumps ahead. When life throws you a curve ball, you adjust your stance.

Other sports where the dangers of multiple concussions exist, with opponents constantly crashing into one another with aggressive velocity, are boxing and **MMA fighting**.

The [63]American Association of Neurological Surgeons, states nearly 90% of boxers suffer from various forms of brain injury, as well as some form of eye injury and dementia. That's a staggering number, yet we find it hard to believe that football concussions have done so much damage?

A study called, [64]**"Boxing - acute complications and late Sequelae**," states, "Ten deaths per year since 1900 can be attributable to boxing; most injuries from the head and neck." The study did not go in to how many boxers suffered from mental illness later in life. To me it's obvious; boxing, fighting, multiple concussions, depression and suicides. Not always, but as with anything done in excess, it can be hazardous to your health. It's not a blown knee; *it's your brain.*

MMA boxers are known for going all out, full speed and looking for the head knockout. A single punch can equal over fifty G's in acceleration. We can see the glazed look in their eyes and mumbles of speech coming out of their mouths. *MMA is just now coming to a point where there is such a thing as veterans.* It's really still in its infancy. We see what's happened to boxers and football players. Is that what the future holds for MMA veterans? Yet, we also see them as entertainers. We want to be entertained. We go to the race to see the crash, don't we?

[65]**Owen Thomas**, 6' 2", 240-pound football captain and charismatic player at Penn State, committed suicide. He was 21. Friends described it as an uncharacteristic emotional collapse. Owen began playing at age nine, continuing on into high school and college. Everyone who knew him knew he was a hard hitter and that he loved to hit. He was also an intelligent young man, who had been admitted into the Penn State's Wharton School of Business. An autopsy performed on him showed he was in the early stages of CTE.

Approximately 3 million children under 13 play football in youth leagues and another 1.4 million play in high school. College football has tens of thousands of players. Owen didn't have any history of memorable concussions, so it's suspected that the thousands of mini and sub-concussions may have been the cause.

Football, soccer, ice hockey, wrestling and karate have the highest number of concussions, consecutively. *Most sports related concussions go unreported, much like warfighters who don't want to leave their team.* They want to stay in the game.

BRAIN PAIN

Concussions in youth sports rose 66% from 2001-2009, while 15% of all sports concussions come from soccer. 47% of concussions occur between the ages of twelve to fifteen.

Young women are seemingly at more of a risk. Researchers aren't exactly sure why, but speculate that it is because of their thinner necks and lower body mass, making females more susceptible. According to the [66]American Journal of Sports Medicine, the number of girls receiving concussions account for the second largest amount of all concussions reported by young athletes. The number one cause is football.

Currently there are over 35 million kids who play organized sports. There are over 3 million kids registered the US Youth Soccer league. *Studies have shown that soccer is in the midst of a concussion crisis.* The number one cause of these concussions is what's called, **"Heading."**

With "Heading," players attempt to use their forehead to direct the ball, often jumping with opposing players, which can also lead to a collision with those same players. A soccer ball can reach speeds upwards of forty to fifty mph. Not only can heading itself lead to neck injuries and concussions, but hundreds of mini sub-concussions. The collision with an opposing player can do the same, if not worse. "Heading" injuries cause anywhere from 4% to 22% of head injuries in this sport.

First, if we're honest with ourselves, we should be able to see the relationship between multiple blows to the head, concussions, slower brain processing, headaches, depression and dementia.

For the most part, we need to admit this relationship exists. But then, there's the other side of our human experience that continually wants to excel and exceed our limitations, and those of our children. Our children are meant to be better than us. Statistics are on our side. *Most people won't get concussions.* Most of those who do, won't get another.

But, for those of us who have always pushed the envelope, we must understand the realities. Did all those blows to the head directly cause permanent brain damage, or were we just prone to mental illness, depression and future neurodegenerative diseases?

Second, the power behind the machine (bureaucracy), whether it is the US Government, or the Major Sports Leagues, there's a fear of the *cost* associated with acknowledging a relationship between these concussions and multiple concussions.

Simply stated, if you're injured as a result of military combat, the US government is liable to support you. Furthermore, if you were injured while participating in a professional contact sport, then the legal team owners are liable to support you. ***Think about the cost.***

The average cost for a senior citizen with dementia, just for housing and care, in a living facility runs $8-$10,000 a month. Think about the living cost of an individual when the war and the sports are over.

Just to be clear, I've been around fighting, practicing Karate all of my life, and I love boxing. I built a skateboard plywood half-pipe ramp in my driveway in the seventies. Never wore a helmet. I'm just saying, maybe late in the game that our brain is fragile and our priorities should be adjusted. Without a doubt, the risk increases exponentially with more hits. We think we're invincible, but I'm living proof that we're not.

We're coming to a crossroad, partially due to the media; where we now know the dangers of contact, especially head contacts, concussions and sub-concussive blows. Knowing this leaves us with decisions to make, the path of less injuries or the path of expensive high-priced front row tickets to watch the blows. We want to be entertained. We go to the race to see the crash, don't we?

Is the risk worth the reward? For most warfighters, it is. Doing my part to protect our freedoms was worth it. I made my choice and accepted the results.

Professional athletes enjoy a substantial financial and celebrity reward. Really? That's rarely the case. The marketing machine has you believing every professional player has millions. That's the fishing lure to attract our youth. Less than 2% of young athletes will ever have a successful professional career. *Yet, so many will seek it.*

When I hear of great athletes falling, my quest to understand this, by putting it down on paper screams to me, ***"How am I going to turn out?"***

I'm doing everything I can to nip this in the bud, but will I become a burden to my family? Will I end up making the same bad choices and bad decisions? Will the anger and irritability push me into making bad choices? Will I end up in a convalescent home?

BRAIN PAIN

Will I have enough money and resources to live on my own if I deteriorate into dementia?

When we see our sports idols injured, their invincibility is unmasked and our mortality exposed.

Will *Chaos* win?

Not if I can help it. I'm "Doing The Work," being proactive in my management strategy, working hard to keep engaged, challenged and purposeful!

In college, riding my skateboard on a ramp I built in my driveway. As most young men, I thought I was invincible. No helmet for me then.

CHAPTER 14

22 A DAY

Simultaneously, Chaos attacked my dad and me. Dad yelled, I yelled, back and forth until he threw me out of his house. Two bulls pitted face to face. I grew up under his anger and spontaneous outbursts and the father / son relationship I so cherished was now edging on domestic violence. The love of my father had been pushed out the door. I got out of there. *"Screw it, I'll show him,"* is all I could think.

Driving home, in the rain, the anger skyrocketed, like a volcano boiling to an eruption. I'd already lost my peripherals. My focus tightened. More and more I thought, "I'm done with this shit. *I can't do this shit! I don't want to do this shit! Screw this pain*!" The explosions in my brain had me seizing and shaking. Vertigo was rocking me back and forth. The screeching voice of *Chaos* told me it would be over quick; just turn the wheel, a quick tug on the wheel. Turn it left. To the left! Just hit that column over there. It'd be quick. It'd look like an accident. The rain was now pouring as my column approached. I changed lanes on a line to my death. The loud startling claxon alert of a "flash flood" came through the radio. *Pattern interrupt*. I was back.

Move through, move through, move through. Breathe. I'm alive. Straight down the road. Never the smoker, I stopped, bought a pack of smokes and had a cigarette, reminding myself that I was worthy. That my life had purpose, had meaning; that we should live a life worthy of those who didn't make it. I can make it. *"I can make it!"*

BRAIN PAIN

I can't even remember what that particular fight was about. I had been on the front lines of this man's anger most of my life. *My mom was on the front lines daily*. I don't know how she's done it. I don't know how they're not divorced. When I moved back to Las Vegas full time back in 1998, I had to assimilate to being around my parents, mostly my dad's ticking time bomb personality, again. You are tiptoeing around everything based on how Dad's doing. *He can go into a full-blown rage in a split second.* When I'm around them, I try to mediate and calm him down. Mostly, when he loses something, or watches politics, his frustration will exponentially burst out and anyone in range will catch his wrath. Usually my mom.

As an example, my brother once got into a politics discussion with Dad over the phone and it got a little heated. Well, when Marcos hangs up, he doesn't have to deal with the consequences. Dad took it out on Mom, just because she's in the *proximity*. I call it "*Being in the proximity of*." If you're in the proximity of my dad when he's in a rage, or if you're in the proximity of me, when I'm in a rage, you're going to be the recipient of my tirade. My brother Marcos wasn't in the proximity of my father, but on the phone, so he just got hung up on. My dad ends up taking it out on the nearest recipient. Usually Mom. I had to call Marcos up and remind him, that Mom's the one taking the brunt of Dad's anger when he does stuff like that. We live here. *We're on the front lines*.

It was 1969; Dad had made it back from Vietnam and we were living in Quantico, Virginia. We were out as a family, everyone in a good mood, and a car swerved in front of us. A few minutes later Dad pulled the driver out through his window and tossed him to the ground. Fast forward to 2009; a driver cut me off, flipped me off then again, cut me off. I followed him, boxed him in, jumped out of the car intending for someone to get hurt. When I saw him crawling into his back seat in fear, I snapped back to reality. I turned around and left. *Was I following in someone's footsteps?*

My first experience with suicide was a young **Marine Officer** and survivor of the Vietnam War. It happened during my senior year, while we were stationed at Quantico Marine Corps Base, VA, headquarters of the United States Marine Corps. He had a wife and children and lived in the Officers' apartments on top of the hill, close to the Officers Club. It was where most of the married Junior Officers lived. *He'd hung himself.*

Although the news spread like wildfire, no one really talked about it. Our parents were warriors, with their wars still going on. We (children) were silently afraid this could happen to our family, and when you're young and don't understand something, silence makes it go away. The peace talks were in play and the war was almost over, but his suicide hung heavy amongst us. We were all the children of war survivors. We couldn't understand their demons.

In the earlier chapter on TBI, I talked about Lt. Col. Ray Rivas, and how his situation mirrored mine. Finally, there was someone taking up our cause and taking it before Congress. Here was another warrior with whom I shared similar experiences. I saved his papers, book-marked articles on him, and planned on contacting him. It was mid August of that year - 2009, and I was working my way through the medical retirement process. Since he had braved those waters, I wanted to contact him for advice. It didn't take me long and what I found kicked me in the gut. *On July 15th, 2009, [67]Lt. Col. Ray Rivas committed suicide.*

Only a year younger than me, he had been diagnosed with rapidly emerging Dementia after being hit. This American hero, who had served his country and survived combat zones around the world, was found dead in his car in the parking lot of Brooke Army Medical Center, in San Antonio. There was a note written to his family, along with an empty bottle of prescription medication.

According to his wife Colleen, *"He did leave us a note that said that he just couldn't take the **headaches** and **pain** any longer.* Earlier that afternoon he had driven to BAMC and had gone to the family clinic and gotten a prescription for Ambien from a PA because he couldn't sleep. (He probably averaged about three hours a night at the most.) I believe he was given a prescription for somewhere around 36 pills. He went out to his car and took the whole bottle of pills with a diet coke. The temperature outside that day was over 100 degrees and he fell asleep in his car."

Just two months earlier he and his wife had testified before Congress, continuing his battle and fighting the fight. Unfortunately, as many Veterans know, the fight is not always won. In death, we remember him for fighting and advocating for wounded warriors and our needs. The cumulative impact of all those explosions and blasts had taken their final toll. ***Chaos* had killed another host**. Clarity to *Chaos* to suicide.

Countless people have committed suicide over their headaches, their, "Brain Pain." Lt. Col. Rivas and NFL football player Dave Duerson, who suffered "Starburst headaches," couldn't take them anymore either. As I worked my way through writing this book, Lt. Col. Rivas' wife, Colleen Rivas saw the movie "**Concussion**," and according to her, immediately stated, *"Oh my God, that was Ray!"*

Can I make it? Chaos? Defective? Move through, Move through, Move through. Breathe.

When you don't have the tools to understand and deal with what's going on, it's easy to fall susceptible to the dark side. So many of us don't have the tools, or even the desire to go get the toolbox. *Defective? Can't be fixed?* Suicide has affected most of us. One that affected me personally and deeply involved a good friend of mine. I mentioned that I spend Sundays with my parents. They live on the other side of town and on the drive over there I pass the Las Vegas Mini Grand Prix Go Kart Track. Every time I pass it, I think of Angelo. He passed away in 1997. Angelo's last birthday party was at this track. He was the son of a good friend of mine.

I had known Angelo's father, Tony, many years since we met in flight school. He and his wife were living in Southern California when job opportunities called them to Las Vegas. In 1990, I was deployed to Desert Storm so I let him stay at my condo. We were that close. As with many friends, we started out in a social environment and then become part of each other's support system. I was a groomsman at his wedding. He was always there for me as I was for him. His wife had a great job offer here in Las Vegas and the couple eventually moved into a nice home in Summerlin, a beautiful suburb in the Northwest. When their son, Angelo was born, they were both so excited and happy for their future.

In the spring of 1997, Tony's marriage was in trouble. We had more than a few discussions about what was going on in his life. He had what would most likely today be diagnosed as fibromyalgia and wasn't able to hold down a job. This guy was no slacker. He was a former Staff Sgt. in the United States Air Force and a very hard worker. *Another veteran suicide.*

A divorce seemed imminent for them. Yes, he was sad and hurt, but Tony seemed to have a plan, which meant to me, that he still saw a future for himself. Although somewhat disappointed, he never actually acted distraught or depressed. I remember spending an evening out, sharing beers and he discussed the plan. He did need a place to stay, since they were separating and I again gave him the keys to my condo. I told him he could stay there until he got on his feet. *He never made it to my condo.*

What happened next was a terrible tragedy. Tony attacked his wife, shot his son and then himself. At his son's funeral, I was angry, stricken with grief and completely filled with loss and despair. Mostly for his son, Angelo, and his wife, who had lost her son. *Diseased? Defective? Chaos?* Maybe I should have felt sorry for my friend as well. I still can't reconcile this one but I can try to empathize with him. I started to wonder if I could've done something to prevent this. ***How did I not see this coming***? He was a close friend. I was in his wedding party. What I did see was how it was over for him, but for everyone else in his world, the nightmare and despair was just beginning. They had to deal with the aftermath.

It's one thing to look at depression on paper, but to know the costs in real-life, jolts you like a taser. I've reviewed it in my mind a thousand times. I just didn't see it coming. Although Tony didn't have a TBI, his *Chain* was weakened due to many issues, including his condition, fibromyalgia. The result was the same. WHY?

The "**Cluster Headache,**" also called "*Suicide Headache,*" is known for the excruciating pain that goes along with it. I can't count the times the pains been so intense that I wanted to put my head through the drywall. Although I've learned to contain it, when the "*Spikes*" occur, *I can't help but TAP hard on my skull*, trying to distribute it's explosions. *Tap, tap, tap, tap, tap, tap. Shocks in my brain, then tap, tap, tap, tap, tap, shakes and tap some more.* The rational part of your brain steps to the side, as your need for relief takes over.

If you understand how a bruise on your leg happens, tiny capillaries under the skin burst and blood is trapped and pools up. This creates an obstacle in the regular flow of blood so therefore; you can then see how the same methodology can apply to the fragile and sensitive brain. The brain is an extremely delicate organ compared to leg muscles underneath our skin. *Once concussed, the normal thought signals sent down our damaged neural pathways are forced to detour around, causing pain and a slower and more befuddled thought process.*

Concussions can lead to depression and untreated depression is the number one cause of suicide. ***Remember my thoughts on TBI being a cause for PTS.*** *The JAMA Neurology study*? When you review the numerous case studies of brain injured / concussed athletes I've discussed here, I hope you can see the clear emotional disarray their lives took.

Defective? Can't be fixed? Where's my toolbox? I'm too tired to go get my tools. Hope is leaving the building to go find Elvis.

Multiple concussions are cumulative, leaving the recipient at a greater risk for long-term side effects. Multiple concussions, just like being exposed to multiple explosive blasts, lead to depression and anxiety, which lead to anger and irritability, which leads to feelings of betrayal, which lead to poor decisions, which lead to a dissolution of family and friends, which leads to poor financial decisions, which leads to personal destitution, which then leads to their perceived last choice, which is often suicide.

When Lt. Col. Rivas was transferred from Walter Reed to BAMC (Brooke Army Medical Center), according to his wife, *"He was sent to the Emergency Department, and I got a call to come and get him. When I arrived, he was sitting there in a room with a huge bag of narcotics in his hand. He recognized me, but he kept getting our children mixed up and calling them by the wrong names. I remember shaking my head and looking at the doctor and asking, 'How could they give a man with a brain injury that has no short-term memory, a gallon size Ziploc bag full of narcotics and expect him to self-medicate?' There was every type of painkiller you could imagine in that bag. I was amazed that he hadn't overdosed before I got him home. The doctor just said 'Ma'am, I don't have an answer to that question. He came in with the medication.' I couldn't believe that they were going to release him to me, but they did, so I took him home with his bag of narcotics.*

His head was killing him, but even with all of the drugs in his possession, there was nothing that would alleviate the pain. He kept going back to the emergency room and finally they did check him in to the guesthouse across the street from the hospital, and that is where he stayed for well over a year. They continued to just treat the symptoms."

After several years of going through my own journey, I've come to the conclusion that I need to take *personal responsibility* for the medications that I take. Inevitably they are entering my body and the risk and reward is mine. *Oh yeah, I'm not thinking correctly.* This is where a *good advocate* can be so very important to back us up. But, as with Lt. Col. Rivas and others like him, how do you take that responsibility when your brain's constantly in pain and deceiving you, moment by moment? When you can't trust your own decisions and the doctors are telling you this handful of pills will work, you more often than not, default to the doctors' advice.

More Pills? 22 a day?

When it comes to TBI and PTS, we have become a "talk the talk" society, not a "walk the talk" one. In other words, we place too much money into bureaucracy, research and development studies, awareness programs and medications, instead of *taking action* and using off label protocols that have already shown some success, such as *holistic* and *alternative treatments*, but are not yet approved by the FDA, to those in danger. Off label medications are prescribed *every day* for maladies that are not FDA approved. Kind of hypocritical, right? *Those with TBI and PTS are in danger now!* They should be given those options that may not be FDA approved. Let them make the choice for themselves if the risk is worth the reward!

[68]**Daniel Summers** was an energetic, intelligent and vivacious young man who played guitar in a band, loved computers, was a car mechanic, who married the woman of his dreams. He was also an Army Intelligence Sergeant who deployed to Iraq twice. He completed 400 combat missions as machine gunner, in the turret of a Humvee. He was also diagnosed with TBI, PTS and fibromyalgia.

When he committed suicide, his family placed his suicide note on the Internet, where it went viral.

Summers wrote, [69]*"My body has become nothing but a cage, source of pain and constant problems. The illness I have has caused me pain that not even the strongest medicines could dull, and there is no cure."* (This is just an excerpt and you can read it in its entirety on-line.) ***The system failed this young man.*** When I say this, I mean the medical support system in place for our warfighters and the Department of Veterans Affairs, which was never brought up to speed in time to help thousands of returning combat veterans. I mean ***the leadership.***

Like many young combat veterans, Daniel was trying to do the right thing; he was "Doing The Work." He was keeping busy, playing in a rock band, working on a documentary related to his time in Iraq and he was trying to seek help from the Department of Veterans Affairs in Phoenix, Arizona. He was also put on hold at the VA, lost in the arteries of paperwork, appointments, and humans who never scheduled his follow-ups.

[70]**Jeffrey Lucey** was a young Marine who had participated in the initial invasion of Iraq in 2003. By his own admission, he had done immoral things. In a letter to his girlfriend he wrote, *"I have done so much immoral shit during the last month that life is never going to seem the same, and all I want is to erase the past month, pretend it didn't happen."* He returned home, transitioning to civilian life, trying college, then to dull his pain turned to alcohol. Finally, his family had him involuntarily committed to the VA because of his drinking, nightmares, violence and threats of suicide. The VA released him after alcohol detox, deciding he was not a threat to himself. *Two weeks later he hung himself.*

We have failed our warfighters. There are literally thousands of these stories. Our military medical system and our Department of Veterans Affairs were ill prepared for the onset of the Afghanistan and Iraq wars. Once more, we have not learned the lessons from our past, which have repeated with war every 10 and 20 years. We finish one conflict, and then decide to downsize the military; then another conflict comes up and we are unprepared for the costs.

When we go to war there are *operational orders* that are put into place to ensure the success of the missions. Hundreds of them, preplanned and developed, to logistically support our ships, airplanes and boots on the ground as they deploy to the hostile zone. In the same manner, we should add to our checklist a **Spin Up Plan**, or contingency plan, for the support medical systems and VA staff, to support those wounded warriors, who will be coming back with the same wounds of war we have seen for hundreds of years.

According to the Department of Veterans Affairs, 22 veterans take their lives every day. Over half the troops who have committed suicide, have at one time or another sought some form of treatment or help. At the onset of these wars the VA was already overburdened with veterans from past wars and now the wars in Iraq and Afghanistan are the longest wars in US history.

Every warfighter is promised the best medical care available during their commitment. The combat veteran returns and becomes lost in the system. One of the major components of his lost trust becomes what's known as, **"betrayal trauma."** This is the social component of PTS and manifests quickly when returning warfighters feel as if they're not getting the appropriate treatment or feeling lost and betrayed by the VA system. The trust they had placed in the US military and the government has been mishandled. In the same way that *finances* are at the top of the list of worries that injured warfighters have, so is the *"loss of trust"* that they have placed in their government. *This betrayal is another link on the path to suicide. I can speak to this myself!*

There are no statistics I can find, but there is a method of suicide that often occurs in individuals who cannot come to grips with their combat experience. Much like "suicide by cop," which is something we all understand, "suicide by crime" is when returning combat veterans find themselves back and feel the need for adrenaline fueled activities and engage in various high-risk crimes.

The most prominent story came out of Fort Carson, Colorado. It stems from the difficulty combat veterans find adjusting to civilian life after being professional killers in combat. The adrenaline high is hard to match. [71]A **group of soldiers** from Ft. Carson, from the 2nd Battalion, 12th infantry Regiment had fought in some of the war's bloodiest battles. From this unit, amongst a laundry list of other violent crimes, ten of these infantry soldiers had been arrested for either murder, attempted murder or manslaughter. They had thrown their lives away for the adrenaline high, and in their own way committed suicide.

We failed in our re-integration process. When you send somebody to war, you know there are going to be consequences when they return. You need to plan for re-integration to society. In these cases, it not only cost the lives of our warfighters, but also the lives of numerous civilians.

There are no statistics for family members of combat veterans who commit suicide. How many wives and children have been lost to suicide because they could not deal with their returning combat veteran loved one?

[72]**Bill** and **Christine Koch** lost their son in Afghanistan, and then their daughter, Lynne committed suicide over the despair of losing her brother. She became a casualty as well. Cpl. Steve Koch was killed at the hands of a suicide bomber. There are many different casualties of war. *Chaos* attacks your loved ones as well.

Since my return home, I had been working with **Crisis Response International**, or **CRI Training** as Director of Training and an Instructor. I was still seeking the adrenaline high. It was my personal method of exposure therapy. This therapy targets learned behavior of avoidance response to memories of past events that were either traumatic or frightening. It is used to treat PTS by putting patients into a simulated combat environment to face their fears. At CRI Training we naturally did all this. Our school trained up Private Security Contractors heading overseas to high-risk zones to provide security and personal protection. We taught hand-to-hand fighting, pistol and rifle shooting, enemy contact drills, tactical medical training, counter kidnapping techniques, tactical offensive driving, etc. You get the idea. I was constantly immersed in my own exposure therapy. For me the constant adrenaline worked well, moving me through my anxieties, or so I thought.

It was May of 2010; I was in Palm Springs, California. As a matter of continuing education for my work, I was attending the **International School of Tactical Medicine**. This is one of the top-notch schools for paramedics and doctors who work as part of either SWAT teams or SRTs, Special Response Teams, across the nation. They are POST (Peace Officer and Standards Training) certified and it's far from a gentleman's course. The school is a classroom and practical skills based program that offers an extensive tactical medical curriculum, which integrates both medical and technical education, hands-on training, scenario-based teaching as well as both pistol and machine gun training. Since I taught our Tactical Medicine class, it was a great refresher. Also, kept me busy.

The training was top notch, as were the instructors. Passing the exams was exciting. It validated that my cognitive ability was improving. *Then came graduation.* Now, in my military career I've been through dozens and dozens of graduations. Some were my own, but most were from the Combat Aircrew Training School, where I was an instructor. Also, at CRI Training, I had overseen dozens more graduation ceremonies.

Out of nowhere, when I walked up to get my certificate, *I started to cry*, having to step away. What just happened? This would occasionally happen in private, but I had never become this emotional amongst colleagues. It caught me completely off guard. After leaving the hotel, out of nowhere the waterworks started again and I cried for the next ten minutes, then spent the next hour trying again to figure out what happened. During the drive home I began to have intrusive negative thoughts. I couldn't stop focusing on the weakness I had just shown and why it happened. *Why? Weak? Defective?*

A storm was building, searching out more fuel.

I was in the middle of the Mojave Desert and finally just pulled over and turned off the truck. I walked over to a nearby rock and watched the sunset. *Pattern Interrupt.*

Having been gone a couple of weeks, I decided to stop by my parents' before heading home. As we were chatting, I was going through my mail and I opened a letter from the Defense Finance and Accounting Service (DFAS). I read through it, and then read it again. I couldn't believe my eyes. *It was a letter stating that I owed the government $74,000 and they were taking it out of my pay starting immediately.* **WTF? Remember Finances? Betrayal trauma?**

The "**Perfect Storm**" was evolving. How could this be possible? My mind went into overload, spiraling. ***Chaos*** was watching, looking to seize an opportunity. I talked it out with my family and came to the initial conclusion, I couldn't fix it now, so I had to just move through, head home and get some rest. It didn't work out that way. My mind was on overload, especially after a day of so many unexplained emotional mood swings.

Earlier I mentioned that at the top of the list for wounded warriors is their *financial future*. My mind had just exploded, the rusty links in my chain were weakening and my perceived future was just thrown in the trash. *I felt my government had betrayed me!*

Arriving home, I unloaded my gear and tossed back my *first shot* of Patron. The more the intrusive thoughts swirled around in my head, the more intense my Brain Pain became. I must have paced around for twenty minutes before I realized I needed to call someone. My first call was to one of my best friends and I received the answer machine. Anger had locked its fingernails into me. They were digging into my skin, manifesting with dozens upon dozens of mini-explosions of pain, bursting forth in my head.

Second shot of Patron and my next call was to another friend and again, I received an answering machine, then with my mind racing still, I called another friend and got voicemail again. *Shit, come on! Somebody answer the damned phone!* Finally, I called the VA help line and was put on hold. *Screw it!*

Earlier, I had unloaded my AR-15 and my Glock and brought them inside. I hadn't gotten around to locking them up. They were sitting on the chair next to the safe, magazines lying next to them.

At first, the Glock whispered over to me, getting my attention. Then it began to speak louder and louder. It seemed to be slowly slithering closer as well. The magazine even seemed to be sliding closer to the gun, like being drawn over magnetically.

"This one's easy. You've seen it on TV hundreds of time. Pick me up, point and pull the trigger. Come on, come on, it'll be quick." *Chaos* was again going in for the kill and the *mosquitoes* were swarming for my blood. My peripherals were gone. In my mind, danger was close. The closest I'd ever been. My focus was on the gun.

Instinctually, somewhere down deep, where clarity resides, I needed to interrupt the stream of intrusive negative and dangerous thoughts going through my mind. I needed to get away from the pain exploding in my head.

I was dwelling on the anger I felt towards the system and the phenomenal feelings of betrayal. *It was overwhelming*!

I knew I needed a Pattern Interrupt, so as quickly as I could, while clarity tried fighting off *Chaos*, I locked up the guns, popped in an adult video tape, changed my mindset, then popped a sleeping pill and passed out.

Masturbation just saved my life.

The stigma in the military is that any weakness in combat is a failing. Warfighters who seek counseling for stress are often looked at as being feeble and weak. Most famously in 1943, Gen. George Patton struck and berated soldiers at a medical evacuation facility. He did so because they showed no obvious physical injuries. They were being pounded by artillery. Come on? Dad's generation called it battle fatigue or shell shock.

Today we know it as TBI and PTS. **The invisible wounds of war.**

[73] Since 2001, more than 2.4 million warfighters have served. Approximately 6,800 warfighters have been Killed In Action (KIA,) 52,000 Wounded In Action, (WIA,) over 100,000 who deployed diagnosed with PTS, 200,000 plus with combat related blast TBI's, and over 1,700 warfighters have experienced dramatic combat related amputations. There were also over 330 suicides while deployed. The suicide rate in the military is at an all time high. *22 veterans per day.*

Being raised a Catholic, most of my life I believed, if you commit suicide you would be damned to hell. But that was before my brain injury and this quest to arm myself against my demons. I often wonder, what if one day my brain turns on me? What if I am on a path towards Dementia, Alzheimer's and Chronic Traumatic Encephalopathy? What if I become suddenly overloaded, and that tight rope I walk on, snaps? Will I break?

The death of Lt. Col. Rivas affected me more than I can say. We were practically the same age, involved in multiple explosions, had a loss of our old self, Brain Pain, memory loss, financial interdiction, loss of emotions and passion. Like other millions, I walk that tightrope.

BRAIN PAIN

Whether you believe we've been here thousands of years or millions, I think we can all agree that *our time here is miniscule* in the larger scheme of mankind. When you're caught up in depression and pain you begin to contemplate your existence, your purpose, your worthiness and your place in this world.

It becomes **overwhelming** as we grapple with the "*why*" of it all. Then because we're in the grips of our injury, our disease, we seek comfort, we seek relief from the stranglehold of "why." Why do I care? Why do you care? Why am I here? Why should I stay? Why, why, why? The quick and easy answer is to let go. To end it.

I believe in our purpose, our worth, ourselves. In the great scheme of humanity, our time here is minuscule. It's only a short distance to our natural death. *I can make it.*

The majority of us have faith, in one form or another. We want to believe we will endure after this physical world. I do. And if I do, what's my rush? Heaven's not going anywhere. I know where the love's at. For me, I know what's waiting. I'm just reminding you. In the depths of my despair, my friend Rick reminded me. No rush. Take the ride. Enjoy the ride. Ride your line. It's not far. Smiles, sneers and frowns. Keep saying to yourself. "*I can make it that far.*"

That's exactly what *Chaos* doesn't want to hear. He's waiting outside in a Limousine filled with your favorite vices and champagne. His ride's free. Take on the simple challenge of making it, the short distance to death. No hurry, no rush. Breathe, move through, and contemplate. We were born fighters. Screw *Chaos'* Limo. I don't need his ride. I can make it that far. *You can make it too.*

Suicide affects us all. Millions of us battle these demons. Our own personal *Chaos*. We have to turn to each other and share the lessons of survival and self worth. Share and care? In an instant, the links in the chain can snap. *22 a day.*

We need to recognize that hope's right there in front of us, just grab some and ride your line. Keep engaged, challenged and purposeful. Remind yourself you're worthy; that your life has purpose. It has meaning.

We should live a life worthy of, and for, those who didn't make it. *I can make it. I can make it. I can make it!*

An active shooter scenario at the Int. School of Tactical Medicine. Teaching and training kept me engaged my first years back.

That's me on the left. This was taken in 2010, the last day of the course at the School. Later that night I came as close as I ever had to committing suicide. ***I made it again! But, the struggle never stops!***

My "Mantra" started with pole vaulting at Quantico High School.

Volunteering at a local school during Nevada reading week. Keeping engaged is so important with a damaged mind. Moving through and moving forward, facing my anxieties.

CHAPTER 15

MOVING THROUGH

Back and forth, back and forth I'd rock. Rocking, processing and visualizing my approach, plant and rise skyward. The pole in my hands followed suit. Most pole vaulters have their own personal psych-up protocol they go through prior to beginning their run. It's a psychological dance they do, rocking back and forth, twitching their fingers and sliding their pole, psyching themselves up and visualizing in their mind's eye: their run, their foot plant, their arm and grip placement, their swing and pull as the pole bends, sending them skyward and over the bar. In my mind, as I was visualizing it I'd say to myself, *"Move through."* Over and over I'd repeat it, rhythmically matching my rocking. For the majority of my adult life, this has been my personal mantra. Before you move forward you have to move through, because rarely is any transition without obstacles. Mine, that day, was the 15' high bar I needed to get over. Our obstacles can bring uncertain moments, but to live is to "move through."

This mantra began in high school, was reinforced in college, Pole Vaulting, from there to Flight School, survival training, flying with my squadron, to Baghdad. *Move Through.*

It's my way of embracing anxiety and reviewing the movements in my mind before they occurred. At obvious lower levels, everyone does this hundreds of times a day. The daily grind up of waking up and preparing for work is the status quo. Moving through. It's a simple process, for situations we're prepared for. But when the unexpected occurs, we're forced out of our comfort zone. The speed with which we're able to move through these, can lead to our survival, or the survival of others.

How many ways does the root of a tree turn and stretch to reach the nutrients it needs to survive? How do the leaves of a tree propagate toward the sky, branching out with limbs as they grow and receive the rays of the sun, photosynthesis, and water? This is nature's way of problem solving and working around resistance. Life is a constant search for connections, searching for what fuels us.

I subscribe to what's called the, **"Constructal Law."**[74] It's a hypothesis by Duke University Professor Adrian Bejan. It's a theory for how the world works. The idea is, everything that moves, whether animate or inanimate, is a flow system. A flow system "wants" to flow more efficiently and effectively, and over time will shape itself to do so. This "Constructal Law" applies to everything from the structure of corporations and our military, to the roots and branches of trees, to our valley streams, to rivers, to the arteries and veins of our bodies, and in my case the neural pathways of my brain. For me, understanding the flow system is at the core of "moving through," "working around," and "staying connected."

Moving through is the force behind life's flow. It keeps us connected in the "moment." How many times have you told someone, or heard someone tell another person in crisis, to just "breathe?" It does several things. It slows their breathing so they don't hyperventilate. It also interrupts their thought pattern, bringing them back into the moment, allowing them to better move through it. As a medic, one of the first things you do as you access a patient is to talk to them and ask general questions. It grounds the patient, while giving you plenty of information, based on how they respond. The connection increases the chances of successfully navigating the moment. That's what my mantra does for me. ***It helps me successfully navigate the moment.***

Life is fraught with what I call, *"Moments."* These are the moments we train and prepare for. We go through dozens, if not hundreds, of these each day; some on autopilot and others that can become monumental. These moments are different for everyone, but the majority of these, "moments" we all can relate to. Moments can be anything from running a yellow light, to giving your first speech in front of a class, to having to figure out how to make fire in a desolate snowstorm. How do you move through your "Moments?"

For a small part of the population, whose careers put them in the frequent path of danger, (military, first responders and athletes) these "Moments" can be epic, even life and death. Whether it's a car crash or a home invasion, your reaction and ability to move through the moment, as well as how swiftly you do it, can have the most seriousness of consequences.

Being human dictates that we ask questions. Part of the learning process is to review, in our minds, different scenarios before they happen. We ask, **"What if?"** We compare the situation against past known scenarios. Our survival instincts tell us to review other scenarios as a means of learning, while not actually having to put ourselves in the situation. We're often caught off guard when the truly unforeseen occurs. It's happened to all of us. *It's how you "move through" these moments that defines you.*

On any deployment, I constantly "what if'd", training my brain for the moment. I was hoping that it would never come, but it did, more than once. *We all hesitate, but training and preparation helps you move through the hesitation.* My mantra helped me revert to my training, believe in my instincts and fight off my anxiety and fear. ***That's the point here, getting over and minimizing our anxieties.***

In most cases, ***fear is a lack of preparation***. If you're prepared, you have a higher probability of success, thus minimizing your anxiety. If you've practiced and understand how to change a flat on your car, then when it actually happens on the side of the road, you'll be less anxious about getting out and changing it. If you've practiced how to do high-speed defensive driving, then when a car pulls out in front of you, you'll be more likely to act faster. Thus the old adage, "Practice makes perfect."

[75]Air Force Military Strategist and combat veteran **Col. John Boyd**, calls the process of "moving through," the **OODA Loop**. This is an acronym for *Observe, Orientate, Decide and Act.* The person, who can process the OODA loop the quickest, is the most likely to be the successful one. Col. Boyd was a fighter pilot. The average time for a combat "dogfight" was forty seconds. He believed that the combatant who most quickly processed the loop would be the victor. Faster processing equals faster predictions, which equal faster actions.

BRAIN PAIN

During the Observation phase, you take into consideration the unfolding circumstances of the event, implicit guidance and control, any outside information that's occurring, and unfolding information/interaction with the environment. This is then fed forward to the Orientation phase. During this phase, your cultural traditions, all new information, but mostly, all the learning and training during your life is taken into consideration. In other words, your developed instincts are then fed forward into the Decision-making process where you make a hypothesis or best guess, which dictates your Action. Observe, Orientate, Decide and Act.

I constantly do this, OODA looping and moving through. This constant mental training allows me to sustain a heightened awareness of my surroundings. I am constantly observing, orientating, making decisions in my mind on the "what ifs," in case I need to act. *I have to maintain my awareness that my memories can be faulty.* I can only trust myself so far.

With my students, I often use a metaphor of driving down the road heading towards a T intersection. When you're driving straight into that intersection, your observation skills are generating new information. Looking left, looking right, looking forward and looking in the rearview mirror. As you close in on the intersection you orientate to the new information and come up with your best decision, then you act. Say the light is yellow; you're forced into a decision to hit the brakes or hit the gas, an action.

With my TBI and PTS, this once finely tuned skill has been challenged within it's newly slowed time constraints. It's about time processing. This is something that I am forced to address. *My mind's processing ability has changed dramatically, mostly misconstrued, askew and slowed. Chaos* has clogged my gears. I can't count the number of times I've had to rely on others memories. One of the biggest moments began with me losing some keys. I was absolutely sure where they were and what I had done with them; one thousand percent sure. I began to rage. I was wrong. My memories were wrong. This happens to Dad all the time also.

Every day is a fight to live. We are all warriors in the battle of life. Some days are easy, some days are monumentally hard. Those hard days are never going to happen when you expect them. It will most likely come on a Thursday morning, when life introduces you to that catastrophic moment or crossroad that will require your call to action. *It will be then, that all the preparation of your life will become the most purposeful.*

We are the sum total of our choices and lessons learned. Knowing that my processing and decision times are going to be significantly more sluggish, allows me to adjust and to flow around my obstacles. Working around my stalemate.

I mentioned earlier, fear is the largest element in lack of preparation. *If you're prepared, you'll learn to control your anxieties, making your "chain" stronger.* Pre-injury preparation meant "succeeding now in my work life," and "succeeding now in my personal life." Post injury preparation means slowing down and managing my life, now and down the road. Whether it's planning out my appointments, or meeting with clients, *understanding my deficiencies allows me to flow around my obstacles.* Knowing my processing can be faulty allows me to have multiple "protocols" already in place, when and if the unexpected occurs. The better you stack the deck in your favor, the easier the transition is.

A clear, sharp mind that can quickly adapt and overcome can do it in milliseconds. No longer having a clear and sharp mind, my "access dyslexia" is a constant frustration. What formerly came natural now requires focus and effort. I needed to relearn my methodology of problem solving. *"**Problem solving**"* could be a whole book on its own, but here we're discussing it in the context of the diminished capacity of TBI and PTS patients.

I was reminded of the methodology I'd been using all my life by a group of kindergartners. Occasionally, I volunteer at a local elementary school in a *"**Watch Dog**"* program. We basically provide security and help, as teacher assistants. One day, I was helping a group of kids put together a puzzle. I hadn't done a puzzle in years. Slowly, I showed them how to break it down into groups, larger to smaller, to get a better understanding. Matching the colors and larger shapes first. In this case the puzzle was of several dancing pigs, with red clothes on. Once they realized the larger shapes and colors were fitting together, they then worked on the sub-problems on the peripherals. It was a basic exercise of the brain's ability to problem solve, moving through the "moment" and not stalling in frustration. I was reminded that there are methods that can help us retrain, exercise and challenge our brains.

Riding my mountain bike, my snowboard, practicing shooting drills, and playing my guitar, are just some of the many things that not only exercise my brain, but they place a **noise** on the "Brain Pain." Dad played golf. They help keep us engaged and challenged.

Throughout the years, I've come to discover that my "spikes" occur more during my mental fact finding missions, when I'm using my mind for deeper research and/or thought processing. As I've mentioned, during debates or arguments, when I have a hard time searching for and accessing my point, the "Brain Pain" erupts to life. At the core of this, is the **frustration** of not being able to retort in a timely manner. The frustrations of feeling inadequate, stupid and unhealed. It is a very, very dark *Chaos* filled space.

My new journey post injuries, is continuous and one that I embrace. They're part of me now. It's my journey to stem *Chaos* and search out my comfort. I'm searching for new methodologies and nonstandard treatments to manage it, hopefully stemming future neurodegenerative disease.

All my new hobbies force me to exercise my brain. They help me "work around" deficits. I believe/hope the pain shooting around my brain are my neural pathways being bypassed, redirected or regrown, as they find new directions and make new connections. When that hurdle becomes too high, you adjust the hurdle. We all need to find our path in life or stay the course to the path we've found. The channel, stream or path has many crossroads, requiring many choices to be made. *Moving through is a choice.*

We must constantly train and prepare for when our paths become most purposeful. For it is in those "moments" of purpose, that we have trained our entire lives for, that we move through. We hold on to what motivates us and we stay the course. How we address our struggles define us, so we must embrace them.

"Moving through" - this is my mantra. I had learned early on, how to **"Pedal Fast."** Now, *back here*, my journey lasts a lifetime. Choose to stay in the fight. ***Pedal. Bleed. Repeat.***

Working as a Special Ops. Air Liaison Officer with Green Beret Reggie Salinas. It was 1984 and I had the whole world in front of me.

Here with best friend, Richard Emanuele, receiving the Key to the City from Las Vegas Mayor Oscar Goodman. If you talk the talk, you have to "walk the talk." **Walking, talking and happy to be here!**

Me in 1985, in Jordan, as a Special Ops. Air Liaison Officer working with the Jordanian Special Forces.

Me in Baghdad with a friend/operator in 2007. My older self, thanking my younger self for listening to him.

CHAPTER 16

LESSONS LEARNED

"Sometimes you must hurt in order to know, fall in order to grow, lose in order to gain, because most of life's greatest lessons are learned through pain." Author unknown.

The only guarantee in life is that time doesn't stop. Years ago, before I deployed, my best friend from college, Rick McMillion, and I pondered about what our *older selves* would tell our *younger selves*, about our journey and lessons our older selves had learned. Rick and I have known each other almost all of our lives. He's traveled the world, exploring our histories and religions. He's not only a successful businessman, but also one of the most existential friends I have. What would you say to your younger self if you had the chance?

Knowing I was headed over there, the question intrigued me so much that I hired a graphic artist to mock up a picture of what I'd look like at seventy years old. I carried this in my wallet the whole time I was deployed and saw it every time I took out my ID or paid for something. *It was a simple way of reminding myself to listen to that **voice** inside me.* It had guided me this far, and I was confident it would lead me the rest of the way.

When I looked at it, I would contemplate my older self speaking with my younger self; counseling, directing, encouraging, approving and disapproving. I was simply listening to myself, reminding myself of how to ride this bike; pedaling as much as I needed, slow and fast, maintaining my balance, headed down my path.

I believe the meaning of life is rooted in lessons learned. Lessons learned in the name of good and righteousness, strengthens our endeavor to persevere. We've been given this gift from our parents and ancestors. The propagation of our species. Lessons learned are the core of who we are, and the spine of our evolutionary process.

As you know, my dad told me, *"Trust your instincts, there's no time for second guessing."* When everything we've ever learned is called upon to address a *"moment"* and our brain makes the decision of action, we have to trust in it. When I was barely four years old, I began my training. I learned how to pedal. Pedaling fast enough to get my balance and fast enough to ride my line. Now, I just have to trust my brain. Clarity or *Chaos*?

I was fortunate enough to have a father who cared, as well as one who took out the time to teach me what he knew. 90% of the time, my father was the dad everyone hopes for. He was funny, kind, involved, generous and always had our back. He was only part time *Defective*.

Dad taught us everything. Not only verbal, but also actionable lessons. It started with learning to ride a bike, then throwing a baseball, bleeding the car brakes, to building a car engine. He made my sister learn how to change a tire before she could test for her driver's license. He'd always say, *"Come over here, let me teach you something."* By learning the lessons of our predecessors we are set up for success. For our entire existence, we are learning. Our life spans are limited, so we pass the torch. We nurture our young and teach them the lessons we have learned, so they can survive and prosper, passing it on and paying it forward.

Two of the most important hypotheses I learned in college were from [76] **Pavlov's** theory of *"Classical Conditioning"* and [77]**Maslow's** theory of the *"Hierarchy of Needs."* Pavlov's theory of Classical Conditioning theorizes that learning occurs through our natural interactions with the environment. This occurred when Pavlov noticed his dogs began to salivate when the attendants showed up with their food. Pavlov's dogs had learned that when the attendants came, so did the food. *Thus, they were "conditioned."* Learning is conditioning.

Maslow's theory of the Hierarchy of Needs is also known as the "Pyramid of Life," because it's well illustrated that way. At the bottom are the survival essentials; food, water, sleep and sex. Next up is safety; the security of morality, a job, family and health. Next up there's love; family and friendship. Then there's esteem; confidence, achievement and respect. Lastly at the top is self-actualization; creativity, problem solving and the realization of one's full potential. All these levels are based on one's mastering of the level underneath, then growing into the next. *Yet, nothing can be accomplished unless you master the first level and survive.* We learn, in order to survive. We are conditioned to survive. ***We learn and grow, to thrive.***

Growing up, I loved reading the **"Aesop's Fables"** series of short stories. They were originally written around 600 B.C. They started with a short story and ended with *"and the moral of the story is."* Morals like; "One good turn deserves another," "It is best to prepare for the day of necessity," "Look before you leap," and "There is always someone worse off than yourself."

The modern versions of these are movies, TV and the Internet. These are becoming the fastest way we are introduced to the lessons of life. Recently, when I decided to pick up my guitar again and learn some new songs, I went to "YouTube." Forty years ago, I was learning songs by playing a 45 record over and over. Times have changed.

The latest in learning methodologies are video games, which are interactive; everything from flight simulators to first-person war fighting. You get all the excitement, without the danger. They entertain, engage and challenge our brains, yet numb us as to the emotional and physical expenses.

Many warfighters are now using these games to overcome their PTS. They are placed back in a combat environment with the use of video games to access their triggers and anxieties. According to my friend, Dr. Valerie Galante, "Exposure therapy" is a cognitive behavioral technique used to treat PTS. [78]"It is not done in isolation; if done correctly, it is paired with Relaxation Therapy including deep breathing and Progressive Muscle Relaxation, perhaps Biofeedback and visualization. As a psychologist, I (Dr. Galante) would never 'expose' someone to an anxiety-provoking stimulus/situation until and unless I had prepared and 'armed' that person with the tools and strategies that he/she requires in order to adaptively manage the 'threat.'" I trained security contractors for several years after my return, using that, as my own form of exposure therapy. It became too much in the end, but it did get me through some tough times.

Brain training. Both Pavlov and Maslow would have a field day on how daily human interaction with a semi-artificial intelligence modifies, possibly healing our personalities, but *it is* the future.

Lessons learned are at the heart of all of our stories. One conversation that helped spark this book hinged on this. It was my colleague **Doron Benbenisty**. He's a former Israeli Military operator, whom I worked alongside with, at his company, CRI Training. He knew me before my injuries and afterwards. He saw firsthand what I was going through.

He felt that telling my story could help others. He argued that everything I teach is always from a lessons learned perspective. Throughout my military career as an operator and instructor, lessons learned were the cornerstone of my methodology. **If you talk the talk, you need to walk your talk.** Time to do the work.

A large part of my post-injury quest was to learn the lessons of others before me. Seeing the loss of Dave Duerson, Lt. Col. Rivas and thousands of others suffering from TBI and PTS, propped up my resolve. Writing this has brought back so much clarity to my life.

Those of us with TBI and PTS seem to be some of the most hopeless people in the medical system, because the system doesn't have a clear answer. Remember, they told Lt. Col. Rivas, "They couldn't fix him." Sad. It's a constant roller coaster of trying this and trying that. Mostly pills! I needed to articulate/show that there are hundreds of thousands of warfighters, as well as the *millions of civilians* out there with these injuries, and that there is HOPE!

My path was changed, as was my journey, and these are my most important new lessons. I'm far from having all the answers, but I have walked this path. *Chaos* is a bitch, but you can work around and move through it. *Change your mindset, change your life.*

"Document everything." This was paramount as I worked my way through the medical system. The first time I was injured, I wandered around the base, rode in a bus for about an hour, before going to the hospital. I didn't care about the paperwork. The second time, I took a helicopter back from the Green Zone to Camp Victory, also without any paperwork. Then I called my parents to let them know what happened. Dad told me to *"Document everything."* He knew this from his experience in Vietnam.

As you transfer from doctor to doctor, especially neurological and psychological, you need to ensure the correct medical explanation is passed on, so you can get the proper evaluation. You're constantly explaining and re-explaining, which can be frustrating. Brain injuries spark memory loss, both short term and long. You may also be fighting other injuries, so I've got all mine broken down into their own files. This helps with continuity and expedites treatment. *Write it down and organize it, so it's easy to recall when you need it.*

Written inside the door jam of my front doors is a checklist. I've forgotten things so many times, I had to place it there. Writing it down also reinforces it in your memory. Your operating system is already damaged so this extra work should become part of your new standard and management strategy.

Modern tools like a cell phone GPS has helped me more times than I can count. I've pulled off the road dozens of times to re-orientate. I've literally forgotten where I was and where I was going many, many times. Tapping on my GPS map reorients me as to where I'm at and where I was going.

For those of us with TBI, our **memory is a weak link** and it is our new standard. For me, that's why using tools, such as yellow stickies, journals, smart phones, calendar, notes and reminder apps is so important.

We *exercise our brain* by reinforcing it with multiple actions. Just because we can't access the folder in our brain doesn't mean it's not there. "Access Dyslexia" is at the core of my *Chaos*. We can't trust our own brain. It's there; we've just got to work a little harder to get at it.

"Find an Advocate." Most of us think we're invincible; Superman, and can handle all of this ourselves. Especially, us A-types. As I have realized, asking for help isn't a sign of weakness; *it's a sign of sensibility*.

With a TBI or PTS, your operating system isn't functioning properly. With me, my thinking was cloudy and my emotions a roller coaster. Having someone to assist you with clarity helps you through the hundreds of decisions you'll need to make. Also, surrounding yourself with those you trust reinforces your confidence and eases your anxieties. In my case that meant my Air Force Wounded Warrior advocate, *Darla Sekimoto*, my parents and my best friend *Richie*. They had my back.

"Do YOUR research." There's so much new information on the brain, but the majority of that information never makes it down to the end user, the injured, us. These new methodologies are stuck in the bureaucracy of research and medical journals. It's up to us to find it. Arm yourself with knowledge and information.

In the last ten years, more research has been done on the brain than in our entire human history. *Treatment options are growing.* Millions are living with this; so don't just accept what worked before. Look for the latest methodologies, protocols and technologies. Every brain injury and trauma is different. No explosion, accident or trauma is the same. Ask questions and seek out advice. Find out as much as you can. Become a pain in the ass, if necessary. I might have never learned about HBOT if I hadn't had a doctor with that experience in one of my courses. But once I learned about it, I did the research and took action. *Knowledge is power.*

"Learn patience." I was in Balad, Iraq, getting a CT scan, a few weeks after my second hit. The kid in the waiting room with me looked nineteen, maybe. He had already yelled at the receptionist twice and was now pacing back and forth spouting off loudly about the guys in his unit and how he didn't want to be here. I asked him to take a seat next to me. He looked at me like I was the enemy and was about to open his mouth and say something stupid, when I stood up, looked him sternly in the eyes and told him I wasn't asking.

While he was deciding what to do, I said, "Two times close, five total." He looked dumbfounded. I finished with "That's how many times I've been hit." "That's why you're here also, right?" He got quiet, then sat down with me. Then he said "Seven times." I sat patiently with him for the next hour, just listening to him. "We're going to be doing a lot more of this, so be patient okay? We did our job, let them do theirs." I told him afterwards.

Individuals with TBI or PTS are prone to over thinking, being easily *overwhelmed*, second-guessing and becoming irritable.

Understand this and learn tools to work around it. Break the pattern, move through, and breathe. I use my phone, a journal, a monthly organizer, newspapers, magazines and whatever it takes to interrupt the "negative spiral" in my brain. I've spent hundreds of hours in waiting rooms, having to remind myself that I'm here to be helped by those who are interested in helping me.

"**Pattern interrupt**." When you're in a meeting with General Officers, there are some things you just don't need to say. Usually, it's not the best time to be brutally honest. I had these meetings often. During one of these meetings in particular, things were getting heated and my headaches were overtaking my sensibilities. I was about to say something stupid. Underneath the table, I jabbed my leg with my pen. HARD. It wasn't to the point of bleeding, but to the point of pain. I had to change my mindset, to interrupt my negative thought pattern.

Growing up with a father with undiagnosed TBI and PTS, my mother used *changing the subject*, to change the direction of his anger. Simply put, changing the subject. I call it Pattern Interrupt. She wasn't aware of any scientific methodology, just that it, *disrupting his anger pattern*, worked. A spark of memory difficulty can send us, instantly, into frustration, then into anger. Situations can spiral out of control fast. I've seen it so many times growing up, that it instinctually came to me when I needed it. Control *Chaos*, don't let it control you.

"**Medications**." After the first explosion, I couldn't get a pain killer. A few weeks after the second, I had bottles of them. When do you call *Bullshit*? At first, because you're being medically evaluated, you have to follow their protocols. Three to four years later, you're in so deep, you don't want to get out. Yes, I'm saying the care our government is giving us, *places us on the paths to addiction. Hmm?*

Opiate-based pharmaceuticals are addicting. After some time on them, your tolerance level rises and rises. What starts out as one pill every eight hours, soon goes to one pill every four hours, then two hours. We know where that leads. Once again, [79]*Each day, 44 people in the United States die from overdose of prescription drugs.* The majority of those are from Opiate-based pharmaceuticals. *Chaos?* Percocets and Oxycodone are no longer part of my strategy.

BRAIN PAIN

I've been through dozens of medications and I still have the Brain Pain and anxieties. Medications, when used in moderation, can help, while you work towards your own personal management strategy, but there are always side affects. With or without the approval of my doctors, I wean myself off, or change to a similar medication, every six months to a year. This is where doing the work comes back into play. The goal is to reduce your medications and take back your life. **Don't rely - reduce.**

I've got my daily medications in a **pillbox**; one color for the day, another for the night. Make sure your evening medications are pre-set and checked. On more than one occasion I've made mistakes. I've also got a **vomit kit**. I've used it three times. It consists of salt, mustard and a toothbrush. I mix lots of salt and mustard in warm water and drink, and then use the toothbrush to induce. Once, I took my sleep meds three times in one night. You've got to have a plan for the nighttime.

"**Botox**" shots didn't help me the first year after getting back, but then, 5 years later, the newer versions did. I can't say enough about this procedure in relation to pain reduction of migraines / brain pain. It's literally been a lifesaver. This journey will trigger frustration, anger and hypervigilance, all which can spiral out of control. Understand that these only occur *because* you're doing the work.

"**Exercise and diet.**" When I started this book I wasn't "out of shape," but I had gotten soft. I was pushing 200 and soft. I felt good about my skills, but my strength had dwindled. Getting back into the gym came after some hard work mountain biking and snowboarding. I'm now 185 and fit. "Doing The Work!" Last year I went for the first run in six years. I was out of the country, so biking, boarding and the gym weren't available. I ran for forty minutes straight. It blew me away. I hadn't run that long since my thirties. All that mountain biking had paid off.

Exercising your body and brain is huge. It's easy to fall prey to sloth, lethargy, smoking, drinking and drugs. Exercise enhances your cardiac performance, leading to better oxygen flow, leading to more oxygen feeding your brain, leading to more natural endorphins. It's also a great way to keep engaged and challenged.

Review your diet. Cut back on sugar and carbohydrates. These have been shown to lead to diabetes and being overweight, as well as decreasing brain performance. We're working towards rebuilding our brain and becoming a lean, mean thinking machine, not falling back into continued sloth and lethargy. Our brain is fueled by sugar, but the right kinds of sugar. Do the research and find out what's right for you. I've also become a *juicer*, everyday. It gives me another, much healthier form of energy, as well as increasing my fiber intake, keeping things flowing properly. *Pain meds can bind you up.* I've also used Omega 3 fish oils everyday since my injury. They've been shown to help with psychiatric disorders as well as fueling the brain with good fats. Remember, the brain is over 50% fat.

Keeping myself in shape, exercising my brain and body, maintaining and even enhancing my skill sets keeps me ready for when everything goes to shit. *Chaos* can take me there in a split second, not to mention the other maladies that come along naturally in life. Maintaining a healthy lifestyle, exercising and watching my diet **prepares me for the inevitable setbacks** to come. It's like a savings account. When those dark days come, you're stronger and more capable of taking them on.

Looking back, this is what Dad did. He was a Marine and looked like the poster in the recruiting office. *He exercised, ate healthy and kept engaged and challenged.* We've all heard this a thousand times, but as I proved to myself, once you click your mindset into action, it can get done.

"**Sleep**." Without **proper sleep**, your brain will be nowhere close to where it should be. Exercise helps tremendously with this. Regular workouts lead to better sleep. I also no longer watch war or violent movies right before bed. Engagement and agitation will lead to hypervigilance of thought, making sleep difficult. In other words, leave the "Bourne Supremacy" for in the daytime.

Often times, my mind doesn't stop and is difficult to slow down, even with sleep medication. There's a form of pattern interrupt that I use at night, when my mind becomes hyper-vigilant. I call this tool, the *"roulette wheel."* I imagine a roulette wheel in my head, spinning, with years of my life in the slots. I stop it on any particular year and try to focus on the good things of that year. It interrupts the negative hypervigilance going on in my head, helping me find more calming thoughts and memories; my modern version of counting sheep.

"Don't re-injure yourself." Once I made the decision to start living my life; getting back outdoors, skiing, snowboarding and biking, the first thing I did was, buy a **helmet**. Skateboarding as a kid, I made my brother wear a helmet, but I was too cool to wear one. I'm not too cool anymore.

I've got four helmets now. When I'm going to do something that may produce a fall, my helmet goes on, just like my shoes. Another concussion and I could be done. Our personalities crave the adrenaline and rationalize that we can still leap those hurdles, but, just like age, getting that adrenaline high can have its downsides. Recently, I fell off my bike hitting my head, which was absorbed by my helmet. Had I not had my helmet on it would have no doubt been a hospital level event. I still crave my adrenaline and endorphin rush, but I have to be smart about it. *Live your life, but protect it.*

"Alternative treatments." Once I did the research, I knew I needed to begin **HBOT**. Army General Maney, who was blown up in 2005 and benefited from HBOT, told me; "I have tried to disseminate the information but the DOD and VA medical establishments were and are resistant to this therapy." I say, look into it yourselves. I think I've made a fairly persuasive argument. Just like amputees have prosthesis, those with TBI should have access to HBOT. With prosthesis you're not going to grow another limb, but you will walk. TBI and PTS patients should be given the same opportunities for clearer and painless thought. *HBOT may not cure the brain, but until better remedies come along, it dissipates the fog and gives me hope.* For me, it was a simple decision, the sooner I get started, the less likelihood I will end up with CTE, a neurodegenerative disease or dementia. I've been doing it for the last five years, and have now written this book. I'm on the path to recovery.

"Supplements." As I mentioned earlier, my experience has led me to three; *Fish Oil* or *Omegas 3, B complex 50* and *L – Theanine*. These help with brain healing and stress. Our brains are who we are.

"Meditation." I started this out of necessity. Fighting off claustrophobia inside my HBOT chamber. When I started, I used music to calm me, and then a friend told me about meditating to *"Binaural Beats."* I downloaded the files onto my cell phone and added this to my routine. The sound is like a Buddhist chant inside my head and it helps place a calming *"noise"* over my pain, anxieties and tinnitus. I often find myself in a clam trance-like slumber after thirty of so minutes. It really helps me relax, and in some cases even sleep when everything else fails. There are also many times when my head and I just need a time out. When the pain, anxiety and tinnitus become too much, I go to my easy chair, turn the lights off, put headphones on and *meditate*. This was far from natural for me. But then, so was horse therapy.

When your brain is in pain, you must look, *outside the box*. For thousands of years, meditation has helped relax the brain, enhancing its capabilities. I meditate while in my hyperbaric chamber and on planes and when the pain gets too bad. The closed and dark environment of my chamber or a dark room, along with listening to the "binaural beats," allows me to slow my minds hypervigilance and places a noise on the pain. I'm working with my head, not against it.

"**Mindfulness**." According to creator [80]"Jon Kabat-Zinn, creator of the research-backed *stress-reduction* program Mindfulness-Based Stress Reduction (MBSR), "It's the awareness that arises through paying attention, on purpose, in the present moment, non-judgmentally." Simpler, it's a **meditative state** to make ourselves be fully aware of who, what and where we are, yet not being *overly reactive* or *overwhelmed* by what's around us. I've heard many good things about how its being used to treat PTS. ***Find your Zen!***

Recently, I tried **float therapy** in a sensory deprivation tank. This is lying down for an hour plus in a tank of salt-saturated water in blacked out conditions. It is completely safe and natural. The water is extremely buoyant and it's a struggle to hold your legs and arms under the water. The lack of sensory stimulation makes the brain go into a meditative state. This results in a reduction in anxiety and blood pressure. Float therapy allows the mind to go into a theta state, which can be likened to state of dreams. For me it gives me a deep relaxing sense of well being, helps minimize my tinnitus and leaves me feeling energized. I'll be adding this to my tool box.

"**Acupuncture**" is the only treatment that has actually worked, to reduce my pain, other than opiate-based pharmaceuticals. The relief only lasted for a few days, but I took my medication daily. One of my good friends, **Jon Eckel**, told me how *acupuncture* had helped his dad. He was right. I was resistant at first; because this was a procedure I couldn't really wrap my head around.

I've had a total of 11 treatments over the last five years, provided to me by the Veterans Administration. I couldn't get any more. My military doctors, under Tri-Care (the military's health care system), couldn't give me referrals either. I ask every time I see my doctors. Yesterday, I asked my doctor for an acupuncture referral. She skipped around her computer for a few moments, before letting me know, they were only giving referrals for musculature skeleton pain and at this time, Traumatic Brain Injuries were not getting referrals.

As I mentioned, I finally got my doctors at the VA to work with me on this and they started me on the new "Battlefield Acupuncture" protocol. The last batch of needles stayed on my ear for three weeks, and I received around two weeks of noticeable pain relief from them.

"**Medical marijuana**." Most research refutes evidence that **THC** is a neurotoxin, and new [81]Israeli research shows it is more of a neuroprotectant, enhancing the brains own protection abilities. If you haven't looked into this you should. I don't smoke now but it's definitely in my future, and looking better and better as I research it. A mentee of mine, has been using it for the last year under a Medical marijuana card issued by a private doctor. The VA doctors won't prescribe it. When he gets over agitated, he slows himself down with it. *He calls it his chill drug.* I don't recall a single overdose or case of suicide by "overmedicating" on medical marijuana; maybe some weight gain?

"**Moving through**." Remember, Professor Bejan's "**Constructal Law**" hypothesis. Moving through is not always moving forward, but staying the course is. The "flow system" is all about *working around* the obstacles and adjusting to the friction. It doesn't get better by following a single path. There will always be paths and crossroads. Some things will work and some things won't work. Things that once worked may not work again. Keep searching!

"**Prioritize your life**." I had to convince myself that my security business was never going to grow into the larger company I once planned. It was no longer my top priority, my mind was. You, your support system and your advocates, need to come up with a *plan of priorities.* Short-term initially, but then long-term. One example from my playbook was buying my HBOT chamber. My mind became a priority over buying material "Bling" things. Life throws so much at us that we need to be able to understand what's really important, so we can make smarter decisions. My goal is to be to be happy, to once again enjoy my life. To smile, laugh and connect. When everything goes to black, what really mattered? Don't wait to find out. *I prioritized what's most important.*

"**Find the middle road**." Being honest with my brother Marcos led me to admitting; I was ebbing and flowing through peaks and troughs, and needed to slowdown and *find the middle road*. This was one of my biggest discoveries. After years of still thinking I was still my old self, I came to realize I wasn't. I may never be. The peaks and troughs of hypervigilance and depression were taking their toll. Once I found that I needed to operate the middle road and managed my life accordingly, my pain became more controllable. Slowing down is hard to do, but it's all part of doing the work. *Just like running a race, I learned to pace myself.*

"**Acknowledge your truth**." If I could do this over, *I would have opened up sooner* to my doctors, advocates, friends and family. I would have been more honest and not have held back so much. What I held in just made it worse. Remember when my therapist asked me about my childhood? I was certain that my childhood had nothing to do with the fact that I was blown up. But then years later, while writing this, I slowly began to realize I was my father's son. He was blown up too, and I had been through all of the "Back here" moments with him. *What I saw in my father was what I saw in myself.* I didn't want that.

*You **don't** deserve more than you were promised.* Don't blame others for what you can fix with your efforts. DTW! It is what it is, and you can't turn back the clock. Yesterday can't be re-written. You survived and only you really know what's going on in *your* head. These injuries affect the core of your operating system, as well as your personality and emotions. ***This is our truth. Make it part of you, don't let it become all you are.*** If you've survived a trauma, learn from it and allow it to make you stronger. The first few years post injury; I dwelled on it compulsively, not being able to let it go. After many conversations with my father, I realized I had to **place it on a shelf**, like other photos and snapshots in my life.

BRAIN PAIN

Anger, irritability and frustration are the seeds to hatred. Forgive, move through and move on. *Don't dwell on the negatives and don't expect a free ride.*

"**This is my new standard**." I'm not the same person I once was. Just like nothing will bring back lost limbs, our brain and emotions have changed. *I am losing memories.* Not just the short-term ones, but also the "life event" ones. Memories like dinners with friends, family visits, the special days. Last week my mom showed me photos of us at a dinner and I had no recollection; empty, gone. What I've seen through the years is that when my dad forgets something, he gets angry. I'm not going to be that person. I'm injured, not stupid. It's not my fault. I'm going to embrace my injuries, and the memories I still have. ***Embrace yours!***

It was extremely hard to interview Dad for this project. He doesn't like to "go there." He's said, "I put those days away in a box." To this day, my dad still fights those demons of Khe Sanh, but he's made them part of who he is and stayed the course. They're part of us, yet don't define us. We shouldn't dwell on them, yet just like high school, college and other milestones in our lives, they're part of us. *The quicker I embraced it, the faster I learned my workarounds.*

"**Keep engaged, challenged and purposeful**." One thing programs like, the Wounded Warrior Project, the Air Force Wounded Warrior Program and the many others like them do well, is give wounded warfighters **extracurricular options to try**, like skiing, hiking, fishing, hunting, biking, etc. Something most of us could never afford. *Keeping busy and engaged is at the heart of our fight against Chaos.* On one of those Wounded Warrior Project getaways I was re-introduced to mountain biking. I took the challenge and found it to be one of my new daily hobbies and smiles. **I'm living my new standard.**

Retraining your brain means learning to accept, adapt and adjust. Multitasking is problematical with a damaged brain. Don't spread yourself thin. Focus on the task at hand. I have specific daily routines that help me move through to the next steps. Simple things like going to bed at a specific time and getting up at a specific time; meds at night, meds in the morning, etc. Focused protocols in the morning give my brain time to warm up. In my case, my routine gives me the best chance for minimal pain and anxiety throughout the day. In my business, I only take on the cases I feel drawn to. I don't want or need the extra stress.

Engage your mind and body. Constantly **challenge yourself**. Remember my concept of *"The Line,"* It simply means using your operating system (brain) to maintain the balance of your path, predicting future possibilities, and making the best decision to ensure your survival and success. *Our brain is the great predictor of our abilities*.

I never thought, pre-injury, about *exercising my brain*. It just happened. But now, I include exercising my brain as part of my daily routine, as I do physical exercise. The gym, snowboarding and biking exercise my body. One hour a day, practicing my guitar, exercises my brain. After my return, I had an extremely hard time reading and absorbing information, having to re-read it over and over, but eventually I got better. Finally, writing this book has been one of my *primary* brain exercises over the last few years. Use it or lose it.

A few years back I downloaded a brain game/training app, *"Lumosity"* for my phone. It allows me to engage and exercise my brain whenever I want. I began using it while in the waiting room for many of my medical appointments, but now it's whenever I have some spare time. It works for me, find what works for you. Search out the obstacles that challenge you and your mind. Your path went in a new direction, so grow and flow with it.

"Find your confidence". I've never lacked confidence. In my mind I was always the most confident person in the room. Then my sensors went bad and *Chaos* started finding its way in. When people talked to me, I didn't always get it. For the first several years after my injury, I was socially awkward, feeling stupid, thinking I had TBI written on my forehead. Thinking everyone knew my brain was slow. I was my own worst enemy.

It took me years to accept my new standard, then to find my confidence. Once I did, my work arounds kicked in. I've lost countless memories, gotten lost hundreds of times, stumbled thousands of times in conversation, but still I get through, learning from each event. *Don't worry about the feeling stupid; just think about the being alive!*

"Rediscover your passions". How do you even describe loss of passion? Passion is almost synonymous with smiles, enthusiasm, excitement and infatuation. It takes over your soul and shines outward for everyone to see. Without passion the world can seem black and white, boring, lack-luster, dull and un-interesting.

One of the traits that have always defined me was **my passion**. I was a musician, college athlete, military officer, entrepreneur, writer, restaurateur and security consultant. *Post-injury, I lost all passion.*

For a long time, my emotional connection to family, friends and the things that I love, were fogged over. Everything seemed dull and un-interesting. A large part of writing this was to try and re-acquire my passions and emotions. *"Doing the work" for me, started with my horse "Buddy."* I started to feel the connection and love. That led to me taking up snowboarding, mountain biking, camping and finding my guitar again; all in attempt to re-ignite my passions. Biking, skiing and guitar playing were all things I loved as a kid. Those days of innocence and bliss, sans the adult responsibilities, put smiles back on my face. I'm trying to find mine, try finding yours.

"Find your mission." Most Fridays my parents and I go to lunch together. I had been contemplating writing this book for a while, but that day I told them I was going to do it. Once I *verbalized* it to my parents, once I said I was going to do this, it was going to get done. I walk my talk. On the 23rd of June 2013 I found my new mission, this book. *Sharing my story and lessons to help those after me, is my new mission; helping others fight TBI and PTS.*

It's a new world "back here." My missions "over there" are completed. What now? Where do I get my adrenaline fix? Where can I be all I can be? Where's my old self? For most of us, it's not within our sights. More than likely it's out there; we're just not able to see it. What are you good at? What do you like?

Search your history, your childhood. Were you athletic? What made you smile? Find your smiles and strengths. Look for good and righteousness. *A new mission will fill the void and darkness, engaging your mind with new goals and crossroads.* This book has been all that to me.

How do I start writing a book? I started by developing a skeleton, a list of chapters. Then I had one rule. Complete one page a day. That sounds do-able. It was. It got me off my ass. "Procrastination" is best friends with pain, depression, lethargy and *Chaos*. They're constantly calling, trying to get back into my life.

Doing the work keeps them away. Come up with your own personal protocols on how to get things done. Start small, setting daily goals, working up slowly to weekly goals, to monthly goals, then to longer-term goals, as you progress in your recovery.

Remember the OODA Loop? Observe, Orientate, Decide and Act. If you don't **act**, the loop fails. Like I tell my students, you're here because you want to learn and prepare, hence, you're at a higher likelihood to **act**, and to "do the work." More than likely, you're reading this for the same reasons. I'm sure as hell not Hemingway and I don't have an epiphany of answers, just my experience. My experience fighting off *Chaos* and I'm still here to talk about it. You get out of it what you put into it. ***Action means DTW!***

"Do the work - DTW." I think I've mentioned this a hundred times. It's so simple, yet so hard. You woke up this morning; you're walking and talking. *Life is short - you're alive, so get your ass going!* Only you can turn the keys and put it in drive. Only you can "do the work." *'Do The Work' to strengthen your mental health 'Chain.'* Otherwise *Chaos* will slip in and bite your ass with his razor sharp teeth. He'll shake you back and forth, ripping out your soul. All the while, you're lying on the couch watching cable, thinking you'll get to it tomorrow.

As a kid we were called "Brats." We moved so much that we developed and hardened our emotional skills every time we left an assignment, then honed our social skills to fit into our new one. We constantly adjusted to our new environment and our new standard. We called it, *"doing the job."* This is my new standard and in order to adjust to it, I've got to do the work. *It's my new lifestyle.*

"Never underestimate Chaos." It's insidious, nefarious, manipulative, self-destructive and has a garage full of tools and assistants. It seeks to control you and those around you. Once it infects you, you infect those around you. You're its host and it feeds on your soul. Recognize it. Recognize it fast. The sooner you catch *Chaos* manifesting, the sooner you can act on finding your solutions to ripping it off of you. Know your enemy. *22 a day.*

The meaning of life is rooted in lessons learned. Lessons learned, in the name of good and righteousness, strengthens our endeavor to persevere.

BRAIN PAIN

For me, comfort comes by way of sharing these lessons with you. It helps seal my cracks. *Chaos* is just like rain on your roof, it's always looking for cracks. It's a never-ending cycle with only one option - do the work.

I had grown up my father's son. I had seen him at his best and at his worst, yet have still always wanted to be the warrior he is. But I also knew the cost he and we had paid. Why would I want to go through that and possibly put those I love through that as well? Not sure, but I did.

Being a bodyguard for the rich and famous can test your values and morals. Prior to deploying my life was becoming askew and my integrity was being put to the test. I needed to redeem my soul and become purposeful again.

At that point in my life I wanted a seat at the table. I wanted to be in the game of war fighting. My choices, my decisions. *I was great at what I did and I thought maybe, just maybe, selflessness and purpose could show me the way to* **redemption**.

It did and in the end I made a difference on the ground. It also made a difference in my soul.

Recently, as I finish this project, I went to my parent's home on Sunday expecting Mom to make dinner, like she always does on Sunday's, our family day. Mom met me at the door, and whispered, "Your father wants to go out for lunch, and he's feeling good." "No problem," I said. They just returned from their annual visiting trip, where they drive around the country visiting family and friends, so it seemed like a good opportunity to catch up. At lunch, dad was funny and engaging the whole time, and when a child, a couple booths down from us kept crying out, (something Dad normally gets upset at and speaks up loudly about,) he just took out his hearing devices and kept on telling his story. *Wow!* He was really patient, maybe even compassionate about the child's distraction.

Moments later, a "Spike" shot through my brain, I blurted out an expletive and began tapping on my skull. He just paused his conversation until my pain passed, and then threw me a wink, as if to say, "I understand," then seamlessly continued his story. ***Wow again!***

We had a really great lunch together that day. It was so cool to see both of them smiling and laughing the whole time. Mom and Dad raised a great family. They taught us the lessons we needed to learn and always had our backs. My sister Pam lives in South Carolina and is a Human Resources Generalist at a corporate bank and has two grown children, Rhianna and Gilbert. My brother Marcos is a Chief US Customs and Border Protection Officer in Chicago and lives there with his wife, Suzanne. They have two daughters, Alexia and Gabriella.

My whole life, as my parents get older and normal health maladies present themselves, I've said *"It's the sign of things to come."* Although subliminally, I've wondered about my dad's brain, hoping that wouldn't be my future. Recently, dad started getting more and stronger headaches. A few years ago, when he got angry, he'd start slapping his head. This year the headaches are getting worse. I watch him, understanding this pain, and helpless to stop it.

My dad is an actor, not re-actor. He stayed the course and has lived an exceptionally purposeful and worthwhile life. My mom has done the same. They've both graduated from the school of hard knocks, so we didn't have to. Now, I walk in their footsteps; learning, growing, surviving and thriving.

This lunch gave me some hope that my future may not be headed in a degenerative direction. ***Dads still doing the work.***

Writing this has strengthened my hope of staving off a future of neuro-degenerative disease. Although hard, exercising my brain to access information, formulate the thoughts, positions and opinions has helped me believe that my brain is "working around" its deficiencies and that my memories are still intact, somewhere.

Keep engaged, challenged and purposeful! Of course, life will continue to throw challenges and obstacles at us. I hope to continue my resolve of doing the work, pedaling as fast at necessary to ride my line, to keep my balance and leave *Chaos* behind. I'm staying the course, chasing my clarity, seeking my comfort, finding my clam, hoping for many more smiles along the way. ***Pedal. Bleed. Repeat!***

Will you do the work? Up to you!

DTW

Team Jones.

*Me, my dad "WK," my mom "Anna," my brother "Marcos" and my sister "Pamela." We're **all** still walking, talking and happy to be here!*

ANTHONY JONES

Taken during a follow-up visit to the Baghdad ER, (28th CSH).

Faith moves me forward, doing the work.

EPILOGUE

HEAVEN IS REAL

In August of 1995, my good friend *Tony F.* died. The events of that week became so monumental in my life that I put them down on paper. I never planned to tell this story, because I knew I could not do it justice. My words could never be eloquent enough to express what transpired. I shared it only with my friends and family, until now.

I was living in Studio City, California at the time, running my retail store in the Arts District of North Hollywood. These were my entrepreneur days. I was full of energy, working the store, going to acting classes, writing my first scripts, and doing reserve duty back in Vegas.

I met Tony through his best friend Dale Nichols. I was living in Fort Walton Beach, Florida and it was the early eighties. We met at the gym and became good friends.

Our workout and beach crew consisted of Tony and Dale Nichols, Bill Klienhelter, Max Maxwell, Randy Moulton, Bill McCoy, Tony Manthey and Rob LeBoeuf. Tony's mother, who we called, "Mama Anne," hosted our crew for many a Thanksgiving, Christmas dinners and July fourth celebrations. Tony's sister, Tonya K., and I remained close friends too.

As I moved to Las Vegas, Tony moved to San Diego, then to Temecula, California. The week prior to his death, we talked on the phone. I was headed down to visit my parents, who lived in Yuma, Arizona and was planning to stop by to visit him.

BRAIN PAIN

It was around 2 am, Monday morning, August 7th, when I received the call that no one wants to receive. It was Tonya K. letting me know that her brother had passed away in a car accident. She was making plans to come out and start the funeral arrangements. Later that day, she would fly into the Ontario airport, in Southern California, where I would pick her up.

That day, I made arrangements to close my store. I packed my clothes, picked her up at the airport, and together we headed to Temecula. There we met Tony's friend and business partner, Steve Saunders. Steve's family graciously let us stay at their home as we went about finding out what happened. Steve brought us up to date on what he knew, and later that evening we went to the Sheriff's office to set up appointments with the police officers that handled the scene.

Later that evening, we also went to Tony's home to meet his roommate. While Tonya K. packed her brothers belongings, I gathered his paperwork, files and folders. We gathered up what we could and what we felt most important and called it a night. Little did we know this was just day one of a long week to come.

The first thing Tuesday morning we drove to the Riverside County Coroners office and met with the coroner. He reviewed his initial findings with us that Tony had died of Traumatic Brain Injury. The Coroner also reviewed the details of making the arrangements for the return of his body.

Next, we drove to the Riverside County Hospital where we met with the attending ER Physician and Medical Chief of Staff, who briefed us about what happened once Tony arrived at the hospital. Our next stop into piecing together what happened the last day of Tony's life was to meet the California Highway Patrol Officer who conducted the investigation.

After lunch, we returned to Steve's house and met with Tony's girlfriend who was in the vehicle with him. She was traumatized, but as considerate and helpful as she could be, under the circumstances. We then went to the accident site, so we could better understand and explain what happened.

The last day of his life was Sunday, the 6th of August 1995. Tony and his girlfriend spent the afternoon together, first having dinner, and then driving through the beautiful backcountry of

Temecula. Tony was showing her several lots of land that he hoped to someday build a home on. She described it as a beautiful summer evening. They were driving his Bronze 1979 International Scout convertible. It didn't have a hard top or a roll bar on it.

Around 9-9:30 pm, they were heading home. The sun had set 30-40 minutes earlier, still with a subtle twilight on the horizon. The road they were on was fairly straight, but then dipped downward, going into a slight right curve, then straightened back out again. Throughout the years, as people drove around that curve and went off the road, hitting the shoulder of the road, gravel had accumulated near the centerline of the road.

As Tony drove into that curve, he saw what the decline had hidden from his view - work cones set up along side the right side of the road. Seeing them unexpectedly, he maneuvered to the center, where he hit the unseen gravel. Losing traction, the vehicle slid through centerline, and then when the tires suddenly gripped the road again, it flipped and rolled twice, finally landing upright. His girlfriend's life was spared because she had her seatbelt on, Tony didn't. The last thing she remembered was Tony reaching over to protect her.

Tony arrived at the hospital just after 10 pm. He was semi-conscious, and his EEG showed only minor brain activity. While on the CAT scan table he flat lined, was brought back once, then passed away around midnight. We now had a clear picture. As the day ended, we related all that we had learned back to his mother. It had clearly been a tragic accident.

Wednesday morning came and our first stop was the coroner's office. We needed to make travel arrangements to return his body back to Florida. It was here that we were met with a major surprise.

The coroner told us he couldn't release the body without a release signed by his wife. His wife? I was aware that Tony had been married years before and had a son, but we thought he was divorced. We conferenced in with his mother, who told us that he may not have gotten around to it, and that we needed to find his wife. That afternoon we spent our time tracking down his wife and reviewing Tony's important papers.

When I was 18 years old, my Uncle Ben, my dad's brother, passed away in a tractor accident. What I remembered most about my father's handling of the details, was that going through all the paperwork, bills, etc. is tremendously important. In that case, there was no will. During my father's review of Uncle Ben's documents, he found an Exxon credit card statement. It showed that his brother had taken out an insurance policy. This could have been overlooked so easily, but it wasn't.

It was a shot in the dark, and specifically because I remembered what my father had done, I went through Tony's paperwork, and bills with a forensic-like comb. There was no will. Hours later, there it was, an insurance policy on a credit card bill. I must have gone over it half-a-dozen times just to be sure before telling his sister.

Then, I received a call from his estranged wife. She was emotionless and direct. There was no negotiation; she wanted the most valuable piece of Tony's estate, his horse. His horse? She would only sign the release for Tony's body, if his horse were deeded over to her. She leveraged this asset, for his remains. The roller coaster continued.

I told her I'd get back to her, and then Tonya K. proceeded to call Mama Anne, Tony's mom, and explained the latest news. She acknowledged that he might have a horse. Further investigation revealed he did, that the horse was stabled at his roommates ranch, and it was worth thousands of dollars. His roommate left out that detail until we confronted her. It was a surreal situation and emotions were running high for everyone.

A mother just lost her son, a sister just lost her brother, a son just lost his father and many others just lost a friend. After discussing it, we drew up a one-page document deeding the horse, "Missy Bar Bingo," over to his wife in exchange for the release of the Death Certificate and Tony's remains. With Mama Anne's approval, we called his wife and set up a meeting. She met us that afternoon, in the Home Depot parking lot, signed the agreement and distributed copies. We were full of loss, despair and trepidation.

The next day Tonya K. and I drove back to my apartment in Studio City, where we had dinner and flew out that night on the red-eye back to Florida. Over the weekend we continued with funeral arrangements for Monday. Sunday evening we all got together again at Tonya K's home. With everyone exhausted, the get together broke up around 10 pm. It was a hard weekend, but we tried to commemorate Tony's life with past stories and anecdotal memories. Tonya K. and I stayed up till around 11:20 talking, I know this because I looked at the digital clock when she went to bed, and laid down to sleep on the couch in the living room.

My body was utterly exhausted, yet my mind was clear. There are those rare times when our mind is at ease and present, not engaged in the past, or the future. Like the innocence of a child's mind, I was weary, but at peace as I began my slumber. *What happened next would change my life forever.* I was lying down with both my arms stretched out over my head, beginning to drift off. Unexpectedly, someone grabbed my forearms, gripping firmly, but not controlling. I jerked, seeming to wake. My body went solid. Time seemed to halt. As I settled from the jerk, I could see Tonya K's cat, "Big Man," scowl and scurry off. Without words, telepathically in my mind, I was told, "It's Okay," and that it was "Tony."

I called out, "TONY!" I remember the feeling of reassurance as I stared at the ceiling, moving through this "Moment." Then audibly, I heard Tony say, "Thank you," as he held my hands.

Next, I felt the weight of a person sit on and through my torso, as I lay there on the couch. I could feel the weight push me down into the foam. As this happened, I was taken from my body to another place. ***This is why I say "Heaven is real."***

I'm not going to try and convince anyone. I'm just going to share the most important moment in my life. There are millions of us who have had Near Death Experiences. There are millions who understand and believe. There are thousands of stories of combat related experiences as well. [82]Bob Woodruff, of ABC World News, had a near death experience, when he was embedded with a Army unit and hit by an IED. It's in his book, "In an Instant."

First, I must reiterate, that my words will never communicate and illustrate the beauty and essence of the experience that followed. I must also remind you that I grew up a Brat, the son of a Marine, rooted safely, in logic and science. As an educated Aviator, all things were clear, black and white, always with cause and effect.

Tony knew me well and knew my warrior/logical mind wouldn't easily accept this and would want to fight back. I believe this is why he gripped my forearms to begin his appearance.

BRAIN PAIN

As I left my body behind, I became an energy, formless, yet complete. Tony was to my left and it seemed as if we were flying in formation, connected, yet separate. He too was an energy form. It wasn't like I could look over and see him, but I knew he was there.

As we entered, I could feel despair and anxiety. I went into a darkness of thick, deep sounds. We climbed up and away from the darkness and into a golden shimmering expanse of sheer magnificence. The darkness dissolved, revealing a heaven filled with golden glittering beams of light. The sounds transitioned from a low bass-like hum, to a higher angelic chorus. The iridescent orbs were sparkling brightly, yet each clearly distinct.

The realization was settling in. I was entering and surrounded by a new realm, the likes of which I can only describe as the most beautiful connection to all life, dimensions and universes. A glorious totality of one. We were enveloped by the light and the sounds of a sea of Angelic voices.

I felt completely self-aware, with laser focus on the present. I knew not of my earth, just of Tony and what surrounded me. As I continued to move through, the twinkles of light revealed themselves. They too were heading towards the Center, the Core. I knew who they were. They were the newly departed, the guides and the angels. Thousands and thousands surrounded me, rising towards a common golden Core.

It was far off in the distance, yet right in front of me. As I gazed into the Core, *I was told by Tony, that he was showing me the love of God, and that this was his way saying, "Thank you."*

It was an overwhelming sense of love, peace and tranquility. I embraced it without question.

It was the mightiest form of love I had ever known. It was here that I was told, ***"It's all about love."*** Those words are the simplest earthy way to describe the most profound message I have ever received. I was basking in the love of all.

As I received this message, I felt my comprehension and intelligence multiply infinitely. I was blessed with the Knowledge of the Universe, instantaneous access to all knowledge. Faster than the speed of light, my questions were asked and answered, over and over. The knowledge of all universes and the Creator permeated my DNA, becoming part of me. For the rest of my life, it would fuel my intuition and instinct.

There is good and evil. Evil exists, but has never or ever will be substantial, in comparison to good and the power of Love. Evil is but a spec of dirt in the desert. It's there so we can learn and grow; to show us that obstacles and challenges can be overcome. Without despair we cannot have moral responsibility. Our growth makes us greater.

We are also not alone. We are each like a single cell in the body of our Creator. Life is everywhere and by no means are we simply singular in the physical world. Like a radio receiver that can tune into thousands of frequencies, which broadcast clear and in depth, there are thousands of other dimensions, layers, frequencies in which life exists. Love and goodness oversee them all.

As we flew closer into the Core, the angels separated themselves from the departed, and came in closer. I could feel their love and kindness grow as they surrounded us. The love surrounded me, held me and comforted me. Longing to continue on, I gazed into the Core, mesmerized by its warmth, beauty and love.

Tony slowed our ascent. I knew this meant I could not continue. I still wasn't aware I was from a terrestrial world, yet I knew I wasn't supposed to advance. I longed to see the Creator, or **God**, focusing my gaze deeply into the Core. Knowing I couldn't stay, I took one last look, basking one last time, in the glory and love.

Abruptly, I was back on the couch, immediately feeling the weight lifting from my torso. Gasping, I sat up, facing the kitchen, my gaze fixated on a sparkle of light, an orb. As I sat, still watching the orb, it slowly manifested into a large bright luminescent glow, which then formed Tony's face, looking back at me, smiling.

He was glowing, lighting up the whole room. Once I had absorbed his smile, and smiled back, he slowly dissolved back into the orb, and then disappeared.

As the logical part of me returned, I accessed myself back into this physical world. I looked over to the clock, 11:37 pm. Was this a dream? Had I had a heart attack? What had just happened? Why had it happened?

As I sat there in the dark, still in bewilderment, the living room in front of me suddenly lit up vibrantly and collected into Tony's form again. This time in full body, with his jacket on, slacks, cowboy boots and long golden hair. His face glistened with a bright white, golden glow. He looked to me, with peace, purity and love, then smiled, turned and walked off, disappearing through the front wall.

The reality of all that had just happened now had me shaking. My heart racing and my adrenaline pumping, my logical warrior mind was overwhelmed. Without thinking, I woke up Tonya K. She was already going through so much, but I had to share this with her. She listened, understandingly.

Still unnerved, I went into the bathroom, splashed some water on my face, then got some blankets and slept on the floor. Even though the experience was glorious, I had to get some sleep. Tony's funeral was in the morning.

The next day, I shared the story with our friends. It was an unexpected blessing in which Tony was sharing with us the love of God and that he was at peace, in Heaven.

I was born and raised a Catholic. My sister, brother and I grew up standing and kneeling through mass every Sunday. As I got older, *my faith dwindled* as my mind was engaged elsewhere. In the Air Force, I distinctly remembered praying during a mission that was going downhill quickly. We survived the mission, but I harbored the guilt of praying only when I needed too. From that point on I make it a practice to take a moment, everyday and pray.

In 1995, this experience left me confused, bewildered and conflicted. I was hit with the guilt of not feeling worthy and asking, "Why me?" I felt that I was a good person and lived my life supporting good and righteousness. But, I was also a sinner, like most of us. Remember the work hard and play hard guy? My morals, values and integrity have been tested and there are many things I am not proud of, so why me?

I was also confused about what had happened. Was this a Near Death Experience (NDE)? I hadn't died, not even close to it. The majority of my adult life was fast-paced; college, flight school, women, being an entrepreneur, rarely giving the afterlife much thought. Was this a dream? I might have believed this myself, had I not looked at the clock, twenty minutes had passed. I sat there, breathing heavy, wide-awake, in wonderment, then watched as *Tony manifested again.*

Afterwards, for the next few months, the experience, especially the "why me?" began to chip away and take over my life. Tony was a genuinely good guy, but we were never church going, bible thumping missionaries. We were workout partners, car enthusiasts, beach lovers, and women-loving single guys, enjoying our youth. Where did this come from?

I also didn't believe in ghosts or aberrations. Yet, I was wide-awake when I stared directly into his gaze. It would have been one thing for him to simply come to me in a dream, letting me know he was okay, but to show me everything the experience encompassed, was quite another.

A major part of me wanted to share this with the world, but to my dismay, most of my friends weren't ready to hear it. When faced with these stories, our mortality surfaces and the majority of us live in the now. We fear that day we all know is coming. Was I shown this to go forth and proclaim? Why? I didn't have a complete understanding of it myself. I also began to sense disbelief and ridicule from others. This, along with my own struggles of worthiness, pushed me to place it in storage. Literally, on the flight home I wrote everything down, put the notes in a brown satchel, then placed them in my garage, only to pull them out twenty years later, to write this.

I stopped dwelling on *why* and just embraced it, making it part of me. I only shared the story with those who needed to hear the words of encouragement. When my Tia Carmen (my mother's older sister) was fighting cancer, my mother, who had flown out to be with her, told her of my experience. She called me immediately wanting to hear it in its entirety. Another great experience of my life was being able to share this with her, in our last conversation.

October 25th, 2007 is one of my "Alive days." It was a cool crisp morning. As I walked to the shower trailer, I could see a tint of the morning light cresting the horizon. Underneath the showerhead, the rain of hot water flowed over me and my mind began to review the day to come. Exiting the trailer, in my gym shorts and T-shirt, I smiled as I could see the warm, white sun forthcoming on the horizon. Moments later a 107 rocket hit the concrete wall, 15 feet behind me, in the open, reverberating backwards, blasting me against another wall. The "107" rocket has a kill radius of 150 feet. *No armor, no helmet. I'm still alive?*

BRAIN PAIN

I remember the all-to-familiar whistling of incoming, the blast, a slow motion movie-clip of hundreds of pieces of shrapnel, bursting out towards me. Time slowed as the concrete and shrapnel headed my way, like a hoard of NASCAR racecars rounding the bend, towards the finish line. I can still see the picture vividly, practically being able to count them.

Simultaneously, the concussive wave threw me against a concrete T-barrier, knocking me out. As I went to black, I felt the presence of my old friend, "Tony." It was during the darkness I felt his embrace. He had returned. I was somehow shielded, and in my mind, I heard the words, **"It's Okay."**

In microseconds, I was reminded and shown again what I had experienced years before. Once more, I heard the angelic voices, saw the "Light of our Creator," and felt the love, peace and tranquility. It was not my time.

Corinthians 13:13; three things will last forever—faith, hope, and love—and the greatest of these is love.

As I arrived at our local Mobile Support Hospital, the Chaplain arrived. He was a friend of mine, whom I had spent many hours with. Not in church, because I never went, but from helping him study for Air Command and Staff College. We'd meet up a couple times a week and I'd quiz him on the objectives.

He asked if he could say a prayer for me. This was probably fifteen minutes after the blast. *As he prayed, the magnificence of this second experience with our Creator became clear. It sank in all at once.* **I realized that I had been protected.**

I rarely talk about this experience, because I remember how years earlier, I was doubted and ridiculed about it. But inside the darkness of that "Moment," with the calmness and strength of "Tony's" voice and grasp, I felt the resolve that I was going to be okay.

I'm sure that there are millions out there who have had similar experiences. I'm also sure there are thousands of Wounded Warfighters who have shared similar experiences. The world is full of small miracles that give us strength, direction, purpose and comfort. They may be as simple as a phone call from a friend in their time of need, or as complex as surviving the unsurvivable.

Afterwards, I was placed on the helicopter and medevac'd out to the Green Zone. The side doors were open, my head lay outward and I felt the rush of the wind over my face. I was alive and feeling the ecstasy of that gift. As I scanned the blue skies above me, I gazed towards Heaven, knowing, undoubtedly, that I had been saved.

I don't dwell in the, "Why?" anymore, just the sharing, caring and finding those smiles along the way. I've embraced it and made it part of my resolve.

Of all the lessons I've shared with you, this is the most important. ***It's the lesson of spirituality and faith.*** I had forgotten mine, and for some unexplainable reason, Tony chose to remind me.

Faith motivates me. Faith ensures I "do the work." It keeps me in check. This memoir is about the lessons I can share with others; the greater good. We are all family in this challenge and blessing of life. We are all connected. Both tragedies and miracles are shown to us to learn from and to grow.

The greatest gift in my life was given to me unexpectedly, when I was shown the Creator, the Center, the Core, and told, ***"It's all about love."*** I continue to learn and grow, to train and prepare, adapt and thrive. Most importantly, I'm doing the work.

My friend Tony. He gave me the greatest experiences of my life. Tony shared the love of God with me from beyond.

FOOTNOTES

[1] 1st Lt. Carlton B. Crenshaw, Letters Home, Another Perspective, http://www.hmm-364.org/warriors-web-site/crenshaw-ltrs.html (accessed 2013.)

[2] Donna Musil, a film documentary, featuring Kris Kristofferson, www.ratsourjourneyhome.com.

[3] Dr. Valerie Glalante, Ph.D., Licensed Clinical Health Psychologist, April 2015.

[4] Christian Benedict, Acute sleep deprivation and neurodegeneration, (Department of Neuroscience, Uppsala University, Uppsala, Sweden.) 1.

[5] Ed Yeates, Soldier fights for care for brain injury patients, http://www.ksl.com/?nid=148&sid=4485466 (accessed 2010.)

[6] Lt. Col. Raymond Rivas, STATEMENT FOR THE RECORD, United States Senate, Committee on Armed Services, Wounded Warrior Policy and Programs, April 29, 2009.

[7] Cindy Dampier, Surviving His Wife's Suicide, http://www.people.com/people/article/0,,20061980,00.html (accessed 2013.)

[8] Camp Liberty killings, Wikipedia, http://en.wikipedia.org/wiki/Camp_Liberty_killings, (accessed 2013.)

[9] Tom Tiede, Operation Awareness helps junkies in Army, Sarasota Journal, Dec 31, 1970, http://news.google.com/newspapers?nid=1798&dat=19701231&id=JBUfAAAAIB AJ&sjid=EI0EAAAAIBAJ&pg=7315,5212191, (accessed 2013)

[10] Chris Roberts, A family's pain: Airman's death raises questions of treatment, El Paso Times, http://www.elpasotimes.com/ci_17428715, (accessed 2013)

[11] Patricia Kime, DoD cracks down on off-label drug use, Military Times, http://www.marinecorpstimes.com/article/20120614/NEWS/206140317/, (accessed 2013.)

[12] Patricia Kime, DoD cracks down on off-label drug use, Military Times, http://www.marinecorpstimes.com/article/20120614/NEWS/206140317/, (accessed 2013.)

[13] HHS.gov, The U.S. Opioid Epideic, http://www.hhs.gov/opioids/about-the-epidemic/#, (accessed 2016.)

[14] H U M A N R I G H T S W A T C H, NO TIME TO WASTE Evidence-Based Treatment for Drug Dependence at the United States Veterans Administration, ISBN: 978-1-62313-1524. July 2014.

[15] Hedegaard MD MSPH, Chen MS PhD, Warner PhD. Drug-Poisoning Deaths Involving Heroin: United States, 2000-2013. National Center for Health Statistics Data Brief. 2015:190:1-8.

[16] Veteransnewsblog, The Seroquel Scandals, March 9, 2010, http://veteransnewsblog.wordpress.com/page/90/?ui=2&view=bsp&ver=ohhl4rw8m bn4, (accessed 2013.)

[17] Cassi O'Brien, Treating PTSD With Omega-3?, October 17, 2015, https://www.intelligentlabs.org/treating-ptsd-with-omega-3/, (accessed 2017.)

[18] Miriam Fishbein, Sahar Gov, Fadi Assaf, Mikhal Gafni, Ora Keren, Yosef Sarne, Long-term behavioral and biochemical effects of an ultra-low dose of Δ^9-tetrahydrocannabinol (THC): neuroprotection and ERK signaling, (Springer-Verlag 2012) Volume 221, Issue 4, pp 437-448.

[19] By Robin Tricoles, The Promise of Progesterone, (*Emory University School of Medicine,Emory Medical - Winter ed.Winter 2007*) 20-21.

[20] Michael C Mithoefer1, Mark T Wagner2, Ann T Mithoefer1, Lisa Jerome3 and Rick Doblin3; The safety and efficacy of   3,4-methylenedioxymethamphetamineassisted psychotherapy in subjects with chronic, treatment-resistant posttraumatic stress disorder: the first randomized controlled pilot study, Journal of Psychopharmacology 0(0) 1–14. http://www.maps.org/research-archive/mdma/ptsdpaper.pdf. (accessed 2017.)

[21] Defense and Veterans Brain Injury Center, http://dvbic.dcoe.mil/, (accessed 2014.)

[22] Cassi O'Brien, Treating PTSD With Omega-3?, October 17, 2015, https://www.intelligentlabs.org/treating-ptsd-with-omega-3/, (accessed 2017.)

[23] MacDonald, Barber, Jordan, Johnson, Dikman, Fann, Temkin, JAMA Neurology May 1 2017 copyright, Early Clinical Predictors of 5 Year Outcome After Concussive Blast Traumatic Brain Injury.

[24] Black Box Biometrics, https://b3inc.com/, (accessed 2017.)

[25] Dr. Valerie Glalante, Ph.D., Licensed Clinical Health Psychologist, April 2015.

[26] Charlie Jane Anders, From "Irritable Heart" to "Shellshock": How Post-Traumatic Stress Became a Disease, http://io9.com/5898560/from-irritable-heart-to-shellshock-how-post-traumatic-stress-became-a-disease, (accessed 2013.)

[27] PTSD: National Center for PTSD, How Common is PTSD? http://www.ptsd.va.gov/public/PTSD-overview/basics/how-common-is-ptsd.asp, (accessed 2013.)

[28] Dr. Valerie Glalante, Ph.D., Licensed Clinical Health Psychologist, April 2015.

[29] Report to Congress on the Use of Hyperbaric Oxygen for Medical Care and Research in Response to H.R. 3326, the Department of Defense Appropriations Act for Fiscal Year 2010, Generated on 2011Apr22 1223, RefID: 1-9B17BF9, March 2011.

[30]Michael Hoffman, Hyperbaric chambers could help those with TBI, Military Times, Feb 2010, http://www.armytimes.com/article/20100204/NEWS/2040313/Hyperbaric-chambers-could-help-those-TBI, (accessed 2013.)

[31] Richard A. Neubauer, M.D., HBOTb7oz, Copyright 2011 g7oz.org, http://hbot.g7oz.org/?page_id=260, (accessed 2013.)

[32] Ginny Paleg, MS PT, Hyperbaric Oxygen Therapy for Individuals with Neurological Dysfunction, Holbach, KH, Wasserman, H and T Kolberg. Reversibility of the Chronic Post-Stroke State. Cerebral Energy 1976; 7(3); 296-300, http://www.our-kids.org/archives/HBO.html, (accessed 2013.)

[33] George Wolf, David Cifu, Laura Baugh, William Carne, and Leonardo Profenna. The Effect of Hyperbaric Oxygen on Symptoms after Mild Traumatic Brain Injury, Journal of Neurotrauma. November 20, 2012, 29(17): 2606-2612. doi:10.1089/neu.2012.2549. (accessed 2014.)

[34] Tom Koch, 09/11/2012, http://www.huffingtonpost.com/tom-koch/bioethics_b_1873995.html, (accessed 2014.)

[35] Media Advisory: To contact author R. Scott Miller, M.D., call Ellen Crown at 301-619-7549 or email jennifer.e.crown.civ@mail.mil. To contact commentary author Charles W. Hoge, M.D., call Debra L. Yourick, Ph.D. at 301-319-9471 or 301-792-3941 or 410-627-5097 or email debra.l.yourick.civ@mail.mil., 11/17/2014, " Effects of Hyperbaric Oxygen on Postconcussion Symptoms in Military Members." http://media.jamanetwork.com/news-item/effects-of-hyperbaric-oxygen-on-postconcussion-symptoms-in-military-members/, (accessed 2014.)

[36] The War Within: Part II - Paths to Healing By Steve B. Brooks, http://www.legion.org/magazine/159052/war-within-part-ii-paths-healing, (accessed 2014.)

[37] Mayo Clinic Staff, Cluster Headaches, http://www.mayoclinic.org/diseases-conditions/cluster-headache/basics/treatment/con-20031706, (accessed 2014.)

[38]Paul G. Harch, M.D., K. Paul Stoller, M.D., William A. Duncan, Ph.D., Using Hyperbaric & Aerospace Medicine in 21stCentury Medical Practice, A National Brain Injury Rescue and Rehabilitation Project ClinicalTrials.gov Identifier: NCT01105962, Power Point, pg. 19.

[39] Richard A. Neubauer, M.D., U.S. VETERAN PILOT TRIAL LSU IRB #7051 HBOT IN TBI/PTSD PRELIMINARY DATA, FEB 2011, Harch Hyperbarics Inc, http://www.hbot.com/us-veteran-pilot-trial-lsu-irb-7051-hbot-tbiptsd-preliminary-data, (accessed 2013.)

[40] Dr Bill Duncan, Hyperbarics for Athletes, Dr Duncan's Power point presentation, slide 21, http://www.slideshare.net/robertinseattle/hyperbarics-for-athletes-dr-bill-duncan, (accessed 2013.)

[41] Steve B. Brooks, The War Within: Part II - Paths to Healing, Oct 2011, http://www.legion.org/magazine/159052/war-within-part-ii-paths-healing, (accessed 2013.)

[42] Colonel James K. Wright, Eddie Zant, Kevin Groom, Robert E. Schlegel,

Kirby Gilliland, Case report: Treatment of mild traumatic brain injury with hyperbaric oxygen, UHM 2009, Vol. 36, No. 6 – Treatment of mild traumatic brain injury with hyperbaric oxygen, Complete article.

[43] Abigail Klein Leichman, Hyperbaric treatment revitalizes neurons in damaged brains, Israeli researchers find, Feb 2013, Israeli 21c, http://israel21c.org/health/oxygen-chamber-can-boost-brain-repair/, (accessed 2013.)

[44] Report to Congress on the Use of Hyperbaric Oxygen for Medical Care and Research in Response to H.R. 3326, the Department of Defense Appropriations Act for Fiscal Year 2010, Generated on 2011Apr22 1223, RefID: 1-9B17BF9, March 2011.

[45] Wounded Warrior Project™ (WWP), Mission, History, http://www.woundedwarriorproject.org/media/42192/wwp_media_fact_sheet.pdf, (accessed 2013.)

[46] Mark Faul, PhD, MS, Likang Xu, MD, MS, Marlena M. Wald, MPH, MLS, Victor G. Coronado, MD, MPH, Traumatic Brain Injury in the United States, Emergency Department Visits, Hospitalizations and Deaths 2002–2006, U.S. DEPARTMENT OF HEALTH AND HUMAN SERVICES Centers for Disease Control and Prevention, March 2010.

[47] Paul Solotaroff, Dave Duerson: The Ferocious Life and Tragic Death of a Super Bowl Star, Mens Journal Magazine, May 2011, http://www.mensjournal.com/magazine/dave-duerson-the-ferocious-life-and-tragic-death-of-a-super-bowl-star-20121002, (accessed 2013.)

[48] Bennet I. Omalu, M.D., M.P.H., Bennet I. Omalu, M.D., M.P.H.; CHRONIC TRAUMATIC ENCEPHALOPATHY IN A NATIONAL FOOTBALL LEAGUE PLAYER, Jul 2005

[49] Daniel Stimson, Ph.D., First cases of degenerative brain disease CTE found in veterans with blast injuries, National Institute of Neurological Disorders and Stroke, June 2012, http://www.ninds.nih.gov/news_and_events/news_articles/CTE_found_in_veterans.htm, (accessed 2013.)

[50] J Mez, MD, D. Daneshevar, PHD, P. Kiernan, BA. Clinicopathological Evaluation of Chronic Traumatic Encephalopathy in Players of American Football, July 25, 2017.

[51] David Leon Moore and Erik Brady, Junior Seau's final days plagued by sleepless nights, USA TODAY, June 2012, http://usatoday30.usatoday.com/sports/football/story/2012-05-31/Junior-Seau-suicide-last-days-sleep-issues/55316506/1, (accessed 2013.)

[52] Terry Long (American football), Wikipedia, http://en.wikipedia.org/wiki/Terry_Long_(American_football), (accessed 2013.)

[53] ESPN.com news services, Study: McHale had developed CTE, ESPN Jan 2009, http://sports.espn.go.com/nfl/news/story?id=3864644, (accessed 2013.)

[54] ESPN.com news services, Police: Ray Easterling shot himself, ESPN April 2012, http://espn.go.com/nfl/story/_/id/7839981/police-say-ray-easterling-former-atlanta-falcon-committed-suicide, (accessed 2013.)

[55]Tyler Conway, Autopsy of Former Ravens Quarterback Cullen Finnerty Reveals CTE, Aug 2013, http://bleacherreport.com/articles/1732157-former-ravens-qb-cullen-finnertys-autopsy-reveals-cte?utm_source=cnn.com&utm_medium=referral&utm_campaign=editorial&hpt=hp_c4&hpt=hp_inthenews, (accessed 2013.)

[56] Associated Press, NFL, ex-players agree to $765M settlement in concussions suit, Aug 2013, http://www.nfl.com/news/story/0ap1000000235494/article/nfl-explayers-agree-to-765m-settlement-in-concussions-suit, (accessed 2013.)

[57] ESPN.com news services, Ryan Freel had CTE, parents say, ESPN Dec 16, 2013, http://espn.go.com/mlb/story/_/id/10142581/cte-present-ryan-freel-killed-self-report-says, (accessed 2013.)

[58] Sports Legacy Institute, Wrestler Chris Benoit Brain's Forensic Exam Consistent With Numerous Brain Injuries, Science Daily, Sept 2007, http://www.sciencedaily.com/releases/2007/09/070905224343.htm, (accessed 2013.)

[59] Tom Llamas, 21 Jan, 2015, http://abcnews.go.com/Sports/wrestlers-file-concussion-lawsuit-wwe/story?id=28369622, (accessed 2016.)

[60] Alyssa Roenigk, May 24, 2016, http://www.espn.com/action/story/_/id/15614274/bmx-legend-dave-mirra-diagnosed-cte, (accessed 2016.)

[61] Chris Nowinski, Sports Legacy Institute, Boston University CTE Center, http://www.bu.edu/cte/about/leadership/chris-nowinski/, (accessed 2013.)

[62] David Browne, Kevin Pearce, After the Crash, Mens Journal, July 2013, http://www.mensjournal.com/magazine/kevin-pearce-after-the-crash-20130617, (accessed 2013.)

[63] American Association of Neurological Surgeons, Sports-Related Head Injury, Dec 2011, http://www.aans.org/Patient%20Information/Conditions%20and%20Treatments/Sports-Related%20Head%20Injury.aspx (accessed 2013.)

[64] Hans Förstl, Christian Haass, Bernhard Hemmer, Bernhard Meyer, Martin Halle, Boxing—Acute Complications and Late Sequelae From Concussion to Dementia, Deutsches Ärzteblatt International | Dtsch Arztebl Int 2010; 107(47): 835–9.

[65] Alan Schwarz, Suicide Reveals Signs of a Disease Seen in N.F.L., New York Times, Sept 2010, http://www.nytimes.com/2010/09/14/sports/14football.html?pagewanted=all&_r=0, (accessed 2013.)

[66] Mallika Marar, Natalie M. McIlvain, Sarah K. Fields and R. Dawn Comstock, Epidemiology of Concussions Among United States High School Athletes in 20 Sports, The American Journal of Sports Medicine, SAGE Publications, Jan 2012, DOI: 10.1177/0363546511435626, http://www.uslacrosse.org/portals/1/documents/pdf/about-the-sport/epidemiology-of-concussions.pdf, (accessed 2013.)

[67] Barbara Starr, Behind the Scenes: Triumph and tragedy for two wounded soldiers, CNN July 29, 2009, http://www.cnn.com/2009/US/07/27/starr.extraordinary/index.html, (accessed 2013.)

[68] Chelsea C. Cook, CNN, Soldier's suicide note goes viral; family demands better for veterans, July 6, 2013, http://www.cnn.com/2013/07/06/us/soldier-suicide-note/index.html?hpt=hp_inthenews, (accessed 2013.)

[69] Daniel Somers, "I Am Sorry That It Has Come to This": A Soldier's Last Words, Gawker.com, June 22, 2012, http://gawker.com/i-am-sorry-that-it-has-come-to-this-a-soldiers-last-534538357, (accessed 2013.)

[70] Irene Sege, Boston Globe, March 1, 2005, 'Something happened to Jeff', http://www.boston.com/yourlife/health/mental/articles/2005/03/01/jeff_lucey_returned_from_iraq_a_changed_man_then_he_killed_himself/?page=full, (accessed 2013.)

[71] D. Mark Anderson, Daniel I. Rees, Deployments, Combat Exposure, and Crime, University of Colorado Denver and IZA, Discussion Paper No. 7761, November 2013.

[72] Survivor Suicides, Tisha Thompson and Rick Yarborough, http://www.nbcwashington.com/investigations/The-Suicide-Survivors-206699561.html, (accessed 2014.)

[73] Anne Leland & Mari-Jana "M-J" Oboroceanu, American War and Military Operations Casualties: Lists and Statistics, CRS Report for Congress, Congressional Research Service, 7-5700, RL32492, February 26, 2010.

[74] Adrian Bejan, Constructal Law, Duke University, Shape and Structure, from Engineering to Nature, Cambridge University Press, 2000, http://www.mems.duke.edu/bejan-constructal-theory, (accessed 2013.)

[75] Wikipedia, OODA Loop, http://en.wikipedia.org/wiki/OODA_loop, (accessed 2013.)

[76] Wikipedia, Classical conditioning, http://en.wikipedia.org/wiki/Classical_conditioning, (accessed 2013.)

[77] Wikipedia, Maslow's hierarchy of needs, http://en.wikipedia.org/wiki/Maslow's_hierarchy_of_needs, (accessed 2013.)

[78] Dr. Valerie Glalante, Ph.D., Licensed Clinical Health Psychologist, April 2015.

[79] HHS.gov, The U.S. Opioid Epideic, http://www.hhs.gov/opioids/about-the-epidemic/#, (accessed 2016.)

[80] Jon Kabat-Zinn, Getting Started with Mindfulness, https://www.mindful.org/meditation/mindfulness-getting-started/(accessed 2017.)

[81] Raphael Mechoulam, Ph.D., General use of cannabis for PTSD Symptoms, 2010, Veterans For Medical Cannabis Access, http://veteransformedicalmarijuana.org/content/general-use-cannabis-ptsd-symptoms, (accessed 2013.)

[82] ABC's "Nightline Primetime" explores NDEs, http://iands.org/news/news/ndes-in-the-news/776-abcs-qnightline-primetimeq-explores-ndes.html, (accessed 2014.)

Made in the USA
Middletown, DE
05 February 2024

49104014R00161